Italian and Italian American Studies
Stanislao G. Pugliese
Hofstra University
Series Editor

This publishing initiative seeks to bring the latest scholarship in Italian and Italian American history, literature, cinema, and cultural studies to a large audience of specialists, general readers, and students. I&IAS will feature works on modern Italy (Renaissance to the present) and Italian American culture and society by established scholars as well as new voices in the academy. This endeavor will help to shape the evolving fields of Italian and Italian American Studies by reemphasizing the connection between the two. The following editorial board consists of esteemed senior scholars who act as advisors to the series editor.

Italy's Divided Memory

John Foot

palgrave
macmillan

First published in 2009 by PALGRAVE MACMILLAN®
in the United States—a division of St. Martin's Press LLC,
175 Fifth Avenue, New York, NY 10010

Where this book is distributed in the UK, Europe and the rest of
the world, this is by Palgrave Macmillan, a division of Macmillan
Publishers Limited, registered in England, company number 785998,
of Houndmills, Basingstoke, Hampshire RG21 6XS.

Palgrave Macmillan is the global academic imprint of the above
companies and has companies and representatives throughout the world.

Palgrave® and Macmillan® are registered trademarks in the United States,
the United Kingdom, Europe and other countries.

ISBN: 978-0-230-61847-3

Library of Congress Cataloging-in-Publication Data

Foot, John, 1964-
    Italy's divided memory / John Foot.
        p. cm.—(Italian and Italian American studies)
    Includes bibliographical references and index.
    ISBN-13: 978-0-230-61847-3
    ISBN-10: 0-230-61847-2
    1. Italy—History—1914–1945. 2. Italy—History—1945– 3. World
War, 1914–1918—Social aspects—Italy. 4. World War, 1939–1945—Social
aspects—Italy. 5. Memory—Social aspects—Italy. 6. Collective memory—
Italy. 7. Monuments—Italy. 8. War memorials—Italy. 9. Political culture—
Italy. 10. Italy—Social conditions. I. Title.

DG568.F66 2009
945.091—dc22   2009023745

A catalogue record of the book is available from the British Library.

Design by Scribe Inc.

First edition: December 2009

10 9 8 7 6 5 4 3 2 1

Printed in the United States of America.

Contents

Illustrations

Acknowledgments

Many, many people have helped with the research upon which this book is based and its writing. I am grateful to numerous individuals and institutions for advice over material and individual cases of "divided memory," as well as monuments, plaques, or ex-memorials. I would like to thank all the following for help with specific questions: Alfio Bernabei, Alan Davis, David Forgacs, Filippo Colombara, Adolfo Mignemi, Enzo Pennone, Roberta Suzzi Valli, Stuart Oglethorpe, John Quick. Carla Giacomozzi of the Archivio Storico in Bolzano was an extraordinary source of help, material and good humor. Her work around the memory of the wartime camp in Bolzano, including the superb guides that tourists can now use to visit the many places of memory in that city, has been exemplary. Eleanor Chiari, Phil Cooke, John Dickie, Maria Novella Mercuri, and Robert Gordon were all generous with their time and read chapters of the manuscript. Dan Sayer and Nick Dines were invaluable in my thinking about memory and place during work in Naples, Venice, and Milan. Thanks also go to Gloria Nemec in Trieste and the staff of that unique institution that is the Istituto De Martino in Sesto Fiorentino in Florence. In San Miniato I was generously assisted by Roberto Cerri, who guided me with good humor through the difficult highways and byways of public and private memories in that small hill town. The Arts and Humanities Research Council awarded me a research leave grant in 2008 to complete this project and the Italian department at University College London gave me a term of leave for the same purpose. Monica Foot was as efficient as ever with the index.

Giovanni Contini's work and insights into divided memories have been a constant inspiration, as has been the work of Luisa Passerini and Alessandro Portelli. Some of the stories told in this book were first aired on Radio Popolare Network in a program run by a brilliant young broadcaster, Paolo Maggioni. At the same time the best magazine in Italy, *Internazionale*, generously hosted a series of ten articles that form the basis of this volume. Thanks to all those at *Internazionale* and to the director, Giovanni de Mauro, for the opportunity to write for a larger public than that usually afforded to academics.

On a hot summer's day in 2008, I visited Guardistallo, the small hill town in Tuscany where a Nazi massacre had taken place in 1944. By the end of the visit, I had understood one thing very clearly: the memories of that massacre had never gone away, and they still divided that tiny town sixty-four years after the event. Memory mattered then, and it still counts today. This book, with all its faults, gaps, and errors (for which the responsibility is mine alone), is a small contribution to the understanding of these divided memories, and the ways in which they have affected politics, history, and identity in Italy since 1915. And this is also a book about my profession, that of the historian, and the ways in which history has played a key part in these debates over time, through important research but also through silences, omission and—sometimes—lies.

I

Divided Memory

Theory, Methodology, Practice

Memory is a battlefield, where nothing is neutral and where everything is
continually contested.

—Luisa Passerini, "Memories of Resistance"

Italy and Memory

Italian memories have often been divided. Events have been interpreted
in contrasting ways, and the facts themselves are often contested. It has
proved extremely difficult, if not impossible, for any group—public or private—to create a consensus around the past, or around ways of remembering that past. Various groups—be they regional, ethnic, political—have
demanded that their memories be acknowledged. Individual events as well
as history itself have been understood in a bewildering variety of ways.
The state and other public bodies have rarely been able to build durable
and commonly agreed practices of commemoration. There has been no
closure, no "truth," and little reconciliation.

This book will use stories, microhistories, and testimonies to explain
and describe some of these divided memories. It will investigate plaques,
monuments, anniversaries, commemorations, and other visible signs of
memorial practice, but also absences and silences. What is remembered is
important, but we must also consider what has not been remembered. This
book is not always interested in "what happened" in a strict sense, but the
debates about what happened afterward and about the facts themselves. I
draw a strong distinction in this volume between the role of the judge and
that of the historian. The former is obliged to come to a conclusion about
the facts of each case; the latter is interested in the ways these facts have
been interpreted, remembered, and contested.

Above all, this book will look at conflicts over public forms of memory. On many occasions in Italian history, public commemorations have been contested, in both their form and their content. Debates concerning these memory-objects have been long-running and heated. Monuments and plaques have frequently been criticized, but also altered, attacked, or removed. They can be seen as "embodying concrete traces of the past, visible and durable signs of its celebration."[1] Memory was—and remains—a battleground for the hearts and minds of the people. Monuments are complicated objects that "call forth multiple contending memory-truths and, eventually, anti-memory monuments or counter-monuments."[2]

While divided memories or narratives about what had happened (and responsibility for what had happened) were there from the very beginning, it was often in relation to memory practice that these divisions became public. Research on wartime massacres, for example, has concentrated on explaining memory divisions while their expression during commemorations—and the effect of these ceremonies on the divisions themselves—has been neglected. Commemorations also created division; they were not just products of debate. These were the moments when private and public memories merged, and where sparks flew. Monuments were not simply the end of a story, but part of the story itself.

Public memory has been largely overlooked in discussions over divided memory in Italy. On the one hand, oral historians have concentrated on the subjective aspects of divisions over the past and have seen public memory as another form of evidence of the ways in which these divisions have emerged or been hidden. Meanwhile, historians who privilege written documents and archives often leave out public memory altogether, or see it in purely descriptive terms. In both cases, public memory has had a harsh deal. In reality, forms of public commemoration are crucial to understanding divisions over the past at a local and national level. Forms of public memory deserve study in themselves, and in an analytical way, and not just in terms of descriptions of plaques and commemorations. This type of work has very rarely been carried out in terms of key events in Italy.[3]

Local debates and divisions have often centered precisely on public memory. Concrete forms of remembering and forgetting were the subject of numerous long-running controversies and negotiations. Many people did not recognize their memories in the types of public memory that were created, and this led to alternative forms of commemoration, protests about those that were there, or simple rejection of what was on offer (the refusal to attend). Thus, public memorials are not just peripheral "window dressing" in terms of the history of memory, but central to the processes whereby divisions were elaborated, explained, closed, or reopened.

Every word was important and was mulled over. Each phrase—on every plaque—told its own story, but also hid other stories. Over time, divided forms of public memory were created that allowed each "side" to tell its own story publicly. Of course, these debates were also political, and it is not by chance that many of the "alternative" public memories that emerged over time were linked to the church, and were often physically located inside churches and religious spaces.

Finally, public memory was where the state showed its face—where it intervened—around local questions of memory and remembering. And this involvement often jarred with local opinions. The state's version of the past was important to those involved in local memory conflicts, but it often failed to satisfy desires for recognition or to close divisions. The state was blamed for its absence (the lack of justice, the lack of recognition) but also for its presence (as with medals for "military valor," which were not always accepted by local populations).

Beyond the state, there were the historians. For many, the final word lay with experts on the past, who—it was argued—would be able to discover "the real truth" (as in one testimony collected by Paolo Pezzino).[4] But historians had their own problems when asked to intervene in communities fractured by conflicts and with their own—fixed—ideas about the past. History was rarely straightforward. There was no "real truth" to be "discovered," although there were versions of the past that could be subjected to various forms of proof. Moreover, although they often did not see themselves as such, the people involved in memory conflicts were also part of history. Protagonists of divided memory debates often saw history as a series of facts. Historians were more interested in interpretation, and thus their work usually failed to satisfy local needs. Written history made things more complicated, while local demands were for simplification. Historians did not always agree, and these disagreements also had an impact on memory divisions.[5]

Public memory conflicts also became part of public memory itself. Numerous monuments were attacked and destroyed by fascists during the "memory war" of the 1920s. After fascism, some of these monuments were reconstructed in the same way, and in the same places, as before. Often, a note would be added to underline the fact of the past destruction. Hence, these monument wars developed into part of public memory. Sometimes, signs of destruction or attempted damage were left as a mark of the "barbarity" of the past and marked by messages or explanatory notes for the visitor. This was also a sign of the power of memory. One of the first acts of the new democratic Italy was not just to destroy symbols of fascism but to replace monuments that had themselves been removed under the regime. The monument war was still being fought in the 1940s, and continued throughout the postwar period.

Studying Monuments

Monuments are critical to an understanding of the past. They tell us about history and about historical change, and about the transmission of memory to the public stage. Alterations to monuments represent a kind of "chronological sedimentation."[6] It is rare to find Italian monuments in their original form. Many have been altered over time—usually through added names from other wars, but also in other ways, as with the removal of fascist features. There is a long tradition of the reuse or transformation of previous monuments, usually for political reasons. Fascism destroyed Austrian memorial sites and reused them for its own symbolic constructions. After 1945, a number of resistance monuments reused parts or material from fascist sites.

Many monuments developed into *palimpsests*—objects that reflected their history as they were written on, partly erased, added to, and rewritten time and again.[7] Thus Risorgimento monuments often became sites of memory for the colonial wars and both world wars. Names were inscribed upon existing lists, or monuments became dedicated to the "dead of all wars." Fascism created separate sections for "fascist martyrs," those who died in Spain, and those who failed to return from the wars in Africa. Sometimes, these names were removed, or their origins glossed over, after 1943. In the wake of 1945, this process happened again, although the civil war aspects of the resistance led to demands for distinct monuments. There were continuities, but also breaks.

Monuments were and are many things at the same time, open to different readings. They are documents that can be seen as historical texts, including the story of their construction and of the commemorative practices linked to them, the ways in which the politics of memory has been "expressed, utilised and ritualised with parties and ceremonies."[8] Public memorials were also the places where ordinary people—victims, the families of victims, partisans, and others—saw their achievements and sacrifice acknowledged in a permanent way. The importance attached to local public memory in particular is an indicator of the ways these objects act as catalysts of public opinion, mourning, and recognition. It is thus not particularly surprising that these monuments have been—and remain—the subject of controversy, negotiation, and often bitter division. The siting of monuments is also important. Monuments become part of the landscape, but are also places of forgetting and silence. For Dogliani, "Monuments and plaques are the most invisible historic traces in existence."[9] Each monument needs to be put in its context; its omissions are as important as what is there. This is thus an "analysis of how memory and forgetting pervade real public space."[10] Divided memories created memoryscapes and geographies of memory where monuments competed for attention in terms of urban space, positioning, and reception.

History and Memory

Subjectivity is as much the business of history as the more visible "facts." What the informant believes is indeed a fact . . . just as much as what "really" happened.

—Alessandro Portelli, in *The Voice of the Past*

What is the relationship between history and memory? There is still a strong tendency among historians—even historians of memory—to draw clear boundaries between the two. History is usually seen as scientific, somehow based on the truth, rigorous and as a good alternative to memory. Memory, on the other hand, is bracketed as unreliable, far from the truth, a kind of flimsy superstructure. Often, memory is seen as unwritten, and history as written. Yet, for a whole series of reasons, these distinctions are no longer convincing. For one thing, memory is part of history. Twentieth century history cannot be written, or understood, without reference to memory. Often, memory is the only way to grasp the lived experience of people, and their relationship with the past. Moreover, history itself is also unstable, flimsy, and unreliable, and often highly politicized. "Memory is presented as spontaneous and unreflexive, [while] history is characterised as critical and scientific," yet "in many cases history is not scientific and memory is not spontaneous, but the result of brooding, suffering and patience."[11] History and memory, as Winter has argued, "overlap in too many ways to be considered as pure categories"; they "infuse each other."[12]

Historians who wish to distinguish their work from memory are frequently attached to the idea of written (and often official) documents. The final answer, it is often said, lies with documents, which are held in dusty archives. What this kind of notion ignores is the fact that most archival documents have oral origins (police reports, phone calls, army reports, investigations using interviews and interrogations, trial documents), and are as unstable and "subjective" as oral history itself. Of course, other documentation can be more "scientific" (such as the reports on bomb damage, or autopsies). But even film of an event does not remove doubts. In fact it often increases uncertainties, as has been seen with the Zapruder film of the JFK assassination, for example, or the filmed material relating to Carlo Giuliani's death in Genoa in 2001.

Given the confusion—or osmosis, in a more positive sense—between history and memory, why should we distinguish the terms at all? Is everything part of a series of conflicting or converging narratives? Many historians argue that we should accept and embrace this osmosis: "Rather than looking for the truth, we need to think about increasing the variety of truths, in order to enrich our possible lines of interpretation, our understanding, our sense of critical approach."[13] Gabriella Gribaudi links the two concepts together: "When we talk about national and local history we immediately are also talking about memory."

This is not an attempt to reduce all history to discourse, to narration. Rather it is a plea to see history as a richer discipline, able to embrace memory studies as an integral part of understanding the present and the past. How can we interpret postwar Trieste without taking into account the divided memories over the events after 1918 and after 1943? How can we understand postwar Civitella Val di Chiana without reference to the memories carried forward by many of the women survivors of the Nazi massacre of 1944? As Portelli has written, "History has no content without their stories."[14]

But not all events are remembered, and thus history and memory need to add other strings to their bows: forgetting and silence.[15] It is through the complicated interplay between history, historiography, memory, and forgetting that we can start to understand contemporary historical events and the ways in which they have been understood. Memory and forgetting constitute a key part of individual and group identity. They have a profound influence on the way that people act (or don't act), individual and collective life-histories, and the history of specific places.

Microhistory, Microhistories

Microhistory and microhistories will form the backbone of this book. The particular, the everyday, and the ordinary are utilized to try to explain the general, the extraordinary, and the exceptional. The scale of research is often reduced to a monument, a plaque, individual life stories, families, events, and places. These microhistories do not replace the big picture or a wider analysis, but are part of the whole story. This is never an automatic process—a series of microhistories do not necessarily make a macrohistory. Smaller stories need to be interpreted, drawn together, and compared. Some of this work is descriptive, but no less historical for that. The historian often benefits from playing the role of reporter, or even detective. Clues, small signs, and traces can be as important as broad trends and national developments. Nonevents can mean as much as real ones. The lack of protest can tell us as much as ten years of street demonstrations.

Narration and description have always played a key role in historical explanation, and these techniques have recently begun to take on more credibility in conjunction with other methodologies and alternative sources. Yet, as Pes has written, "No description is neutral," and "the reporting of concrete facts is a way of understanding the real functioning of society . . . which otherwise would end up as simplified or distorted by quantitative calculations or excessive generalisation."[16]

Microhistory is not just a reduction of scale. Born as a radical alternative to big, schematic historical methodologies, whereby history moved along straight, ideologically defined, teological tracks, microhistory is interested in everyday life and necessarily entails the breaking-down of disciplinary boundaries.[17] As such, microhistory naturally allies itself with anthropology, as well as ethnography. It also rejects the old hierarchies and the old categories—and thus links well with oral history. As Portelli has put it, "The death of an obscure factory worker in an obscure industrial town is a historical fact of great significance and deep implications."[18] This is true for memory as much as it is for history. Stories also need to be told, as part of history.

Oral History, Oral Histories

Oral history work forms the basis for many contemporary debates and research about divided memories in Italy. It has a unique ability to understand as well as collect memories, bringing history and the subject together. A further strong feature of the work of oral historians involves the desire to bring history alive through the voices of ordinary people. What is the relationship between oral history and traditional history? It is now well known that oral history is extremely unreliable concerning a simple reconstruction of the past—when events and history are seen as a series of facts.

Yet oral history gives us a lot more than the facts. First, it tells us about how people remember the past. Second, it gives us an insight into subjectivity, and into self-representation. Third, the errors and exaggerations that appear in interviews are themselves indications concerning the forms of memories and the ways in which politics, collective narratives, and time can transform and distort our memories of the past into myths and stereotypes around which narratives can be shaped.[19]

Oral history is not just about memory, but about ifs and buts, utopias, missed opportunities, might-have-beens, invention, the imaginary—it is a history of betrayals, dreams, and desires. Interviewees will often muse about where they and where history went wrong, and they will write themselves into that history, move events around to fit certain more coherent versions of their story, or develop memories that coagulate around certain key stereotypes, commonplace stories and iconic images, photographs, or films. Interviewees are not another kind of source but a completely different form of source. They help us to understand the past, not to uncover it. Historians cannot, as Benjamin argues, describe the past "as it really was."[20]

Divisions over memory—over plaques, monuments, commemorations—are also, always, divisions over history, over how to interpret and understand the past, and how to transmit that understanding to others. The historian's task is to interpret and understand this material as history. This book will attempt to follow Passerini's lead and "combine history and memory in new ways and in hybrid genres." What is important is to recognize that "the memory itself has a history"[21] and that "telling and remembering are themselves events, not only description of events."[22]

Divided Memories

This discussion of divided memories in Italy will make reference to different forms of division. First, there are the gaps between national narratives and local or individual narratives. National versions of the events of World War I, for example, or those linked to the resistance, have often jarred sharply with local or individual stories. Sometimes, local memories have been seen as countermemories, or as counterinformation. A second set of divided memories can be seen within individuals. For Portelli, "Memory is divided, lacerated, within itself, within the unreconciled double consciousness of individuals and social groups."[23] In each case, the influence of politics and manipulation is never far away. Historical work has also had difficulty in dealing with "uncomfortable" areas from the past.

Divided Memory: History of a Concept

The term "divided memory" (*la memoria divisa*) as used in historical debates in Italy can be traced to the 1990s.[24] In that decade historians made a "surprising" discovery. They began to pick up on and study alternative memories, which had been carried forward largely by the families of victims of local massacres perpetuated by retreating German troops in Tuscany in 1944. Research on a massacre at Civitella Val di Chiana formed the basis of Giovanni Contini's book *La memoria divisa*, published in 1997. Contini's book was preceded by a conference organized in Civitella by Leonardo Paggi that also led to an edited volume, and where the term "divided memory" appeared.[25] Paggi's father had been killed in the massacre in Civitella, an event he had witnessed as a child. *Anatomia di un massacro*, Pezzino's study of another Nazi massacre in Guardistallo in Tuscany (on the same day as that at Civitella) and its consequences, also appeared in 1997. This research into two 1944 hill town massacres has since inspired a number of similar studies across Italy.[26]

What was the substance of these alternative and "surprising" memories? In short, many people who had lost relatives and friends not only blamed the partisans for provoking these massacres (and often for failing to protect the population), but had carried forward this hostility to the actions of the local Resistance for over sixty years. Put very simply—and these narratives are neither straightforward nor lacking in internal contradictions—for these survivors and their families (and others) the principal responsibility for some of these massacres, while obviously perpetuated by the German troops, lay with the partisans. According to these accounts, the latter had carried out irresponsible and useless attacks that had left the civilian population defenseless and had provoked German ferocity. Since 1944, commemorations have been contested, and a geography of divided memory has emerged in these small towns. There has been no reconciliation of these versions, although changes have taken place over time.

These "scandalous"[27] narratives not only flew in the face of traditional left-national discourses concerning the Resistance, but also tended to create problems for much of the historiography of the partisan movement published during the cold war, as well as its numerous myths. Many historians also refer to these memories as antipartisan memories, although this seems a somewhat reductive (and politicized) way of understanding them.

Contini's study (which is mainly but not entirely based on oral history interviews) reconstructs the events leading up to the massacre (which was probably not a reprisal at all) and examines in detail the competing memories that have divided Civitella ever since. His explanation for these divisions lies in a combination of historical and geographical factors and sociopsychological (and gender-based) features linked to the isolation of Civitella and the particular way in which mourning and narratives relating to the massacre were created and carried forward over time (leading, for example, to court cases, clashes at public ceremonies, and even violence). Other research on massacres in Tuscany and elsewhere discovered divided memories in many cases, although each particular massacre had its own history of memory.[28]

Portelli's work on the Nazi massacre of 335 people at the Fosse Ardeatine in Rome in March 1944 came to similar conclusions. Many Roman citizens were led to believe—and remain convinced—that the partisans whose attack inspired the Nazi reprisal should (and could) have given themselves up. Antipartisan memory contaminated a whole generation, despite the fact that it was linked to a demonstrably false version of events: the partisans could not have prevented the reprisal by handing themselves in to the Nazis. To some extent, the story of the failure of the partisans to give themselves up was part of a propaganda effort, led by the Vatican at the time, that blamed the anti-fascists for Nazi reprisals. In part, however, these false versions of history are also linked to doubts about the role of the partisans themselves, even on the left. These uncertainties tell us much about the divisive nature of the war and the ways in which the politicization of memory has led to bitter disputes over what had happened and who was to blame.[29]

So the idea of divided memory relates to a specific set of events and historical research, emerging in part from a post–cold war opening out of research into the past. Research on other comparable massacres turned up different stories and different memories—but also similar patterns in many cases. The breakdown of partisan-community relations depended on a series of factors, such as the strength of local political traditions, the ability or otherwise of partisans to set up lines of communication with communities, and the military strategy of the Allies and the Nazi army. (Bad) luck also played a part, and massacres did not need specific justification (beyond that of war strategy). Not all partisan attacks led to reprisals. But the civilians on the ground didn't have the benefit of the wider picture, as they struggled to make sense of the holocaust and the horror that had enveloped their lives. Anthropologists have pointed to the natural tendency to look for a scapegoat within these communities, the search for an "internal foreigner" or "internal enemy."[30]

Since Contini's book appeared, the term "divided memory" has become commonplace among Italian historians, particularly those dealing with World War II and the cold war, but little attempt has been made to build on the concept, or even to extrapolate it from specific historical moments and events. Quite often historians use the term "divided memory" without talking about memory at all.

A Wider Definition

Following the existing studies, I would like to elaborate a more general idea of divided memory, moving the concept away from its origins in discussions of 1943 to 1945.

Divided memory is the tendency for divergent or contradictory narratives to emerge after events, and to be elaborated and interpreted in private stories as well as through forms of public commemoration and ritual. These memories are often incompatible, but survive in parallel. Politics, historical research, and cultural change affect the ups and downs of the conflict. Sometimes, reconciliation takes place, and the memories "merge." Local historical, social, and political factors (including the work of historians) contribute to the survival, or otherwise of the divided memories. Divided memories are also reproduced as public memory in local memoryscapes.

In this sense, Italian history has been marked by divided memories ever since the nation took shape in the nineteenth century. Different sets of memories have surfaced from and about events, shaping both public and private memory. One aspect of this divided memory is that certain accounts were excluded from historical discourse for long periods of time. In many cases, official and unofficial commemorations, interpretations (including those of historians), memorials, and private memories and stories have competed at an everyday level. There have been moments of rupture when "old memories simply could not be contained . . . [and] official symbols could not make shattered memories whole."[31]

Why? Explaining Divided Memories

At the macro and national level, divided memories are linked to two features: the series of civil wars that have marked Italian history ever since the formation of the nation in the 1860s, and the weakness of the state and the nation. At a micro level, local, personal, psychological, and other specific factors come into play.

A History of Civil Wars

Italy has experienced a series of high- and low-level civil wars since unification, when the country was fused through civil conflict as well as military struggles against foreign powers. The early unification period was marked by intense internal strife and the army and martial law were used to repress social rebellion. As the twentieth century took shape, Italians fought Italians at various points, from the street battles after World War I,[32] to the struggles over Fiume, to military clashes during the Spanish civil war, to the Resistance and World War II (1943–45), and finally during the "years of lead" marked by terrorism and political violence in the 1960s and 1970s.[33] Strikes, riots, and protests were often resolved at gunpoint, and not at the negotiating table, although the peninsula never degenerated into the full-scale "autonomous" civil wars (outside of world wars) that divided Spain in the 1930s and Greece in the 1940s.[34] Many have often seen the entire cold war as a form of civil war. Italy's edges and their shifting borders were particularly volatile, as places where divided memories also took on ethnic connotations. Fascists and landowners in 1945 were often attacked as much for their activities twenty years earlier as for their actions during the war.[35]

Italy's civil wars also contributed to a strong politicization of historical practice in Italy, limiting debate over what happened and how history was experienced. Historians have often felt the need to line up behind set versions of history, dictated by political considerations. Individual identity and the past were intimately connected—and this included the identity and the past and present political choices of historians themselves. The memories of these divisions were slow to fade, affecting subsequent conflicts.

History has tended to be written by the winners of wars—often as a series of myths, and through the exclusion or demonization of the defeated. Fascism constructed the myth of the "fascist martyrs," excluding the far greater numbers of victims on the other side of the barricades. After 1945, it was the fascists themselves who were cut out of the story, along with the majority of Italians who had lined up on neither side of the fence. This "gray zone" was removed from most (but not all) accounts. The so-called Resistance *vulgata* (*vulgata resistenziale*) developed. This *vulgata* (a commonly accepted text or reading) came in many different forms, which played on the various overlapping "wars within wars" that had been fought by protagonists (sometimes at the same time).[36] Nonetheless, while these official versions of the past imposed themselves at levels of public memory, education, and public discourse, alternative versions were carried forward from below, and often created hidden forms of local and private memories. Silence did not mean that the past had been forgotten. Histories and experiences that didn't "fit" were ignored or played down, such as the Allied bombings of Italian cities.[37]

Many underlined the unified, democratic, and antifascist aspects of the resistance, but above all stressed that there had been a war of national liberation, and not a class or civil war. The very term "civil war" was taboo (particularly for the communist left), until the late 1980s. Meanwhile, the more revolutionary parts of the left (and many ex-partisans) pointed toward moments of class and revolutionary war. Neofascist historians attempted to "denationalize" the Resistance, and promoted the concept of civil war (which underlined how many Italians had fought on the "wrong side"). This work was largely ignored by mainstream historians, but was able to build on the uncertainties of those who had remained in the gray zone. Commemorations, memorials, anniversaries, and monuments drew on the heroic, national, and unifying aspects of the Resistance, with occasional forays into more revolutionary symbolism. Each "school" removed from its accounts the uncomfortable parts. Historians were as guilty of this as anyone. Few wanted to hear the stories of those returning from the concentration camps after the war, while the crimes committed by the Italian occupying army in Greece, Albania, and Yugoslavia were ignored for years.

While the formation of the republic was a brief moment of unity, divisions remained—hidden, unresolved, and festering. It was often left up to novelists or filmmakers to draw a more realistic and complicated picture of the resistance, as in Rossellini's *Paisà* (1946), Bertolucci's *La strategia del ragno* (1970) and the novels of Calvino, Fenoglio, and Meneghello. As the cold war came to an end, the field began to open up. Pavone's *Una guerra civile* (1991) laid the basis for a revisionist approach to the Resistance from the left, while Renzo De Felice's work on fascism revisited the years of the regime. New methodologies began to confront previously taboo subjects— antifascism among Turinese workers, the support among the peasantry for the partisans, and the memory of the war of its victims. In particular, the combination of oral history and microhistory opened up a Pandora's box of alternative and surprising memories and narratives. It would be difficult now to attempt an account of postwar Italy without reference to the key work of historians in the 1980s and 1990s—often based on oral history and microhistorical methodologies.

The end of the cold war also brought back into the fold the neofascist historical accounts that had been in "internal exile" for the whole postwar period. Some were reproposed, with great success in terms of sales, by a journalist with antifascist credentials. As the Resistance generation disappeared, the antifascist paradigm began to fade in importance, if not to enter a deep crisis.[38] Anti-antifascism (or post-antifascism) became the vogue, from both left and right. Attempts were made to highlight events from the war that undermined the resistance narrative—above all on the edges of Italy (the massacres known as the *foibe*) as well as the postwar *resa dei conti* (settling of accounts). Plaques were changed and new ones put up. Rival days of memory and remembrance were instituted.

The reaction to this shift was twofold. Some simply restated the *Resistenza vulgata*. Others took the opportunity to open up new lines of inquiry—into Allied bombings, total war, civilian memories of Nazi massacres, conflicts within the Resistance, and injustices perpetuated by "partisan justice." A richer, more human and less heroic version of the resistance emerged, which extended the idea of civil resistance itself to large zones of the South. There was a flourishing of work into, and interest in, the holocaust in Italy. A historiographical revolution took place, which mirrored, and affected, forms of public and private memory. Politicians were slow to adapt to these changes.

Legitimation Crises
Institutions cannot govern, survive, or function properly without significant degrees of legitimacy. A political system "requires an input of mass loyalty that is as diffuse as possible." [39] Citizens must have certain levels of faith in the right of the state to govern, collect taxes, enforce law and order, fight wars and educate their children in order for these institutions to work. It could

be argued that the Italian state has been in the throes of a semipermanent legitimation crisis ever since its inception. The basic "rules of the game" have never been accepted by many Italians in terms of a "rational" management of the state and the political system. They have, instead, been partly replaced by other, unwritten "rules" that have institutionalized patronage, clientelism, and informal modes of behavior and exchange.

In short, "mass loyalty" has never been achieved. The evidence for such a state of affairs is easy to obtain. Legitimation crises are at their most evident when citizens refuse to vote, pay taxes, fight "for their country," or obey basic laws or when the state resorts to violence to regulate "normal" economic or social conflicts. But this crisis can also be seen at everyday levels in the normal set of relationships between the citizens and the state and in attitudes among Italians toward the state. The crisis has always been there, but its intensity has risen and fallen, in various ways, through time.

This ongoing crisis has had profound implications for the ways in which events have been remembered and commemorated. The Italian state has been unable to create a consensus over the past, and this has been reflected in forms of public memory. Fascism imposed its own particular version of the past through force, and through the exclusion of other possible memories. Even in democratic Italy, certain memories were taboo (on both the right and the left). This is not to say that these memories were not carried forward in other ways (for example in local opposition to the centralized state). They were, and this is precisely where the concept of divided memory becomes useful as a key for understanding these issues and conflicts.

Monument Wars
Conflicts over the past, and how to remember that past, exploded at various times into full-scale monument wars. Memorials were attacked, replaced, and defaced as part of a political strategy. This was seen with contrasting war monuments and plaques after 1918. A further "monument war" took place after July 25, 1943, with fascist symbols and statues being torn down all over Italy. Finally, another battle over memory marked the end of the 1960s, with the renewal of clashes between neofascists and the left, and a concerted series of attacks on resistance symbols. The rebuilding of previously destroyed monuments was often the first real act of what was seen as a new beginning, and a new relationship with the past.

Alongside these full-scale memory wars, there were a series of lesser (but intense) conflicts over local monuments—in Trieste in 1915 after war was declared by Italy, in Bolzano and Alto Adige in the 1920s and 1930s and then again in the 1960s. In these border towns and regions, the role of ethnic policies and denationalization played a strong part in the construction of monuments, which were often designed to divide local communities.

But no city or region was free of tensions over memory and commemoration, and the content of these conflicts depended on local factors linked to politics, the ways in which events were played out over time, and the power of those able to decide to impose their own versions of the past.[40]

People expected forms of memory to be constructed for them. They demanded recognition for themselves, or relatives, or fellow countrymen, in terms of commemorative objects and events. Memory expectations were often very high, and this created concerns about a "lack of memory." This rhetorical form often refers to issues that are not about memory at all. Memory has often been seen as part of personal, regional, municipal, political, and ethnic identity. In the era of nationalism, the possibility of being remembered after dying "for your country" took on major importance. Memory developed into a lay patriotic version of the Christian afterlife. People expected recognition, solemnity and above all unity over this "sacrifice." And when these expectations failed to materialize, anger and frustration were quick to take over.

Definitions of people's role in war—and in peacetime—were crucial in terms of legal recognition and official commemoration. What had you done in the war? Had you been a "soldier," a "combatant," a "partisan," a "terrorist," or some combination of these categories? Those soldiers who fought in the Italian army before September 1943 were usually given official recognition but those who sided with Mussolini after September 1943 were not seen as official soldiers. This definition was contested by rightwing and neofascist representatives in the postwar period. With a divided state, and a loss of sovereignty, the whole question of who was fighting and for what was a gray area that left space for divisions and arguments over memory and commemoration. On the edges of Italy, where many fought for the "wrong" side, these issues were particularly divisive.

Eliminating the Past, Preserving the Past

New regimes tried to eliminate traces of uncomfortable pasts, but they were never entirely successful in doing so. Fascism's *monumentmania* was difficult to wipe clean, and remnants of the regime remain all over Italy. Sometimes, the extent of removal of the traces of fascism was to do with chance, but local factors were usually crucial. A fascist mural or a quote from Mussolini could be wiped out by a new lick of paint, or be restored thanks to a council vote. On the road toward the Val Rendena in Trentino, there is a beautifully restored mural with an incongruous message: *Noi sogniamo l'Italia Romana* (We are dreaming of a Roman Italy). The mural on the school in the nearby town of Pinzolo, however, was removed sometime in the 1970s. Many fascist monuments, signs, and traces survived in Rome. The same is true of Bolzano and Trieste. In Bolzano a huge fascist *bassorelievo* was completed after the war, in postfascist Italy. In part, this reflects the ambiguous (and ubiquitous) nature of fascist architecture, with its presence in most Italian cities, as well as with entire cities constructed in "fascist style." Fascist symbols had different meanings in different parts of Italy, and these meanings changed over time. No law was passed about the removal of fascist symbols, something that was not carried out in a systematic way. In some cities, the removal of these symbols was an expressly political act, as in Bologna where a statue of Mussolini was melted down and transformed into a resistance monument.

Wartime shifts in alliances affected the status of public memory. In Gorizia, for example, a World War I monument was blown up by Germans and Slovenians in 1944. The German army—officially still an ally of Mussolini—felt free to damage or destroy a number of national Italian monuments after 1943, a fate that befell part of the infamous "Victory Monument" in Bolzano, or a memorial dedicated to Italian war hero Enrico Toti on the Carso that was smashed up in 1944. In World War II, Italy's Nazi allies were often uncomfortable with the public memorials they encountered in the peninsula, especially if they harked back to previous conflicts. This hostility increased after Italy changed sides in the war in 1943.

Border disputes created geographies of divided memory that spoke to each other across the frontier. When the territory of Gorizia was cut in half by the 1947 peace agreements, the city of Gorizia remained on the Italian side of the frontier, while the countryside and province were assigned to Yugoslavia. Nova Goricia was built ex-novo just over the frontier, and a mural in the town hall, in socialist realist style, told a tale of national liberation and the horrors of fascism. On the other side of the border, different kinds of memories were preserved and transformed into monuments and other forms of public memory. Italian Gorizia built its memories around World War I, Nova Goricia around World War II. Bolzano's borders were internal, dividing the German-speaking and Italian populations. Fascism had constructed a "new city," and the clash between these "two cities" was symbolized by the hated (or loved) "monument to victory." In these areas the whole question of fascist symbolism, architecture, and memory was extremely contested, and it continues to be so up to this day.

Traces of Conflict and Monument Wars

How can we analyze these conflicts? In many cases, memory wars had an impact in the media (or the debates themselves were played out in the press). Often, this was the intention of the perpetrators. Attacks on monuments left physical traces or absences—a smashed plaque, graffiti, the space where a stolen lamp once hung. Those interested in the defense of the original monuments usually restored the damage. On occasion, this ritual was repeated time and again. The monument war of 1919 to 1927 only left traces in terms of documents, archives, newspapers and in private memories. No single antiwar monument from that period survived. Things became more complicated—as ever—on the edges of Italy. During the bomb campaigns carried out by separatists in Alto Adige in the early 1960s, numerous monuments—often linked to fascism—were destroyed. This left the Italian state with something of a dilemma. Should fascist monuments be rebuilt, with public money, by a democratic government? A discussion took place (which was interesting in itself), but in the end, most monuments were not reconstructed.

Memory could and often did play a part in violence. Recent memories of fascism were the context for the *foibe*-killings and deportations in the northeast in 1943 and 1945, as they were for the *resa dei conti* in the rest of Italy. A desire for revenge lay behind many terrorist acts in the 1960s and 1970s. Anniversaries and commemorations were often—as we shall see—an occasion for further violence and bloodshed, creating further events to be commemorated and remembered.

Myths, History, Memory, Lies, Counter-Memories

Any more than a superficial understanding of Italian culture and politics since Unification requires an understanding of the myths that have served as the lens through which recent Italian history has been seen and interpreted.

—David Kertzer, "History as It Really Wasn't"

Myths play a large part in history. Mythical creations of the past and mythologizing about what happened, and why, are some of the key ways in which we understand historical processes. I see myths in this book as "narratives that have a sacred character, that link past to present to future . . . a tissue of interlinked beliefs that are beyond direct empirical refutation, that express basic values, that emotionally and cognitively unite people who adhere to them. Through such beliefs people interpret both past and present events, and create their own sense of identity."[41]

Narratives of this kind can be created from above, or below—and their success depends on diffusion through numerous channels—the media, historical scholarship, cinema, literature, art, and music. Myths are powerful ways of mobilizing public opinion and consensus. Italian fascism was extremely successful in creating a myth that linked itself to victory in World War I and to the fate of the nation and the state. Much scholarship in recent times has shown how myths and invented traditions are at the bases of many local and national identities. Myths are believed—they are part of and fit in with people's subjective experience.

Myths are almost always linked to real events, but they also extrapolate from those events and modify their meaning. With time, in some cases, the myth substitutes reality, becoming the guiding force around which a certain story is told and transmitted. In these cases, the myth has become history—it has taken on a life of its own, ready to be reproduced in various forms of literary and visual media.

"Myth is a fundamental component of human thought."[42] It is not enough—and it is not even particularly useful—for historians simply to dismiss or unravel myths—to prove them wrong. Such an act tells us very little about the way myths influence and create history and memory, and act as ways of interpreting the past. It is through myth that the past is remade and understood—and claimed. But myths also remove other windows on the past—leading to absences, silences, and gaps. We can learn much about history by studying myths—about a nation's image of itself, for example. Myths provide a powerful set of indications concerning Italian national and political identity, and the stereotypes that have marked that identity.

In a seminal article written in 1988, Tim Mason unpacked the ways in which the strikes of March 1943 in Turin have since been interpreted and understood largely through mythical accounts. He wrote in that article that he would analyze the different accounts of the strike, before "finally arriving at what we shall perhaps never know: what really happened."[43] In many ways, in this book, I am least of all interested in "what actually happened." Myths are not side issues or distractions, but central themes for historians to explore. As Mason argued with relation to March 1943, "The accepted versions, which expunge the disputes, the doubts, the false starts and the manipulations that accompanied the struggle, may well weaken the inspirational effect of the Resistance that can still be stirred today; but a painstaking study, such as a medievalist might attempt, can restore these events to their true grandeur."[44]

Recognizing plural and divided memories in this way is the opposite of accepting a bland conservative revisionism. In the revisionist project, the dead are all the same and the intended goal is national reconciliation. Bringing out divided memories allows for a deeper understanding of history. The dead—and the living—are never all the same. That is one of the starkest messages provided by the study of divided memories.

Judging Divided Memory

Is divided memory a problem? Different versions of "what happened" and how to remember the past are often seen as healthy, as democratic, and as preserving the idea of a historical dialectic. Sergio Luzzatto has written a "eulogy to divided memory,"[45] while Paggi has argued that memory should remain divided, "in the sense that discussions over the origins of events should remain open" but that they should cease to be "a form of division at a personal level."[46] Divided memories are also a crucial part of free speech. Often, the suppression of different or countermemories has been violent—a pretext to censorship and even to dictatorship.

Others see these divisions as a sign of failure, as a kind of original sin that prevented Italy from moving forward. A nation, for Nucci and Galli della Loggia, requires "a common history and . . . memory."[47] In recent years, leading politicians from both left and right have made constant calls for the creation of a shared set of memories. This is thus also a debate over whether memories should, or should not, remain divided. It has also been argued that reconciliation can be achieved only through the acknowledgement of division.

Other Countries: Pacts of Silences and Syndromes

Every country has its own history of divided memories. Spain's "pact of silence" (pacto de olvido) took hold during and after the transition to democracy in the late 1970s. This unwritten pact meant that the civil war was not discussed or raised as a political issue during the 1980s and 1990s. The pact started to unravel in recent years, as a spontaneous movement (made up of the "grandchild" generation as well as those with direct memory of the conflict) began to (literally) unearth the past. Mass graves from the civil war were dug up and calls were made for those executed during the war to be given memorials and proper burials.[48] This culminated in the historical memory law of 2007 (passed by Zapatero's socialist government) that led to the final removal of most fascist monuments and official support for the digging up of mass graves. The end of the pact of silence caused some conflict and disquiet and to some extent reopened old wounds.

Did Italy have its own "pact of silence" after 1945? Yes, and no. Talk of a "civil war" when discussing World War II was taboo for many years, apart from among sectors on the neofascist right (who were themselves "untouchable" politically) and some antifascists and novelists. A pact of silence that covered every political shade and color also related to the activities of the Italian army between 1940 and 1943. Left and right conspired to cover-up or play down war crimes committed by the Italians in Greece,

Albania, and Yugoslavia. There was no Italian Nuremberg. Not one Italian was extradited for crimes committed in that period. Thus, all sides collaborated in reinforcing the powerful myth of the "good Italian," a myth that only began to come under serious criticism some sixty years after the end of the war. A political decision had been made to close all legal procedures against Nazi war criminals for their activities in Italy, with a few exceptions. The files were closed, and only reopened in the 1990s. Yet, as in Spain, these various pacts of silence did not resolve questions regarding divided memories and feelings of injustice. On the contrary, these problems were left to fester, leading to long-term trauma and open wounds among many different types of victim. History also suffered, as a mutilated historiography emerged. A final pact of silence was in relation to the activities of the Allied armies as they liberated Italy—such as the bombings and the mass rapes of Italian women. These uncomfortable episodes were largely omitted from official accounts of the war, while remaining important to local and private narratives of the conflict.

In France, the "Vichy syndrome" has led to incessant debate over the events of World War II and how to remember them.[49] After liberation in 1945, the issue of Vichy became a permanent and running sore, emerging time and again to haunt the new French republic. The attempts to deal with Vichy led to the creation of a series of myths—most notably through De Gaulle—of national resistance and struggle. These myths unravelled at various moments in French postwar history, as the "Vichy syndrome" took hold. Again, as with other nations, the conflicts were exacerbated toward the end of the cold war, with a series of trials of Nazis and collaborators, many of whom had been living (and working) quite comfortably in France for the whole postwar period.

Has Italy suffered from its own "Vichy syndrome," which we might call the "Salò syndrome"? There is no doubt that Salò as a mark of shame (or as political smear) has emerged time and again in postwar Italy. As in France, the purging process in Italy was short-lived and superficial. State and public institutions experienced considerable levels of continuity. Many officials from the fascist period were still around in postwar Italy and still in their posts: generals, judges, police chiefs, bureaucrats. But in Italy, it has not been Salò as such that has created a syndrome, but the whole period of fascism (the *ventennio*). Salò was sufficiently short-lived, understudied, and geographically limited for its long-term effects to be relatively constrained. Fascism, on the other hand, had touched the lives of many (if not all). Time and again, in the postwar period, documents turned up that showed intellectuals (in particular) caught in some sort of compromise with the regime. These documents would be used to smear these figures. Many people had an interest in not digging too deeply into the fascist past.

Italian elites supported a version of the past that merged with the few certainties of postwar Italy.[50] The Nazis had been the bad guys, aided by some Italian fascists. Italy had united to drive the invader out of the country. There had been passive and active resistance across the country. The Allies had only dropped bombs when they had to. Little comment was made on the conduct of the war before September 1943, apart from a depiction of the Italian soldier in the role of victim (as in the retreat from Russia).

This version of the past worked well. It exonerated Italy from guilt for the great crimes of Nazism—above all the Shoah. It drew a veil over any possible complicity of communists in the crimes of the USSR (although this "complicity" was often used against the communist left during the cold war). Moreover, the vast majority of Italians who had not taken part in the resistance were able to identify with this past. In this way, many other experiences and histories were absent, covered up, and glossed over. Those left out carried forward alternative versions of history, stories that were (in the end) "discovered" by historians.

Elsewhere, Ireland's memories have long been divided on religious and political lines.[51] In Greece, civil war and occupation led to silence and memory disconnections.[52] Germany was divided in two by the Cold war, and this had a lasting effect on memory.[53] Eastern bloc countries had extreme difficulty in relating to their past, both before and after 1989.[54] Yugoslavia's civil wars and her break-up in the 1990s was in part thanks to deeply divided narratives about the past, which imposed themselves in the various new countries after the war.[55] Europe as a whole also "suffered" from clashes over visions of the past.[56] Italy's divided memories were not unique and comparisons with the experiences of other countries will be drawn in this book. As we have seen, Italy had her own "pacts of silence" and "memory syndromes," and the cold war was a crucial influence on narratives about the past.

* * *

As Carlo Levi once wrote, "Italy is a great, mythological artichoke, a green and purple flower, where every leaf hides another, every layer covers another, which is jealously hidden. Who is able to pull off the external leaves will discover unthinkable things, in a difficult journey through space and across time."[57] This book will be a journey through Italy's divided memories, an attempt to unpeel some of these skins of memory. My journey begins and ends with two exemplary stories, from two places where divided memory has become public memory. These two stories have each ended up (but they have not by any means "ended") with two plaques, side-by-side, bearing different versions of the same event. The telling of these stories will take us to the center and north of the peninsula, to San Miniato in Tuscany and then to Milan (at the end of this book).

In both these stories, we will see ways in which recently, Italy has started to institutionalize divisions over memory. The state (seen in a wide sense as public authorities of various kinds) has decided to acknowledge division, even to the point of allowing different versions of events to become part of public memory. Multiple or divided memories have become the only way to tell the story. Divided memories have come out into the open as history—leading to forms of memorialization that allow winners and losers to tell their own stories of the past. This conclusion is also part of (and thanks to) a historiographical shift that has moved from the macro to the micro, from big explanations to oral history, from a politically inspired championing of one side of the story to an understanding of the contradictions of memory.

One City, Two Plaques: San Miniato, Tuscany (1944–2008)

Between 1943 and 1945, more than 10,000 Italians were victims of massacres carried out by the Germany army. Of these, nearly half (over 4,400) were killed in Tuscany. The hill town of San Miniato runs along a crest dominating the plain above Empoli and Pisa in the Tuscan plain that stretches to the sea. In July 1944, the German army was withdrawing upward and across Italy, after months of heavy fighting. San Miniato was packed with refugees looking to escape from the bombing and hostilities in Livorno and Pisa. All political and state authority in the town had vanished, leaving just the bishop—Ugo Giubbi—and the Germans.

On July 22, 1944, the occupying and retreating German army ordered the local population to gather in the small, main square in front of the cathedral. In other circumstances, such an order had been the prelude to the massacre of civilians. Bishop Giubbi, it seems, suggested that the people move into the church, as the city was being shelled by the advancing U.S. army. As the Germans prepared to leave, they mined a number of houses and the ancient tower above the city so as to impede the Allied forces.

It was the morning of July 22, and the cathedral was packed with something between 700 and 1,000 people (many of them older men and women and children). Giubbi blessed the congregation before leaving to preside at Mass in another church. German soldiers guarded the cathedral doors. As Giubbi was on his way back, at around 10 a.m., an explosion inside the church caused chaos and panic. At least fifty-five people died and many more were injured. Giubbi was unhurt. In the Taviani brothers' film *The Night of San Lorenzo* (1982) "the massacre of San Miniato" is depicted in a scene near the middle of the film. With the Duomo full of terrified civilians, smoke emerges from the building, before people begin to run for their lives. A young woman escapes from the church and is faced with the bishop, with whom she exchanges an accusing glance.

Almost immediately in the wake of these events, differing versions of what had happened in the church began to emerge. The dominant version—that of most of the survivors, the Allied army and many others—blamed the Germans for the massacre. Many thought that a German time bomb had been placed in the church, others that a Nazi shell had hit the building. However, evidence also pointed to another possible explanation. The U.S. army had been bombing the town, and the remains of a U.S. mortar were found inside the church.

A series of inquiries were set up to decide the truth—the most important being a local government commission that reported in 1945. After listening to witnesses, the commission presented its findings to a Florentine judge (Carlo Giannattasio) for a final decision. The judge concluded against the time bomb hypothesis and concluded that "the cathedral had been hit by two shells—one German and one American—but the killing was only caused by the German device." The massacre had been "premeditated." Giannattasio had created a story to fit the crime—a story that merged well with local narratives and memories. This remained the official truth in the town for the next sixty years. The "massacre" of innocent civilians, inside a church, with the connivance of the clergy, was the shocking story that divided San Miniato for six decades, and continues to do so.

Bishop Giubbi's role was crucial to the whole story. He was accused by many of actively collaborating in the massacre. In short, he became a local scapegoat. Anthropologists and historians have explained these narratives through the search for an "internal enemy" within the community as part of a way of understanding tragic events. The German army, after all, was no longer around. It had no human face. Giubbi was the leading religious figure in San Miniato—highly visible and an easy target. In other places, the partisans often became the scapegoats, especially where massacres were interpreted as reprisals after partisan actions, as at Civitella and in Rome (with the Fosse Ardeatine).

Despite the fact that the council enquiry of 1944 to 1945 cleared Giubbi of any responsibility and had praised his actions before, during, and after the massacre, doubts remained in the town. The bishop was threatened physically by relatives of the victims and he died in 1946 unable to clear his name. A popular story relates that during his funeral in 1946 a fire was lit on the hill above the town in celebration. Giubbi had been a strong sympathizer with fascism and had no time for the partisans—whom he called criminals. The divisions in the town were also political.

In 1954 a plaque was placed on the wall of the town hall—a Palazzo in the center of San Miniato—to commemorate the tenth anniversary of the deaths of 1944. The importance of this event can be seen by who unveiled the plaque: Ferruccio Parri, one of the leaders of the Resistance and Prime Minister of Italy in 1945. It was the first and most important act of public and official memory regarding the massacre. It read, and still reads, as follows:

THROUGH THE CENTURIES THIS PLAQUE WILL COMMEMORATE
THE COLD-BLOODED KILLING OF 60 PEOPLE CARRIED OUT BY
THE GERMANS ON 22 JULY 1944
THE UNARMED, AGED, INNOCENT VICTIMS WERE PERFIDIOUSLY
ENCOURAGED TO TAKE REFUGE IN THE CATHEDRAL SO
THAT THE EVIL DEED COULD BE CARRIED OUT FASTER AND
MORE HAUGHTILY
IT WAS NOT ANY NECESSITY IMPOSED BY WAR THAT DROVE
THE MURDERERS TO LAUNCH A LETHAL SHELL INTO THE CATHEDRAL,
BUT PURE FEROCITY
AS BEFITTED AN ARMY THAT WAS DENIED VICTORY BECAUSE
IT WAS THE ENEMY OF ALL LIBERTY
ITALIANS WHO READ THIS, FORGIVE BUT DO NOT FORGET!
REMEMBER THAT ONLY THROUGH PEACE AND WORK IS CIVILIZATION
ETERNAL

THE COUNCIL ON THE 10TH ANNIVERSARY

This plaque replicated one version of the massacre (that was also known as a "killing") but the debate over the facts and the battle over memory became part of an intense political struggle in cold war Italy. When the Taviani brothers made a documentary (their first film) about the massacre in 1953, they were not allowed to film inside the cathedral.

It was the plaque and the 1954 anniversary that encouraged a local priest, Don Enrico Giannoni, to produce his own detailed counterreport arguing that the killings had been caused by a U.S. bomb. The priest in question refused to bless the plaque. Doubts and alternative versions had been around ever since the massacre itself. In the early period after the war, Petrizzo argues that there wasn't divided memory, but a deep–rooted silence about the debate itself.[58] There were moments of conflict, such as 1954, when the two versions came out into the open, but also long periods of a kind of stand-off. The U.S. bomb story had always been there, but had never won over the majority of the town. The postwar resistance consensus forced these doubts underground until a new commission of inquiry was set up in 2002.

Divided memories about the events of 1944 were carried forward and expressed in private narratives, public memorials, and debates. These divisions were layered with politics, class, ideology, and psychology. The Taviani brothers (who are from San Miniato) brought out their film out in 1982, reopening debates about the massacre. The film was ambiguous over the events of 1944, but it certainly pointed the finger at the Germans. Paolo Taviani, the brother's father, had been on the original commission.

Other historians began to unearth new documents that pointed toward the U.S. "version." Meanwhile Battini and Pezzino set aside more than thirty pages to the controversy in their *Guerra ai civili* (1995) and concluded that the balance of evidence (and of probability) pointed toward German responsibility (in the form of a time bomb or mine).[59] In 2000, a new book by Paoletti laid out documentation that pointed back to the Allies, and claimed there had been a cover-up.[60] Paoletti dedicated much space to an attack on Pezzino's book. Other publications also backed the U.S.-bomb version of events, and this was supported by a strong local press campaign. Paoletti's book had a deep effect on local narratives relating to the massacre, and even on memories.[61] In the meantime, other plaques and monuments had appeared that reflected divided memories, or were more conciliatory and "neutral." Through the 1980s and 1990s, San Miniato created a memoryscape that—in the small town center—reflected different versions about the past, and specifically about the 1944 killings.

Pressure came on the local council to look into the case again. They decided to act, calling on a group of local academics to reexamine the old evidence, as well as the new evidence that had emerged over the years. Paggi and Contini—two of the first historians to use the term "divided memory"—were on the commission. Instead of a dreary report, they produced a fascinating book, which included studies of the massacre, of the commemorations over the years and new interviews with witnesses and survivors.[62] In terms of the facts, the conclusions of the commission were clear. The bomb, according to the commission, had been American. The massacre had thus not been a "cold" act of the Nazi army, but pure chance, an unfortunate by-product of war.[63] Almost immediately this conclusion had an effect on the way the massacre was described. Words changed. From a massacre (*strage*) the event became a more neutral *eccidio* (killing). The title of the commission report had already made this change.

The outcome of the report had a number of other consequences. First, it reclassified the massacre. Should San Miniato still be included in the list of Nazi massacres, with all that entailed (in terms of memory, commemoration, history, and meaning)? If San Miniato had been a mistake, a stray bomb, friendly fire, then it was similar to thousands of other cases of "collateral damage" across Italy at that time, and didn't deserve the exalted status of a Nazi massacre (and one of the best-known Nazi massacres at that). Historical lists thus needed to be changed, but it was also true that commemorations needed to be altered, as did the attribution of responsibility (or the very idea of what the word "responsibility" meant). At about the same time as the historian's commission, a new inquiry was also set up into Bishop Giubbi's activities in 1944, which again cleared his name in terms of responsibility for the massacre.[64]

According to the commission, the most likely account of what happened is this: an American missile, a delayed explosive device, came through the rose window on the south of the church, hit the bas-relief, and bounced up over the crowded pews in the main part of the church where it exploded right above the waiting refugees. Other historians remain convinced that the Germans were directly responsible, or that doubts remained over the cause of the deaths in the church. What we are interested in here, however, are the ways in which these developments affected the memories of the events of 1944.

As experts on divided memory, the historians on the commission came to an original conclusion. They argued that the "memory" of the survivors and others who had believed in direct Nazi responsibility needed to be respected. In short, they called for an acceptance of the divided memories emerging from the San Miniato tragedy, and tried to avoid any political exploitation of their findings.[65] The commission rejected the idea of a constructed lie or cover-up after 1944, calling the anti-German version of memory "spontaneous." This collective narrative blended well with local and national narratives about the war and its aftermath. San Miniato had constructed its antifascist identity around the massacre, which linked in with the transition from fascism to democracy.

Contini looked at the witness accounts from the 1940s and also carried out his own series of new interviews. After sixty years there was much confusion—layers of interpretation had become part of the story. Contini talked of a *Rashomon* effect—a reference to Kurosawa's 1954 film where different versions are given of the same event. He argued that these interviews were not "useable" in terms of the commission's conclusions concerning the origins of the bomb that caused the massacre, but that they were essential in understanding the power and birth of the "German" version of events. A "German bomb" had been a way of explaining a confusing and shocking event.[66] For the revisionists or "fact-historians," on the other hand, these issues are not even taken into consideration. The author of a key volume on the San Miniato massacre, for example, ignores the whole question of divided memories. For Paoletti, "History is truth and truth is history."[67] In this way, historical debate was reduced to a "document war." But surely San Miniato proved quite the opposite—that memory and history were linked at every stage of the debate, and it was impossible to separate them?

Debate shifted toward the idea of German responsibility in a wider sense. The population had, after all, been forced to gather together in an exposed part of the town at a time when San Miniato was under fire. Moreover, the Germans (and Italian fascists) were responsible for the war itself. There are others who still argue that a massacre had been planned. Other killings had taken place in cathedral squares. Round-ups often took place before such massacres. Politics played a part in these divisions. The "revisionist" campaign was often supported by those on the right, while many on the left tended to back the Nazi massacre version of events. Nonetheless, these divisions over memory were not purely political, but were also linked to history, culture, and the work of historians.

Beyond the 1954 plaque, the memorials installed in the town in the 1980s and 1990s reflected the ambiguities over the facts, and the different positions among various residents. Divided memory had already become public memory in the town, well before the latest commission began its work. Three separate but linked monuments or plaques were put up in or around the Duomo after the 1980s and 1990s. None of them takes a clear line on the responsibility for the deaths in 1944, unlike the plaque on the town hall nearby. The 1984 monument is abstract and simple. It takes no position at all. Its inscription gives no information about the killings, apart from its date: *San Miniato 1944–1984*. 1994's monument is similar, although it makes more explicit statements about the massacre. Both of the monuments in the piazza were examples of the stand-off in the town, a kind of pact that acknowledged the conflict over the past but also created a kind of silence.

The 1994 plaque inside the cathedral ignores the question of who caused these deaths, and concentrates on the dead as "innocent victims of war." It might be possible to read this plaque as an explicit challenge to the 1954 plaque (that doesn't carry names). Finally, the small plaque at the base of the 1994 monument lies somewhere in the middle of the debate, with its reference to victims as "killed by the barbarity of war." San Miniato's complicated and ever-growing memoryscapes reflected local unease about what had happened in 1944, and why.

The council took the 2002 commission's report at its word, and decided to dedicate a second, "correcting" plaque to the events of 1944. The delicate issue of the wording of the new plaque was handed over to the ex-president of Italy, Oscar Luigi Scalfaro. In February 2007, he came up with this version:

MORE THAN 60 YEARS HAVE PASSED SINCE THE TERRIFYING
MASSACRE OF 22 JULY 1944
WHICH WAS ATTRIBUTED TO THE GERMANS.
HISTORICAL RESEARCH HAS NOW SHOWN THAT THE ALLIED
FORCES WERE RESPONSIBLE FOR THOSE DEATHS
THE TRUTH DEMANDS RESPECT AND MUST ALWAYS BE DECLARED
IT IS ALSO TRUE THAT THE GERMANS WERE RESPONSIBLE FOR
THE WAR, FOR SHAMEFUL AND UNJUST REPRISALS AND THAT IN THIS
AREA, WITH THE COMPLICITY OF ITALIAN FASCISTS, THEY SOWED
DEATH, DESTRUCTION AND TRAGEDY
THIS IS WHAT HAPPENS IN WAR
FOR THIS REASON THE ITALIAN CONSTITUTION PROCLAIMS IN
ARTICLE 11: 'ITALY REPUDIATES WAR'

THE TOWN COUNCIL ON THE 64th ANNIVERSARY

In this new plaque the responsibility is now shared, between "war" in general, the Germans, the Italian fascists and the "Allied forces." No mention is made of the victims in a specific sense.

One further—crucial—question remained. What was to be done with the old plaque? The council stated that the second plaque would be put up on the walls of the Town Hall, while the first one would be left in place. The two plaques directly contradicted each other but were also symbiotic: they talked to each other. As the commission report had argued, the memories of the "German version" of events, still strong in the town, needed to be respected. By adding the second plaque, the council had also fixed the first in place. The second text made no sense on its own (see Figure 1.1).

But this decision was attacked from a number of sides. Pezzino called it "hypocritical." If the bomb was American, the old plaque was simply wrong, a "historical lie." More predictably, the right were extremely critical of the 1954 plaque. The mayor of San Miniato, Angelo Frosini, called the old plaque "an historical document" and reminded people that it was protected by law. Others claimed that the 1954 plaque had been an expression of "what was felt" in the town after the war. Some said that the truth lay in the cemetery, in the fragments that had penetrated the bodies of the victims. Perhaps only with a macabre reexhumation could the story finally be laid to rest.

The story of the "two plaques" of San Miniato—side-by-side, and contradictory (although with some common ground) forms one of the frameworks for this book. Two plaques—that relate to the same "fact"—but with contrasting versions and interpretations of those facts. San Miniato provides us with a perfect example of divided memory, of the way in which in Italy it has been difficult to reach a consensus about what happened,

SONO PASSATI PIU' DI 60 ANNI
DALLO SPAVENTOSO ECCIDIO DEL 22 LUGLIO 1944
ATTRIBUITO   AI   TEDESCHI.
LA RICERCA STORICA HA ACCERTATO INVECE
CHE LA RESPONSABILITA' DI QUELL'ECCIDIO E' DELLE FORZE ALLEATE.
LA VERITA' DEVE ESSERE RISPETTATA E DICHIARATA SEMPRE.
E' ANCHE VERITA' CHE I TEDESCHI
RESPONSABILI DELLA GUERRA E DELLE IGNOBILI E INIQUE RAPPRESAGLIE,
CON LA COMPLICITA' DEI REPUBBLICHINI,
PROPRIO IN QUESTA TERRA
AVEVANO SEMINATO DISTRUZIONI. TRAGEDIE E MORTE.
E' LA GUERRA.
PROPRIO PER QUESTO LA COSTITUZIONE ITALIANA
PROCLAMA ALL'ART. 11
L'ITALIA RIPUDIA LA GUERRA

IL COMUNE NEL LXIV ANNIVERSARIO

Figure 1.1   San Miniato, Tuscany, 2008: New plaque dedicated to the 1944 killings.

about the facts. The idea that it was a U.S. bomb in 1944 that killed fifty-six people does not cancel out the memories and the identities of those who believed—or who continue to believe—in another version of those events. Divided memory in San Miniato has become public memory—official—etched in marble. Only through an analysis of these divisions can we understand the postwar history of San Miniato. As one local councillor said, "In any case there can never be only one truth."

2

World War I

Monument Wars, Unknown Soldiers, and Open-air Cemeteries

Italy between the wars became a huge backdrop for a large-scale and collective recital.

—Mario Isnenghi, *L'Italia del Fascio*

Forced to leave the fields and the factories
to fight in a four-year long fratricidal war
the best of Cardanese's youth
died
on the cursed battlefields of
Trentino, the Carso and the Piave
May 1915 *November 1918*
Plaque, Cardano al Campo (Varese)[1]

Two stories will be used in this chapter to illustrate the ways in which memories of World War I were elaborated, made public, or silenced in Italy. First, we will look at the "monument war" that raged in Italy (and in particular in the north and center of the country) roughly between 1915 and 1927. The second story will recount the transformation of a battlefield on the Carso into two very different types of monument.

This chapter has no claim to be a definitive or comprehensive history of the memory of World War I in Italy. It will attempt—through microhistories of places and stories—to draw out some of the ways in which divisions over the past and the present became translated into public memory, as well as looking at the transformations of this public memory over time and in relation to space over a period of some ninety years or so.[2]

Studying Monuments, Studying Memory

How should we study war monuments and commemorative practices? They are texts, works of art, but also places whose gestation, birth, and management were usually the outcome of complicated negotiations between the state and local elites, as well as the interplay between politics, ideology, and the needs of the veterans. As Winter has written, "War memorials are collective symbols. They speak to and for communities of men and women."[3]

Place and geography were also important. Once constructed, memorials were often altered, added to and—especially during the "monument war" that exploded after 1919—attacked and destroyed. Monuments were sites of commemoration, collective and individual rituals, political debate, speeches, and campaigns. What was left out was as important as what was there. For Mondini, monuments are "extraordinary examples of how the processes of remembrance . . . are a chorus of voices, and not a unambiguous monolith."[4] These sites, monuments and ceremonies were palimpsests, with layers of memory being added (or taken away) over time. They were also—as many have pointed out—as much about forgetting as about memory.

Winter has recently introduced the idea of "modes of collective remembrance" that he describes as "activities shared by collectives, groups of people in the public domain."[5] The term "remembrance" (instead of the catch-all word "memory") helps us concentrate on the question of agency—"who remembers, when, where, and how?" Remembrance links history and memory, which in any case "overlap in too many ways to be considered as pure categories."[6] In this chapter, remembrance practices will be the main focus of the analysis. As Dogliani has argued, for most places in Italy *the* monument was that dedicated to World War I, and this centrality continued throughout the twentieth century.

Story 1: The Monument War, 1915–1927

We will massacre / those who had us massacred

—Hymn of the *Lega proletaria mutilati invalidi reduci orfani
e vedove di guerra* (Proletarian League)

Close to six million Italians were called up to the army between 1915 and 1918, to fight a ferocious series of battles over a relatively small area of land. Nearly 600,000 men were never to come home, and 450,000 suffered serious injuries. The war was a powerful unifying force for the new Italy, but it was also a "factor of division."[7] The "great war" developed—almost immediately, while it was still being fought—into a vicious source of arguments and debates over memory. For the socialist and anarchist left, and also for many Catholics, the war had been a "useless slaughter," as Pope Benedict XV called it in 1917. For the nationalists, many of whom were to become fascists, the conflict had been heroic and glorious. These two visions of the past, and of the world, clashed in every corner of the country. World War I thus divided Italians in profound and long-lasting ways. Hundreds of thousands rebelled, in many different ways; 150,000 soldiers deserted. Between May 1915 and September 1919 more than a million military tribunals were held for infractions of military law.[8] Others, however, viewed the conflict as the opposite of disaster, as an opportunity to reinvent Italy's image in the world and restore (or create) nationalist aspirations and identities. These deep fissures ran right through society.

Caporetto

The breaching of Italy's lines on October 24, 1917, at the town of Caporetto was a traumatic event for both sides of these aforementioned divisions. Italy was invaded for the first time since unification, and the threat of overall defeat seemed very real, as foreign troops occupied much of the Friuli-Venezia region. Hundreds of thousands of troops were captured and whole villages razed to the ground. Refugees flooded out of the occupied zones and fled from cities close to the new front line, from Treviso to Venice. The image of defeat was an apocalyptic one, a vision of total collapse.

Military elites and nationalists blamed the left for this retreat and defeat. For them, Caporetto was a deliberate act of cowardice and sabotage. Soldiers and socialists had worked together to create defeat, they had planned a "military strike" as General Cadorna put it. They were not merely shirkers (imboscati) but defeatists (disfattisti).[9] Thus some Italians, it was claimed, had actively sought military disaster, just as Lenin had called for "revolutionary defeatism" in Russia during the war. This case of blame for a defeat—that a disaster had been organized for political reasons—was to return later in the century, with the bitter debates around September 8, 1943.[10]

Some took pride in this label, happy to call themselves disfattisti. They rejoiced at the news from Caporetto, or looked to recapture that defeat as an active revolt against authority. Malaparte called Caporetto a "revolution . . . a form of class struggle."[11] Others told of joy during the retreat, of widespread relief that the war appeared over, of cries of "Long live peace!" or "Long live Giolitti!" Yet the reality of Caporetto was that a poorly motivated, badly led, and ill-provisioned army had ceded to a rapid and well-planned attack.[12] The separation of Italians into those who had "run away" and those who had "stood and fought"—into the courageous and the *vigliacchi* (cowards)—was a constant one in the postwar period, when these wounds were ever-present and as the *Caporetto Inquest* raged on throughout 1919.

Mussolini and the fascists later presented themselves as the *antidisfattisti*, brave, nationalist, and willing to defend Italy at all costs. Mussolini's first words to the king on taking power in October 1922 were "I bring you the Italy of Vittorio Veneto." By definition, the Italies of "Caporetto" were excluded from this historic moment—these people had "never seen a trench in their lives."[13] They were the *antination*. The fascists used war metaphors well into the postwar period and painted themselves as those who, in Mussolini's words, "were not tired of fighting . . . and were ready to restart the war and to dig . . . trenches in Italian cities."[14] The fact that the Italian army was able to reorganize and win a victory (thanks in part to the internal collapse of the Austro-Hungarian armies) could not cancel the shame of Caporetto and its power to divide. For Procacci, "The use of Caporetto as an event linked to defeatism . . . created a climate of fanatical division between friends and enemies, which helped to prevent a reformist and democratic solution to the crisis created by the war after the conflict was over, and became the main element of propaganda behind the rise of fascism."[15]

Finally, Caporetto was also a place, which became part of Italy after World War I, and where a huge *sacrario* was constructed by the regime in the late 1930s and which then "disappeared" into Yugoslavia in 1947 (changing its name to Kobarid), before finally becoming Slovenian in the 1990s. The complicated history of this place (and the semidisappearance of its important name as a place, but not as a leitmotiv for disaster) seems to mirror the myriad and confused meanings of the concept of "Caporetto" itself.

This experience was not unique in Europe—much greater (and real) defeats were experienced by Russia, Germany, and Austro-Hungary. Yet the divisions in Italian society despite war victory led to intense conflicts that the liberal state was unable to heal in the postwar period. The horrors of war remained ever-present in many people's minds. There was a strong desire to punish those responsible for the conflict, and also to gain reward for the suffering and sacrifice of the war: hence the rapid growth of ex-combatant movements, of land occupations and of socialist organizations during the *biennio rosso* (the "two red years," 1919 and 1920). For many on the left, the war had been a criminal act of folly and violence. Symbols of the war became targets.

Many were vehemently opposed to the very idea of war memorials, or symbols linked to patriotism and the nation. The Italian flag was torn down and burnt. People in uniforms were attacked in the street, as during the so-called "hunt of the officers" in December 1919.[16] Prowar groups and individuals also utilized violence that had often been honed on the battlefield, as with the *arditi* (the shock troops). War militarized (and brutalized) a whole generation. Nationalists exhibited their wounds as trophies, as examples of their heroism and national pride. The greatest symbol of all was one-legged soldier Enrico Toti, who had apparently carried on fighting despite his disability and had even thrown his crutch at the enemy. Toti's funeral in San Lorenzo (Rome) in May 1922 was the scene of violent clashes between left and right.[17]

The Memory War: "Purified with the Hammer"

After 1918, the war continued to influence Italian society. Visible evidence of the conflict was everywhere. *Mutilati* paraded through the streets demanding their rights and displaying their injuries. The mark of the trenches was a powerful sign of belonging and of anger, from Mussolini's war injuries to the protests of blind soldiers. Socialist cartoons depicted war veterans as gruesome victims of oppression; fascists idealized victims and *mutilati* as heroes.[18] Fascism called for a *trenchocracy*, based on the suffering and "heroism" of the troops.

The memory war began early. Before the conflict itself was over, there was already a debate over the interpretation of the events of the war, and about how to remember them. Caporetto—as we have seen—produced contrasting theses almost as it was taking place. Hatred of the *imboscati* (those who "did not fight," the "shirkers")—a category of "internal enemies" that was applied very widely—pervaded large sections of public opinion, but was strongest within the army itself. "Sharks," those who had made great profits during the war, such as industrialists and shopkeepers, also developed into symbolic hate-figures. Certain figures and moments were perceived by many as betrayal—Claudio Treves's speech in parliament in 1917, the activities of the future deputy Francesco Misiano, the comments of the Pope, the pacifist propaganda of left-Catholics such as Guido Miglioli.

Italians generally agreed that the war was to be remembered, but disagreed over how (and why). For the socialists and many others, the war had been a massacre produced by capitalism. For this section of public opinion, the war was to be remembered as a disaster, as an international event, and as something that must never be repeated. Often a class-based interpretation was also involved. These narratives thus highlighted the dead of every country, undermined nationalist and heroic rhetoric, and made reference to the proletarian origins of the soldiers (thereby excluding many officers). This interpretation was carried forward with force by an organization created by the Socialist Party in 1919—the *Lega proletaria mutilati, invalidi, reduci, orfani e vedove di guerra* (The Proletarian League of invalids, veterans, orphans, and war widows).[19]

Historians have generally viewed the setting up of the Proletarian League, and the left's use of antiwar propaganda, as a disastrous tactical move, which turned away (it is argued) many of those veterans who were not enthusiastic about fascism.[20] However, what these discussions ignore is the ways in which the Proletarian League interpreted the narratives shared by many Italians after the war, and the sense in which the touchstone for conflict was very often a debate over the recent past. Moreover, the destruction of the traces of this memory by fascism led to these alternative narratives being excluded from the history of memory of the war. The myth of the "defence of the Piave river" began to dominate.[21] Fascism's increasing monopoly on public memory did not allow other stories to survive. A final part of the left-pacifist strategy was to propagate a wider vision of war and its victims. Sometimes, deserters were included among the war dead, or those who died of disease, or those who had been killed on the home front. Victims of other countries were also—implicitly—included in the call to commemorate "all victims" of the war. Thus, this alternative view of the past formed a critique of official (and later fascist) narratives in terms of who fought, who died, and why.

The power of the pacifist-socialist interpretation of the war can also be gauged in various ways. In Milan, antiwar feeling was high both during (in 1917 antiwar riots raged through the city) and after the conflict. Moreover, the left often attacked patriotic events, such as the award of medals. It was not possible to erect a monument to the war dead in any part of Milan until 1921. This antimilitarism could also be seen in the flags and banners created by the left, as well as in the frequent use of the white flag.

One of the activities of the Proletarian League (but also of other proletarian organizations after the war) was the creation of public memory that propagated internationalist ideas. The socialists, and many of those who joined the Proletarian League, were not pacifists. On the contrary, they were ready, they said, to take up arms in the cause of revolution. They expressed an "anti-militarism" that was both "negative and positive."[22] Very often, this public memory took the form of plaques and monuments (this form was universal, but not its content). Some research has been carried out around this phenomenon, but most of it has remained locked in local history, and there has been no systematic study of these conflicts across the whole of Italy. By bringing together some of these local studies we can begin to paint a clearer picture of the "memory war" that raged from 1919 right up to 1927 (and sometimes beyond).

What was the form of these conflicts over public memory? On the one hand, the plaques and monuments proposed by the Proletarian League and other organizations clashed with official ideals, and the official line on the past. Thus, potential plaques were often censored, or banned altogether, on the orders of local prefects (who had to give permission for all public monuments). On other occasions, plaques were altered or taken down by the authorities after they had been put up. Symbols were important in postwar Italy and could get you killed. Socialists cried, "Down with the warmongers!" and attacked those seen as responsible for the conflict, while nationalists and fascists flew the Italian flag and exalted the "heroes" from the trenches. A second level took in the fascists, who made it their policy not to allow "subversive" plaques to remain in place. One of the key aspects of early fascist activity was to physically destroy these monuments. Violent clashes often marked inaugurations of such plaques, or marches by fascists took place in order to demolish them.

Fascist agitation around issues of memory was not merely destructive. Fascism's ultimate aim was to construct national narratives of memory that made strong connections between fascism, the war, and the nation. Unlike socialist and pacifist interpretations of the war, fascism saw the conflict as heroic, necessary (and not "useless") and to be repeated. The two sides agreed only that the war should not be forgotten.

A whole series of intermediate monuments and memory strategies stood on either side of this divide. All over Italy, in town squares and cemeteries, memorials sprung up to the war dead. These memorials were a way of remembering the "fallen" but also crucial to the mourning process for those who had survived—families and friends of the victims, and the soldiers who had come back. Here, the messages were simple and often repetitive.

For those who came back, these monuments sent out a simple message: *that could have been me.* These plaques and monuments inspired feelings of guilt and sometimes trauma, but also were the source of pride and belonging (to the *Fatherland*, to the community, to the army, to a "glorious past"). They thus transmitted many messages, which were intimately linked to the subjective experience of the war. This was also true of the hundreds of thousands of spontaneous memorials created on the battlefields themselves, during the war. Often, memorials linked to the soldiers' associations were far less heroic and "active" than those created directly by fascism.

In general, the first processes of memorialization usually began with the outbreak of the war itself, with the collection of names of the war dead as well as photographs. Official lists, however, were not drawn up until 1920, when medals were awarded to the mothers of the victims. These lists were important for the construction of monuments, which usually contained names and images. Many local councils (if they were not already in socialist hands) saw the election of radical socialist administrations in 1920, which often set about putting up their own war monuments, and sometimes dismantled those from the past. There are good reasons for thinking that the monument war was peculiar to Italy, at least in terms of its scale and its violence.[23]

Socialist plaques were marked by differences in language, in the dates used, in the symbols and in their tone. The war was "European," not national; the dead were "victims," not "the fallen," and they had not "died for the patria." The final texts were often the result of compromise. In Barengo, for example, a small town in the province of Novara, this was the original proposal of the left for a war monument (with its darkly ironic message): "The People of Barengo for its sons who gave up their youth for the progress of capitalism." After a long debate the final version—in 1922—was this simple text: "Barengo for its sons."[24]

As Mignemi has shown in his pioneering local research, "the monument war began in 1919 and went on until 1927."[25] In some cases there were political protests against fascist attacks, state censorship of the plaques, or both. In 1921, the Socialist Party in the Biella zone in Piedmont threatened to call a general strike if plaques were altered or removed. Often, these subversive memorials were specifically directed against other forms of commemoration, as with this inscription on the *casa del popolo* in Cossato (another small town in the Province of Biella):

> the injured and the veterans of the Proletarian league, the socialists, the
> organisers, do not take refuge in the fiction of posthumous tears for those who died
> in the barbaric conflict of the world war
> but remember the agonising waste of human life . . . and await calmly the final
> victory of the working class

Today, we might call such an inscription an *antimonument*, with its criticism of other forms of commemoration (as the "fiction of posthumous tears") and its positive message of the final victory of the working class. These inscriptions were not designed for mourning, but were calls to action.

Another difference in the socialist vision of the war was a wide sense of the idea of "victimhood." Antimilitarist interpretations of the conflict included—in this category—not just those who died on the battlefields, but also those who were victims of military justice and of the army itself. The Proletarian League looked to remember the entire war experience, from the barracks to the front line. These narratives were far richer than those on the other side of this divided memory, interested, as they were, mainly with the final act—the death—of the soldiers.

One conflict over the very definition of "war dead" exploded at Prato Sesia, in Piedmont, a town to the northwest of Novara. Here, before the war had even begun, a twenty-four-year-old man called Achille Baraggiotta was arrested after—it was said—he was heard singing antiwar songs in a bar. He was later found dead—hung—in a *carabinieri* barracks. For Mignemi, "In the collective memory of that area . . . his name was remembered from that moment on as one of the first innocent victims of the conflict."[26] For many locals, Baraggiotta had "been hung"—while for others it was suicide—but the substance of the event was little changed. Baraggiotta's funeral was attended by hundreds of people with red flags and banners, and this message placed on his tomb: "He killed himself so that his conscience would remain pure."[27] It was natural for the left—after the war—to want to add Baraggiotta's name to the local plaque dedicated to the conflict, and also natural that such a decision would meet with opposition from the fascists, and others.

Moreover, Baraggiotta's name was right at the top of the plaque (where the word *Pace* [Peace] could be found) and was accompanied by this phrase: "His life was crushed by blind partisan hatred." Legal proceedings against the plaque (inaugurated with music and thirty "red flags" in June 1920 in the presence of the mayor) came to nothing, but the protests continued. In October, however, the mayor was sacked by Royal Decree. The decree, signed by the king and Giolitti, made direct reference to the plaque, "which offended the holy sentiments of the love of the nation." The plaque itself was also later removed. In other cases, deserters and those suffering from shell shock were added to lists of war dead. If the war was seen as a disaster, then all of its victims needed to be remembered. But if the conflict was interpreted as a triumph, only the "glorious dead" were worthy of mention. The left extended the war experience way beyond the battlefield, while the nationalists and fascists confined that experience to the trenches.

Sometimes, different political groups held separate ceremonies around the same monuments. Socialists or members of the Proletarian League occasionally complained that the names of "their dead" were included on patriotic monuments, and threatened to remove them. During the local election campaign of November 1920—which was marked by violence and violent language—in a climate of near civil war, three socialist sympathizers visited the local cemetery in Tollegno, a town to the northwest of Biella. They claimed to have a "mandate" from some families and proceeded to cancel thirteen names from the official war memorial with black paint. A trial followed and the men were fined.

The "war" was not always waged by fascists against the left. Nationalist (or more neutral) plaques were blocked by socialist administrations and there were cases of attacks on traditional monuments. Sometimes individual families used plaques to contest the war and contextualize the death of their loved ones. This plaque, for example, was put up in the cemetery of Recetto, to the west of Novara:

*A perennial infamy, people please take note that on the 15 June 1918 Giuseppe
Beltrame (36 years old) was murdered on the Piave for a cause to which he was opposed
He was a person of rare intelligence, respected by all for his noble character
his wife and relatives place this in his honour.*

In the area around Biella—with its strong socialist and working-class
traditions—the monument war was a bitter one. According to the detailed
research carried out by Moranino, at least twenty-four plaques were put up
by the left (including many by the Proletarian League) in the postwar period
between the end of 1919 and 1920.[28] Most of these were destroyed by fascists
between 1920 and 1922, or removed (sometimes on the day of inauguration
itself) on order of the authorities. A monument in Coggiola, to the northwest of Biella, which was described as a "beautiful work, by the architect
Crippa di Varallo and the sculptor Cantoni di Novara," was inaugurated on
Sunday, May 29, 1921, and then "purified with a hammer," as the fascists put
it, during the night of August 22, 1922. Many of these inaugurations were
well attended, and were intended as demonstrations against the war (and
those responsible for it) *and* against any future war. In some cases, the money
to pay for the plaques was collected by popular subscription, but usually the
funds came from the local government coffers.

These monuments were meant to divide, and their texts were in contrast with what the socialists called "the usual lying forms of rhetoric"
(while using their own rhetoric). In many cases the strongest contrast was
with Catholic commemorations of the war dead. Although Catholics and
socialists had often "agreed" about the war, and their opposition to the
conflict, in the postwar period ideological differences on both sides prevented any alliances between these two forces.

Central government also became involved in these disputes, and asked for
changes to the texts of a number of plaques. Some plaques lasted less than a
day. By 1922, the local fascist movement had crushed the socialists in Biella
and the surrounding area, and their actions had all but destroyed all forms
of local democracy. Fascist newspapers applauded the removal of "15 Austrian plaques that insult the memory of our heroes who died for the fatherland as well as the national sentiments of the good citizens of Biella." Here
the fascists were looking to stigmatize the socialists as "internal enemies" by
using the term "Austrian plaques." By the end of that year, most traces of this
attempt to create an alternative memory and narrative of the war, in terms
of public memory at least, had been forcibly excised from the landscape. In
Biella, at least, the fascists had won the monument war.

Often the proposed plaques preached class and civil war, and violent revolution. One text, written by maximalist leader Ercole Bucco, was banned
by the Prefect in the Province of Mantua. It attacked those who "bless and

exult" war—and was thus also a critique of other forms of memorialization. What was at stake was not just a historical and political understanding of the conflict, but the ways in which that conflict was to be remembered. This was a battle over memory itself, and its meaning.

The Memory War: Victims, Final Acts, Legacies

Fascist attacks on plaques and monument often took place at night. In Cecina near Livorno, during the night of January 24, 1921, eighteen fascists attacked local government offices and put up a plaque dedicated to the war (this same plaque had just been removed by the newly elected socialist city council). The next day the council decided to take the plaque down again. This re-removal led to more than thirty fascists from Livorno turning up in Cecina. In the clashes that followed a fascist was shot (Dino Leoni) and another was injured. Leoni died of his injuries three weeks later. According to Abse, "The episode gave birth to a bitter debate between left and right about the desirability of commemorating the war dead."[29]

This event also marked the local memory of Cecina. After 1923, what had been known as Piazza della Dogana was renamed Piazza Dino Leoni. In 1943—with the fall of fascism—the original name returned in place of that of Leoni, and in 1946 the piazza was renamed again after a partisan, Ero Gelli, killed in 1944. The Mayor of Cecina, Ersilio Ambrogi, who had been arrested and charged with the murder of Leoni, had escaped trial thanks to his election to parliament. He subsequently went into exile in Germany. The long memories of the fascists were revealed again when Ambrogi was put on trial in 1942 for the same murder, condemned and this time, deported to Germany.

In Muggiò, a small town near Milan, a socialist (and war veteran) was killed by fascists as he tried to defend a plaque in 1921. In Milan itself nobody was able to build a war monument for years after the conflict. The left were strong in the city and there was widespread hostility to the army (and especially to officers). The first public plaque dedicated to the war (apart from those in the cemetery) was only unveiled in the Fontana neighborhood in 1921. The population in that zone were, according to the local priest, "mainly workers and in the past they have been easy prey for subversive propaganda." Fontana was "the reddest zone of Milan" where the population were "Bolsheviks right down to their little fingers."

An Italian flag had been flown there "for the first time" in October 1919. For the committee who constructed the monument, their work represented "a duty which will last for all eternity . . . [the monument] will talk to our children and grandchildren and transmit the language of discipline and brotherhood." The local Catholics were those behind the monument (not the fascists, who were still relatively weak in the city). In this way, the monument remained "apolitical" and survived at a time of strong political and social tension.[30] Fontana's monument—with its 350 names—was inaugurated on October 16, 1921, with 4,000 people in attendance. Many other monuments and remembrance parks followed in other areas of the city, although a city-wide structure was not completed—after much debate—until the late 1920s.

Conflicts and controversy of this kind continued right up to 1927, with the removal of entire monuments, or the adaptation of texts. The "monument war ended with the destruction of many of these monuments, by fascists or radical nationalist ex-combatants, who wanted to substitute them with new monuments which celebrated and exalted the war."[31] Beyond the violence of the monument war between the left and the fascists, a whole range of other memorial practices and forms had emerged right across the country. Many early monuments had no real connection to the idea of the nation—they were simple and funereal mementos for the dead, often to be found in cemeteries and churchyards.

The Fascists Win the Monument War

Traditional monuments for the dead were intimately linked to forgetting. People needed a place in which to mourn. Remembering their sons was a way—eventually—of forgetting them, of overcoming the trauma of their loss. Meanwhile, fascists and socialists—who disagreed so violently about the content of this memory—agreed about one aspect of the monument war: memory was active. Monuments were not places for mourning, or for forgetting. Trauma was not to be overcome, but ever-present. For the socialists, this meant revenge for those who had created the slaughter. For the fascists, the war dead were always *presente*—never forgotten. Trauma— and memory—for both sides in the monument war, were operative. Memory was designed to act in the present. It was important, not a side issue, and that is why both socialist and fascist monuments were different from the others, and why these two sides clashed so violently over memory. It was, in fact, central to their (opposing) political projects.

Fascism's victory in the monument war led to a specific form of monument being imposed across Italy. Around Turin, the monuments constructed in the 1920s and 1930s were geographically central, nonfunereal, "vertical" (often with stairways), and carried a heroic message, almost always this one: *ai nostri figli caduti per la Patria* (to our sons who died for the Fatherland). In this way the "cult of the fallen" was disseminated—with its idea of a death donated to the nation. These were places, as Mosse has argued, where "the nation worshipped itself."[32] Of 168 such monuments examined in the Turin Province (and not in the city itself) only two carried even mild criticism of the conflict.[33] With Mussolini in power after 1922, and the end of democratic debate, the fascist version of the war began to suffocate what was put forward by the socialists and pacifists. All antiwar plaques were removed. We only know of their existence through newspapers, archives, and testimonies.

Despite this victory, commemorations of the war were still marked by conflict and division throughout the 1920s. Fascists were extremely intolerant of the autonomy of the ex-combatant organizations, which were violently attacked on various occasions (and often on key anniversaries) before they, too, fell into line. As the work of Baldassari has shown, moreover, there was rarely consensus over which anniversaries were to be used to remember the war. November 2 is the "day of the dead," a religious festival when people visit local cemeteries. After the war, this date often became an occasion for the commemoration of victims of the conflict. November 4, however, was the official date—the anniversary of the victorious end of the war, a date that was made a national holiday just before Mussolini became head of the government. After 1922, however, the fascists in power tried to privilege October 28, the date of the March on Rome.[34]

By collapsing the March on Rome anniversaries with those of the war, fascism looked to equate itself with the victory of the nation. November 4 was silenced. There had been "just one victory," according to the fascist state. But this imposition was not always accepted at a local level, where there was a "geography of dissent." In Lucca, for example, there was a "plurality of identities and memories" and a citywide monument was not created before 1930.[35] With the end of the violent phase of the monument war, fascism set about constructing its own memories of the conflict.

Evaluating the Monument War

The monument war was a struggle over the interpretation of the past, but it also evoked debates over responsibility, and about what the conflict itself had been for. The Caporetto enquiry in 1919 made these divisions crystal clear. The socialists put the war "on trial," along with the military command and the political class who had been in charge of the conflict. Often, the pacifist-socialist idea of what the war had been was quickly transferred into forms of memorialization—above all into words on the plaques and monuments erected by many of the thousands of socialist administrations who governed Italian cities and towns after 1919 and 1920. There was a "spontaneous spread of plaques which, by separating themselves from the official rhetoric, linked the commemorations of the fallen to a clear condemnation of the war, of those who were responsible for it and its logic."[36] The peak of the violence against these forms of memory was in 1921 and 1922, the *biennio nero*.

Many of these texts were never actually converted into real plaques, with censorship preventing proposals becoming reality. Negotiations often took place over the final wording of these monuments, although in some cases the socialists ignored official warnings and went ahead regardless, and censorship took place after plaques had already been laid. The memory war was one part of what was a civil war—with the socialists being viewed by the fascists as internal enemies (as they had been during the war itself).

Fascism, as Gibelli has argued, "silenced all criticism of the war and its costs, and amplified the myth of a heroic conflict."[37] The socialists and the pacifists thus lost their battle against the war twice, first with the intervention and then with the rise of fascism and the monument war. These defeats had a number of consequences, one of which was that the monument war itself was forgotten.[38] Fascism reunified the memory of the war. Their strategy was to eliminate all other versions of the past that did not agree with their own.

These debates were only reopened with the emergence of the "new history" in the 1960s, although antiwar sentiments remained underground (and could be discovered through oral history or work on—for example—popular and subversive songs) throughout fascism. It could be argued that the lack of enthusiasm for the war after 1940 might also be attributed to strong and resistant memories of World War I.

Story 2: On the Killing Fields: Memory on the Carso

On the battlefields, the monumentalization of war sites began during the conflict itself, and continued apace after the armistice in 1918. Small cemeteries, crosses, and makeshift monuments had been constructed ad hoc as soldiers fell, and even as battles raged. War left behind deep traces—trenches, barbed wire, unexploded bombs, bullet holes, and rubble, and of course bodies (of men, but also of animals). Large parts of northeastern Italy were strewn with this debris. For years, this material was gathered (and often sold) by collectors who became known as *recuperanti*. Many private collections were created by walkers and mountaineers, as well as some official museums. Bodies from the war are still turning up in the mountain regions that hosted the white war. Each year, in Trentino, there are military funerals for those who have been found as the glaciers melt. New graves are still being dug.

In Meneghello's *I piccoli maestri*, the partisans of World War II find themselves on the battlefields and trenches of World War I. Meneghello's group leaves a message for their friends written on a relic of the previous conflict: "Before dark I chose a white tibia bone and I wrote on it with a pencil 'Lelio, we are in the shack: north-east.'"[39] Fields covered with the remnants of war became instant memorial sites, especially for the soldiers who had spent so much time in the trenches there.[40] Hills were particularly significant, as they had been fought over time and time again. This was especially true in the Isonzo region, or on the Carso, or in the white war zones of Trentino and Lombardy.

The "cult of the fallen" was intimately linked to these battle sites.[41] They represented "an enormous stage upon which the war, with its ammunition and its horrors, was represented as a holy tragedy."[42] These spontaneous memorials were part of the mourning process, especially as so many bodies were unknown and thus so many of the dead were "missing," and destined to remain so. Hundreds of thousands of mourners were never to be free of their pain, they were condemned to "mourn endlessly, an eternal bereavement."[43] Closure was hard to achieve, with no body to bury and little news on the means or even the place of death. Their men had simply left home, forever. "Communities in mourning" were created across Italy, from Sicily to the battlefields themselves.[44]

The lack of a body, the lack of a funeral, the lack of closure created a deep psychological need for monuments, commemorations, and memorial sites for the families of the victims. For the ex-soldiers, these locations played a role in mourning, but were also important in the reevocation of the war experience. Over time, most of these spontaneous, semiprivate cemeteries disappeared, as bodies were moved to bigger, more monumental *sacrari*, or were taken back to their hometowns. The memory of the war was monumentalized, taken under the wing of the state, and after 1922, of fascism itself.

In recent years, many projects have looked to conserve traces of the war in the landscape, and provide more ways for people to visit these places. Sites at the former front have been reopened and signposted, "pathways of peace" created or recreated, forts renovated and turned into museums. Often during these projects tiny crosses or monuments have turned up, some with real sculptures made by soldiers in the trenches. Climate change is also revealing remains of the war that have long been covered in ice and snow. On the Adamello Mountain in Trentino, for example, the melting of the Mandrone glacier is beginning to uncover the ruins of barracks and constructions from the war itself. All these elements made up—and still make up—what has been called "the immense mosaic which is the memory of the Great War."[45]

Monuments on the Battlefields: From Sant'Elia to Redipuglia

I watched the disappearance of the humble crosses, the abandonment and
the decline of those makeshift cemeteries, which were essential for the pull
they had on people's souls and the variety of memories which they were able
to envoke.

—G. Stuparich, in *La Metamorfosi Della Memoria*

Battlefields had developed into spontaneous cemeteries during the war,
dotted with bodies and human remains. Over time, there were attempts to
normalize and organize these makeshift graves and burial grounds. A first
step was to place simple plaques or signs near to graves. In a second phase
these became small military cemeteries. Under fascism, many of these cemeteries were removed and the remains collected in vast, institutional *sacrari*.
In the postwar period there was an incessant reorganization of these cities
of the dead, these *necropoli*, in line with the needs of politics, the veterans,
and through constant negotiations between local and national interests.

Unlike in other, previous, wars, thousands of these dead were name-
less, unknown, and unable to be mourned directly by their families. These
anonymous remains required some kind of collective commemorative
form, a need that was in part met by the "unknown soldier" monument
in Rome. Other procedures were in place for bodies with names. Families
were given the right to bring their relatives' bodies back home, with the
state footing the bill. This process was completed by 1928. After that, the
military cemeteries were reorganized and then, in the 1930s, huge *sacrari*
were constructed at Redipuglia, Asiago, Rovereto, Caporetto, and Monte
Grappa (and in many other places). Bodies were constantly on the move
in line with the needs of politicians, families, and monument-makers. The
"varieties of memory" that Stuparich had seen in the small and spontaneous sites all over Italy were slowly leveled out into one, dominant version of
the past. Fascism was in favor of the "near-elimination of private mourning . . . in favour of a monumental display of those who died for their
country, who were often confused with those who died for the regime."[46]

In 1923 on the Carso, a monument-cemetery (known as the "cimitero
degli invitti") was created. It resembled a kind of futurist Dante-like pur-
gatory, on a small hill suited for the purpose in terms of its conical shape.
Two years of work were needed to blast the space for containers of the
remains of about 30,000 soldiers (of whom over 24,000 were "unknown")
into the Carso stone, and to create pathways up to the summit. This huge
site was conceived as a series of circles around the hill, with a labyrinth of
monuments, gravestones, barbed wire, abandoned arms, rusting bombs,

and crosses. Four hundred and sixty-three officers were buried on the top of the hill, with the commander of the third army (the Duca d'Aosta) destined for a chapel on the summit (although he was to die in peacetime, in 1931).

Colle Sant'Elia's cemetery looked like a battlefield, and the individual tombs and names were important. This monument had its age—and its memory—built into its own structure. It rusted and deteriorated naturally. All this marked a distance between the past and the present, something fascism was anxious about denying. Although this monument was opened officially by Mussolini and the king in 1923 (on May 24, the anniversary of the declaration of war) the fascists were never particularly fond of its form. Mussolini criticized what he called "whining and pitiful monuments." To the fascists, Colle Sant'Elia seemed a monument to pain, to suffering, almost to defeat, out of keeping with the triumphalism and imperialist rhetoric of the regime. Colle Sant'Elia looked back to an unrepeatable and apocalyptic conflict; Redipuglia (its replacement) would be a call to arms for future wars. The former was a collection of individual stories; the latter would highlight the collective sacrifice of a united people.

Sant'Elia was a complicated place. It separated the past from the present, but it also brought back to life the horrors and sacrifice of war. Tombs on the hill were linked to the present by writings that appealed to visitors to think and interact with them. For example, one epigraph read, "What do you care about my name, shout to the winds Italian Infantry and I will sleep happily." Other epigraphs were connected with the relics of the war itself, as in this example that was accompanied by a roll of barbed wire: "This rusty wire is no longer the colour of our blood which is now scarlet red!" These quotes almost seem like forms of oral history, testimonies, and dialogues, written for all to see.

The Sant'Elia hill was thus a palimpsest, a living monument, a cease-less series of signs and messages and a place of pilgrimage. Objects and other kinds of memorials were being added—continually—to the site. Ex-soldiers, school children, and many simple citizens made pilgrimages to the Carso, often in organized groups (complete with ceremonies and even publications linked to these trips). Veterans would often go with their old companions, and much alcohol would be consumed.

As Todero has pointed out, the Colle was a mixture of the classical and the modern, the individual and the collective, the literary and the material, the Christian and the pagan. It was a place that was sad and uplifting, trau-matic and cathartic. Visitors to the Colle were faced with "a bombardment of patriotic messages."[47] Many tombs were unique, and there were con-tinual reminders of the materiality of war. It was a community of the dead, which interacted with those who had survived. Like Redipuglia afterward, this was also a theatrical place, where ideas of national identity were given both mythical and material form.

In the 1920s a series of proposals were put forward for a new monument at Monte San Michele, and the physical decline of many older sites was used to justify their destruction. The fascist state thus decided to dismantle the Colle Sant'Elia cemetery, despite the work and care that had gone into it, and its success in attracting visitors, and construct an entirely new monument. A hill opposite the Colle was selected, mainly for its scenic possibilities, but also for its proximity to the spot where one of the great Italian war heroes, Enrico Toti, had died.

Fascism wanted a different kind of monument, and the Colle Sant'Elia was dismantled, toward the end of the 1930s, and replaced with the massive Redipuglia site. This decision was criticized by many, even under the regime. In a project that took years to complete, thousands of human remains were moved across to the new site. Soldiers from the Sassari brigade were assigned to this task. Using explosives—in a kind of macabre recreation of the war— they blasted their way into the hard Carso stone once again. The idea of the private fallen was replaced with that of thousands who had died exclusively for the nation. Fascism's vision of the war had no role for the ordinary soldier, and the past was linked to its vision of the future.

With Redipuglia, "a Carsic hill disappeared, to be covered with white stone."[48] When Redipuglia opened (although it was not quite finished) it was intended to be part of a system of monuments covering the main battlefields and sites linked to the war. One of the first acts of fascism had been to transform the ex-battlefields into "national monuments." Redipuglia represented the end of a long mission to "clean up, order and discipline places of worship." [49] Redipuglia had little or no private dimension. It was clean and orderly, "a choice which was directly opposed to the hell-like image of the war which had been represented by the Sant'Elia hill."[50]

At Redipuglia and in the whole Carso area, the ghosts of the past were everywhere. Fascism wanted them to be *presente*, ready to fight another war, but also absent. There were to be no real traces of the war, no bodies, no barbed wire, no blood. This idea was not particularly popular with many ex-soldiers. Even at the end of the 1930s, Fabi argues that there were still differences between the fascist view of the past, and that of the ex-combatants. Fascism "aimed to propagate, above all for the future, the idea of the Nation's 'inescapable destinies,'" while veterans were "imprisoned by the epic and painful memory of the war which they had lived through."[51]

Redipuglia was an immense undertaking. An entire hill was covered in clean, white marble, stretching for some 100 meters. The remains of 100,000 men were placed underneath, 60,000 of whom were "unknown." You can only go one way up the monument at Redipuglia, with its stunning white marble and huge steps, which are not designed to be climbed, but rather to be seen from afar. As a monument, it has many similarities with the *mise en scène* of the *Altare della patria* in Rome. It is a staircase toward the sky.[52] At the top of the series of huge steps stand three crosses, "as if it was a modern Golgotha."[53] On every step the word *Presente* was etched in the marble time and again. Slovenian inscribers were used—on very low pay (seven *lire* for every letter)—to etch *Presente* in the marble 748 times. The use of this word was in line with the many monuments to the so-called fascist martyrs that had sprung up all over Italy in the 1920s and 1930s. Fascism was to be fused with the nation, and the army, and the state. Italians were urged never to forget their "glorious" past, and that past was present in the wars that fascism had fought and was still fighting. Redipuglia was an archetypal example of fascism's attempt to create a civil religion.[54]

This was also a monument with its own built-in hierarchies. It is set up as a military formation—but in an opposite sense to Colle Sant'Elia. At the base of the steps is the tomb of the Duca d'Aosta, Commander of the Third Army, surrounded by those of his fellow generals. Twenty-two massive "steps" then led up the hill, with 39,857 named victims from the war. On the last step, in two large tombs on either side of the chapel, are the remains of the 60,330 unknown soldiers. From a monument that was a mix of individualism and the collective experience of the soldiers, at Redipuglia "collective death took on a meaning which was merely heroic and abstract."[55]

Redipuglia was only completed in 1938, and opened toward the end of that year (along with a number of other similar monuments and sacrari). By then, a new war was just months away. This was also a recognizably fascist monument, with its typical symbols linked to the regime—eagles and *fasci*. But Redipuglia had no time to develop as a "fascist" monument in terms of its links to commemorations and memory activity, and World War II changed its meaning forever.

Redipuglia after 1943

By 1943, the monument at Redipuglia was largely defunct, in terms of its fascist message. For one thing, it glorified an alliance between the monarchy and the regime that had been shattered by the events of July 25 and September 8. Neither monarchists nor Mussolini's new fascist republicans could take pride any longer in these words of the Duca d'Aosta (inscribed on the monument): "I die serenely, safe in the knowledge that a magnificent future awaits our fatherland, under the illuminated leadership of the King and the wise government of Il Duce."[56] Moreover, the short time span between the opening of Redipuglia and the outbreak of a new war never allowed the monument to take on the collective symbolic role that the regime required.

But the monument itself—as a monument—has been singularly successful. Redipuglia is easy to visit, it can be seen from the motorway, it has its own train station, and it attracts some 500,000 people every year. Its "imperial and self-celebratory" message has been partly transformed by its use in the postwar period. Redipuglia has become a place of multiple meanings in a democratic country—an important place for fascists, but also for pacifists, for nationalists, for anticommunists and for monarchists. It has adapted rather well—despite its "fascist" nature—to postwar Italy.

In the 1950s, attempts were made to save what was left of the Colle Sant'Elia, which became a park of memory and is today part of the complex series of sites and monuments. In 1964, a Roman column from the museum of Aquileia was placed on top of the hill (in the same year as Trieste became Italian, again) and was dedicated to the fallen of all wars, "without distinctions of time or fortune." Sant'Elia became an open-air museum, with a cypress tree-lined pathway leading up to its peak. Scattered across the site were remnants of the war.

With the end of the war, Redipuglia became something of an embarrassment for a time. But it soon took on a different role, that of a monument to peace. As the war commemorations themselves began to assume—in postfascist Italy—a more solemn and pacifist tone, so the monument itself was still a site for commemoration, but no longer hosted the bombastic celebrations that had been the norm under the regime. Most, but not all, of the fascist symbols were torn down, and although the monument as a whole remained "fascist" in style, its message was no longer so equivocal. By 1946, the fascist eagles had had their wings knocked off, and the fasci symbols had also been removed. To some extent, the monument had been—like so many others in Italy—spontaneously *de-fascistized*. This process was not complete, however, and certain fascist parts of the monument have survived, such as the long inscription at the top of the stairs. But it was as if these words no longer had any meaning; they were ignored, unread, invisible.

The monument continued to evolve after the war, and it now also hosts remains from World War II. One of its rooms is reserved for remains of Italian soldiers from the ill-fated Russian campaign. It is thus a monument not just to victory, but also to bitter defeat. In the past, Redipuglia had offered a view over the battlefields, but the landscape has now changed thanks to rich vegetation.

During World War II the area was occupied by Yugoslav troops, and then fell under the control of the Allies until September 1947 (with the actuation of the treaty signed in February of that year). Italian postwar politicians reinvented Redipuglia as a symbol of reconciliation, but also as a place of national identity. Prime Minister Alcide De Gasperi visited in 1948 and Italian President Sandro Pertini in 1978, but there were still debates over the meaning of the site, with some viewing the monument as a hymn to militarism. Occasionally, the annual celebrations were an opportunity for political mobilization, as in 1976 when they saw protests against the Osimo agreements with Yugoslavia.

Economically, the monument attracted many visitors to a depressed region. In the 1950s, buses still came from all over Italy, including the south, on November 4. The area was "incessantly visited by veterans and their families."[57] But over time, with the decline in numbers of veterans (from 1.6 million in 1962 to none today), the typical visitor has changed. Tourism and educational visits have become more important than a sense of "pilgrimage."

In 1953, with negotiations at a delicate stage over the city's future, Trieste celebrated Italy's victory in World War I. The ceremony was marked by tensions and violence. Allied military administrators banned the flying of the Italian flag on public buildings but the mayor refused to obey this order. On November 3, police took down the Italian flag from the front of the town hall and the next day the local *Comitato per la difesa dell'Italianità* (Committee for the Defence of Italianness) organized a "national flag pilgrimage" to nearby Redipuglia.[58] A huge crowd of 150,000 people turned up.

On their return, the demonstrators moved toward the town hall in Trieste, determined to fly the flag there. After clashes with police, more demonstrations followed on November 5. Later that day, the police fired on a crowd of Italians, killing two people and injuring thirteen. A general strike was called in the city. On November 6, the violence reached its peak; the police killed four more demonstrators and there were attempts to storm the prefecture. Big crowds turned out for the funerals of the six victims, who became the "fallen of Piazza Sant'Antonio and Piazza Unita d'Italia."[59] In November 1954, with Trieste now secure of its place within Italy, President Luigi Einaudi visited Redipuglia. The monument, for many locals, had become a symbol of "being Italian" (in opposition to the East). This time, the atmosphere was one of celebration—and the event was compared with the end of World War I, when Trieste (for the first time) had become part of Italy.

Today, Redipuglia is part of an itinerary of memory. School children are taken there as part of a tour that includes an ex-Nazi death camp in the city of Trieste and a nearby site where Tito's partisans executed some prisoners in 1945, accompanied, for example, by readings of Primo Levi, Anne Frank, and Italian war poet Ungaretti. But the monument also attracts groups of ex-soldiers from World War II, veterans' families, and many tourists. It remains a spectacular place that has retained its ability to shock and impress visitors. A bar and restaurant serve coffee and lunch, and sell kitsch souvenirs and books. Nearby, in the local town, there is an Austrian cemetery that is beautifully maintained, with its simple gravestones and inscriptions, in stark contrast with the white marble of Redipuglia.

Memory can play some strange tricks. In August 2001, a fire destroyed 120 hectares of vegetation around Gorizia. The flame damage seemed to return parts of the Carso to the period of war. Trenches became visible, again, especially from above, and some explosions were heard during the fire, presumably thanks to bombs still unexploded from the conflict. The geology of the Carso meant that the traces of the war there were destined to remain. Unlike the mud of the Somme, the hard stone of the Carso kept its shape—and can still be seen and visited.

In recent years, there has been a flourishing of projects dedicated to the battlefields around the Isonzo. Battles have been revoked, and paths and trenches have been restored to their former state. During the restoration of one of these areas, the so-called *Dolina dei bersaglieri*, a unique relic turned up: a large head of Christ carved, it seems, during the war itself. Later, this artifact was placed inside the Redipuglia monument. Much of this work of promotion and renewal has been made in the name of peace, with the idea that these places should also serve as warnings against future war. Thus, the tracks and itineraries around the Isonzo are known as *Pathways of Peace*. There is a conscious attempt to recognize all the victims of war, with trips to Austrian-Hungarian cemeteries as well as Italian ones, and the creation of a peace event linked to Redipuglia, with representatives from a number of countries.

Yet the idea of Redipuglia as a generic homage to peace creates an image that jars somewhat with both the look of the place and some of the messages that are still there (such as the references to *Il Duce* and to the empire). By ignoring or playing down these visual messages, and through the reinvention of the monument, the addition of further material, the organization of tours and a number of publications, the message of universal peace has been linked to a place that was intended to promote a message of glorious war, imperialism, and Italian national identity. Today, Redipuglia and its surrounding monumental sites, the battlefields (real and reconstructed) form a complicated and fascinating palimpsest that interacts in different and complicated ways with the many visitors who arrive here each year.

Nature, the Environment, Time, and Memory

In the areas of the "white war," the rapid melting of glaciers revealed a series of structures that had been built in tunnels within the ice. But just as soon as they were "rediscovered," these war constructions began to crumble and collapse, as the land beneath them literally fell away. It was only in the 1990s that projects aimed at cataloguing and restoring these traces of the war were promoted by local authorities. Before then, the initiative had been left to local enthusiasts and dealers. The vast bulk of what had been there was lost, although much was still hidden under the ice.

Global warming threw up some surprises. In the mountains above the Val Rendena in Trentino, excavations began in 2007 into a frozen cave known as the *caverna di cavento*. This cave had been occupied by both the Austrian and Italian armies during the war. Using fans to melt the ice, and working at over 3,300 meters above sea level in the summer months, a group of workers uncovered a frozen moment from the past, with blankets, lamps, newspapers, hats and a whole living quarters, much of which is still being catalogued and collected. Some of this work was motivated by serious historical concerns, but tourism was also important. Certain decisions were rather questionable, as with the reconstruction of a broken cannon (in a different position from its original site) on the mountainside. The same criticism could be made of some of the more kitsch aspects of tourist-war promotion, such as special trains to Redipuglia, complete with dressed-up "soldiers," "trench-soup" lunches, and reenactments.

The *caverna del cavento* was closed off to the outside world for the winter with a door and a padlock. But in the summer of 2008, those working at the site found that the doors had been forced open. Conflicts were growing locally over the ownership of these sites, and the material found up on the mountains, which for years had been free pickings. There have been a number of thefts from mountain refuges in recent years. Memory was also a business, and a business that created new divisions over the past.

3

Fascist Memories, Memories of Fascism

Here lies Giovanni Amendola, waiting

—epigraph on Amendola's grave in Cannes, 1926[1]

Fascism and the Memory of Fascism

Fascism sought to create a collective memory of itself, right from the start. This memory was to be part of a civic religion, an all-encompassing ideology that would stand beside and merge with the nation and the state.[2] To this end, the March on Rome was reinvented as a revolution, complete with a new calendar (1922 was redesigned as *year zero* of the *Era Fascista*, and many buildings all over Italy still carry dates linked to this conception of time).[3] After that of the "fallen" of the war, the first and most important fascist memory was linked to those who died during political clashes after the war. These people became known as the "fascist martyrs."[4]

The Myth of the "Fascist Martyrs"

Those 3,000 dead are the guarantee, the great guarantee that fascism will not fail to reach its destiny.

—Benito Mussolini

Fascism constructed a myth of its own past through these "fascist martyrs," militants who died during clashes with the left, or the forces of law and order, in the run-up to the assault on the capital in 1922. The exact numbers of these "martyrs" varied according to how "martyrdom" was calculated. Fascist estimates were very high: it was claimed that 3,000 fascists died between 1919 and 1922, but the real figure was probably closer to 100 or so.[5] Registered "martyrs"were given the full status of war dead—and in fact they were awarded even greater standing than most of those who died between 1915 and 1918.[6] Their families received full war pensions and monuments were dedicated to them across Italy. Special recognition for the "fascist martyrs" was also added to war monuments, as at Redipuglia, or near the monument to Guglielmo Oberdan, in Trieste. In the Oberdan crypt, built in 1935 on the site of an ex-Austrian barracks, you can still read the names of the *Caduti per la rivoluzione* (the fallen of the revolution).

This myth was not simply a way to exploit the past for political ends, but also part of an attempt to eliminate all other memories from the postwar period. For the fascists, "intervention, war and fascism are successive moments of the same revolutionary fact."[7] Alongside "creative" uses of memory, fascism attempted to wipe out all reference to socialism, apart from in a negative sense. All socialist symbols were banned. May Day was abolished, certain "subversive" public holidays were altered and streets were renamed. Fascism's martyr cult was a way of imposing its own version of history. This was another battle in the "memory war" that continued throughout the 1920s and 1930s. For the fascists, the postwar period had been a civil war, which they had won, but also a moral crusade. This civil war was presented as part and parcel of the struggles of World War I.

Fascists depicted the postwar period as one of social chaos, where Italy had been saved by the courage of a few militant heroes, some of whom had fallen victim to "red barbarism." Postwar and war were merged, and this slowly led to the commemoration of the March on Rome taking over from the other possible dates linked to the war: November 2 and 4.[8] For Gentile, "With the passing of time, fascist symbolism increasingly substituted the rites of the 'reborn fatherland.' In many cases the ceremonies came together in a single rite, the cult of the fallen for the fatherland and the cult of the fallen for the fascist revolution."[9] The cult of the martyrs was a reminder of "the tendency of the *squadristi* to translate their political actions immediately into epic and religious terms.""[10] The obsessive use of the word "Presente" in the monuments dedicated to the "martyrs" mirrored that of war monuments like Redipuglia.

Every city had its own "martyrs" monuments and plaques, but some martyrs were more important than others. Tensions had been high in Florence in 1921, and a number of socialists and fascists were killed during violent clashes in the city. That year, Giovanni Berta became the most celebrated of the fascist martyrs. He was supposedly thrown into the Arno, and legend has it that his hands were cut off, or stabbed, an act that forced him to fall into the river and drown. The image of a man with his hands cut off was reproduced in numerous murals, and Berta had bridges, schools, and streets named after him. Berta's story—about which there is still some debate—was perfect for the fascist martyr myth. His death was blamed on the "barbarity" and lack of humanity of the subversives, and he was also a young war veteran. The "blood-stained bridge" itself became a relic, part of the civil religion constructed by fascism, appearing at the Mostra della Rivoluzione Fascista with "BERTA" in huge letters above it in 1932.[11]

A figure representing Berta was included in a huge bas-relief in Bolzano. The image itself of a man hanging from a bridge was enough on its own to identify Berta, an indication of the level of importance afforded to this event by the regime. But despite these bombastic sites of memory, fascism's version of the civil war did not convince everyone. Berta's death inspired many different versions, which were all highly politicized. At least two contrasting songs had the Berta death at their center. Both songs spoke of revenge. The kind of rhetoric in the songs—on both sides—reproduced the language contrasts seen during the monument war.

One of the most elaborate of the public memorials to these "martyrs" was constructed in Florence in 1934, in a crypt below the Santa Croce church. This was how one woman—at the time a schoolgirl—from Florence remembers the "Sacrario dei martiri fascisti":

> The Sacrario was a deep and austere crypt which had various wings, a bit like a labyrinth. Huge stone sarcophagi contained, I think, the remains of the fallen. On each one there was simply the name of the "martyr." Along the walls there were stone *fasci* with the word Presente! repeated many times. Dante Rossi, presente!—Giovanni Berta, presente! A silent guard stood by made up of *avanguardisti* and young fascists, in black shirts with muskets. This whole scenario provoked a sense of proud participation in us, of religious respect. It was all we knew. It was what we had been taught. This was how we had been brought up.[12]

Thus, an elaborate site of religious-fascist memory was created in a place that was already designed as an Italian Pantheon of heroes. Hitler and Mussolini visited the Sacrario in Florence together in 1938, as if to underline its importance as a form of fascist public memory. Much effort was put into the complicated ceremony that inaugurated the Sacrario and a permanent fascist guard stood watch over the "thirty-six martyrs."

The model for these *sacrari* was laid down by the iconography of the 1932 exhibition in Rome with its special section dedicated to the "martyrs." Fascism was extremely interested, therefore, in public memory as a means of creating consensus, just as it had been concerned in the destruction of all alternative forms of memory during the *biennio rosso* and in the period running up to the establishment of the dictatorship. Having won the destructive battles of the memory war, the fascists set about building a series of sites of memory. The myth of the martyrs looked back to the Risorgimento, to World War I and the postwar social struggles. These "martyrs" were seen as "heroic fighters for an idea, who died in order to defend that idea in a war against subversive forces."[13]

Siena also constructed an expensive and intricate Sacrario for its "fascist martyrs" (ten of whom were buried there), which was opened in November 1938 after nearly four years of work. The Sienese sacrario was positioned in the enormous crypt of San Domenico, and opened with the full permission and collaboration of local Catholic elites. After the war, this fascist sacrario, as with Florence, was dismantled, with some sculptures being moved elsewhere, and other traces removed (but not until the 1950s in both Florence and Siena). Siena's fascist sacrario was "consigned to history."[14] The same fate befell the small monument to the "martyrs" that was added to the huge *Altare della Patria* in central Rome, as well as the larger structure built on the Campidoglio for the "martyrs," and removed in 1944. The names of fascist martyrs, and those who died in Spain, were often added to war monuments, with phrases used to describe their "sacrifice." These names were usually (but not always) removed after 1945, creating further reasons to read these monuments as palimpsests, as documents with texts that have been added and removed at various times.

Fascism's myth of its own martyrs did not survive beyond 1943 and 1944, and there were to be no serious attempts to revive it in the postwar period. Apart from a small minority of neofascists, the memory of these martyrs thus disappeared completely after the war, and very few of these monuments remain (despite their claim that they would "remember down the centuries—those who fell in the cause of the black-shirted revolution"). There seems to have been considerable embarrassment about the very presence of these *sacrari*, which are barely mentioned either in church histories or official documents. The same fate befell the thousands of streets and squares named after the fascist martyrs all over Italy. In Parioli (Rome) *Viale dei martiri fascisti* eventually became *Viale Bruno Buozzi* while *Piazzale dei martiri fascisti* was renamed after another antifascist martyr, Don Minzoni. Despite fascist rhetoric, there had been far more "martyrs" on the other side of the divide. A new set of "fascist martyrs" would later be created around those who died in the *resa dei conti* after 1945, yet these memories (at least until the 1990s) never obtained official recognition from the state.

Fascist attempts to create and influence historical memory went way beyond the idea of its own "martyrs." Most effort was concentrated on the memorialization of World War I, but fascism also constructed entire cities or parts of cities in its own image, using its potent combination of the past and the future to try to create a new order that covered every aspect of society, from architecture to daily life to education to work to leisure time. Rome was reinvented as an imperial city, with connections both back to the Roman Empire and forward to a new Italian empire. History books were rewritten, and older monuments embellished with fascist symbols. Fascism also attempted to link up its ideology with the memory of the Risorgimento. School children were given special courses on fascism and the history of fascism was merged with that of Italy in general. Italy was reinvented as a "massive stage"[15] where the fascist past and present could be played out.

The Other Side: Remembering the Socialist Martyrs of the *Biennio Nero*

On July 24, 1921, at least seventy fascists descended on the small town of Roccastrada near Grossetto to impose the flying of the Italian flag. They came in two trucks, and were singing *Giovinizza*. This "expedition" was accompanied by the usual rites of beatings, the enforced drinking of castor oil and the destruction of socialist and union property. As they were leaving, a blackshirt was killed by a gunshot. This sparked off an orgy of violence: crops were burnt, and ten people were shot dead by the fascists, more or less at random, including two sixty-eight-year-old peasants, a young married couple, and a twenty-four-year old woman as she tried to protect her father. The police report wrote that "people were killed with wild fury, with no regard for the age or the condition of the victims." As in so many other cases, no action was taken against the perpetrators of these crimes. The fascists involved were identified but never arrested.[16] In 2001 the massacre was "commemorated" in Roccastrada in a ceremony with various politicians and members of the public.

Fascism tried to obliterate the memory linked to the thousands of socialists, anarchists, communists, and trade unionists who had died as a result of *squadrista* violence after 1918. Were these dead nonetheless remembered after 1943 to 1945? To some extent, they were—especially the more celebrated victims—such as Matteotti, Amendola, Gobetti, Don Minzoni. But public memory of the more normal "martyrs" was and is much more rare, as it seemed more urgent after 1945 to remember those who had died during the Resistance, or at the hands of the Nazis. Local factors also affected the ways in which the victims of fascism were given public recognition after the fall of the regime. Communist activist Spartaco Lavagnini, for example, who was shot dead in his office by fascists in February 1921 in Florence, had a plaque dedicated to his memory, but only in 1958.

For Maurizio Gribaudi, "silence" over a socialist past was one of the outcomes of fascism.[17] Under the regime, subversive and socialist memory had to survive underground. It could not create lasting public memory. Activists resorted to short-term, spectacular forms of protest, such as Lauro De Bosis's "antifascist" flight over Rome in 1931 or the flying of a red flag alongside individual forms of protest such as wearing a red tie or refusing to have as many children as the regime required. May Day was an important moment for a reaffirmation of socialist principles. On May Day 1931, three red flags were flown on the hill of San Lorenzo, above Prato Sesia in Piedmont, at a point from which they could be seen far into the distance. Ritually, the fascists climbed the hill to take the flags down. A man in Prato Sesia continued to sing *Bandiera Rossa* on his bicycle—as he delivered bread to the town—right through the 1930s. During other May Days, people would simply not go to work, while some antifascists refused to stand up during Mussolini's speeches on the radio. The memory of fascist violence was transmitted down the generations by local militants.

Memories of what fascism had done in the 1920s survived in people's minds. Many acts of civil resistance in the 1920s and 1930s were linked to symbols. Occasionally, silence itself became part of the myth of the resistance. When the FIAT workers greeted Mussolini with silence and not the usual cheering on May 15, 1939 at Mirafiori, they revealed "that they were outside of the nature of fascism in a way that was wider and more radical than simple political dissent."[18] When the chance came, the continuities with the past took the form of active and collective antifascism, after September 8, 1943. In Prato Sesia, a worker beaten up by the fascists in 1922 became a local resistance leader, and the mayor, who had been sacked over a subversive plaque by Royal Decree, was renominated mayor in 1945.

In terms of memory, during the regime, no myth could compete with that of Giacomo Matteotti.

The Martyr and the Myth: Giacomo Matteotti

In order to bring Matteotti back into history, where he deserves to be, we need to look for him in his myth.

—Stefano Caretti

During his last, celebrated speech to parliament on May 30, 1924, Giacomo Matteotti was constantly interrupted by fascist deputies. Farinacci, one of the most extreme of all the fascists, threatened Matteotti with violence: "We will have to finish off that which we have not yet done." Eleven days later, five fascists bundled Matteotti into a car as he walked along the Tiber in Rome. As the car drove off, Matteotti was stabbed to death. His body was hidden in a wood at Quartarella, twenty-five kilometers from Rome. The corpse was not "discovered" until August 16 (a "choice" that represented a first attempt to diminish the impact of Matteotti's posthumous myth). Even before his body turned up, Matteotti had become a martyr. He was buried in his hometown of Fratta Polesine on August 21, and, as a satirical paper wrote at the time, his body was already part of a political struggle over memory: "Matteotti's body is argued over, hidden, purloined."[19] The battle over Matteotti's memory began early, even before his body was discovered outside Rome. Flowers were left at the spot where he had been kidnapped by fascists, and homage was paid at the spot by all the leading antifascists.

In the wake of Matteotti's murder, his wife employed a photojournalist to document events in Italy, in secret. These exceptional photos later formed part of a travelling exhibition, *Matteotti: Storia e memoria*, which has been seen across Italy in recent years. The Matteotti myth was, as Caretti has written, "very operational." Matteotti's memory brought people out onto the streets, it made them act differently. It was this level that most concerned fascism, the power of the imaginary provoked by Matteotti's martyrdom.

Filippo Turati's celebrated speech at Matteotti's funeral was a conscious creation of a myth, and memory. Matteotti was dead, but he was also still alive:

> We are here for a rite, a religious rite, the rite of the fatherland. Our brother, who I do not need to name, because his name is in our hearts . . . has not been defeated, he is not a murderer. He lives. And he is part of us all. He is an individual and he is the people. The dead person gets up, he talks. And he repeats those holy words . . . which are true, because they are his soul. The words that will be carved in bronze on the plaques which we will put up as a warning for the future: you are killing me, but you will never kill my ideas . . . my children will glorify their fathers. The workers will bless my body. Long live socialism.

Two phrases uttered by Matteotti became legendary, and were reproduced on monuments and photographs of the dead socialist. One was a kind of premonition of his death. It was after his last speech to parliament that Matteotti supposedly pronounced the words "and now, you can prepare my funeral." The other "words" attributed to Matteotti often appeared on monuments or other forms of memorialization, and were a kind of manifesto of his martyrdom, and the power of his sacrifice: "Today you are killing me, but you will never kill my ideas." The fascists tried to prevent protests arising from Matteotti's huge funeral (an estimated 10,000 were there). The power of this event worried the regime, after they had banned the family from holding a funeral in Rome. Fascist violence later forced Matteotti's elderly mother to move her son's body to a different part of the cemetery.

The material collected by Caretti shows how far and wide the cult of Matteotti spread and its quasi-religious aspects. People kept small photos of Matteotti in their wallets, erected shrines in their homes where they would pray "every night," and frequently compared Matteotti to Christ. The language itself was often religious—martyr, sacrifice, apostle, visionary, saint, and even "God." Matteotti's image was "conserved and venerated with the same devotion reserved for a holy relic."[20] Matteotti's myth was powerful, long-lasting and was spread through songs, anecdotes, and memorials. Children were named after Matteotti, as were offices, party sections, and other institutions all over Italy (after 1943) and in the rest of the world (after 1924). Anniversaries and commemorations—despite fascist repression—were also celebrated, often in private. In Italy, this collective memory survived largely in the private sphere.

Elsewhere, Matteotti's image was often used to raise money for the left. Special issues of newspapers were produced, and the anniversary of his death was commemorated. Throughout the *ventennio*, strict measures tried to prevent all public commemorations of Matteotti, but the regime could not control events beyond Italy's boundaries. Monuments to Matteotti were created in many antifascist emigrant communities, and a housing block in "Red" Vienna was named after him. Public memory in Italy was much more difficult, for obvious reasons. Cesare Battisti's wife draped a black cloth over the monument to her own dead husband in Trento when she heard of Matteotti's death. This was an example of the use of a national monument to commemorate a socialist martyr, and was thus an extremely subversive act.

Fascism used all the power at its disposition to crush all memory of Matteotti. Flowers were banned and removed from the place where he was kidnapped and where his body was found. Fascists attacked and defaced the cross placed on the spot where Matteotti's body had been recovered and Mussolini personally ordered the press to "reduce reporting" of the farcical trial of his murderers in Chieti to a bare minimum. Mussolini insisted that the trial "must be ignored by the nation as a whole so that we can avoid that Italy starts to matteottiise itself after two years of healing." Spies followed the Matteotti family at all times, and even checked up on his mother's funeral, as well as preventing a planned move abroad by his wife.

One of the key moments in fascism's struggle against the Matteotti myth came on September 12, 1924. That day Armando Casalini, a fascist deputy, was shot dead on a tram in Rome by a carpenter (Giovanni Corvi) who claimed that he wanted to avenge Matteotti. This murder allowed the regime to draw parallels with the death of Matteotti (both were deputies, both had families) and to repropose the "fascist martyr" myth. Fascism now had its "own Matteotti" to celebrate and mourn. In 1926, the failed attempt on Mussolini's life by Violet Gibson was also linked to Matteotti. Gibson, an Irish woman with mental health problems, had witnessed part of the absurd trial in Chieti. But repression and the "countermyth" of Casalini failed to cancel the power of the Matteotti myth.

Matteotti continued to exercise power over both his supporters and his opponents for years after his death. For one antifascist from Rovigo, Matteotti "was a life long project."[21] The writer Leonardo Sciascia remembered how his aunt "kept a portrait of Matteotti . . . every so often she would show it to me and would say that 'that one' had had him killed."[22] Often, these reminders of Matteotti contained explicit promises that his murder would be avenged, promises that were to become reality after 1945, with the *resa dei conti*. As Luzzatto has written, "In the Italian anti-fascist imagination the Duce began to die with the recovery of Matteotti's body."[23]

As Caretti puts it, "Fascism was very sensitive to the power of myths, symbols and rites, and therefore it looked to prevent access to the places linked to the Matteottian cult."[24] Matteotti frightened the regime; the power of his myth was something they could never deal with. As *La Voce Repubblicana* wrote in 1924, "It really seems they are scared by the shadow, just the shadow, of Matteotti."[25] But Matteotti was also a case of divided memory. Some fascists evoked his death and celebrated it as part of the ongoing civil war.

After July 25, 1943, the first name to be shouted from the streets was Matteotti's, and many place-names were changed—unofficially, and then officially—in his honor, from Trento to the south of the country.[26] In all, more than 3,200 place names carry Matteotti's name today, making him seventh in the list of the most popular names in this sense. After 1943 to 1945, Italy was *Matteottized*. Piazza Nuova in Genoa was called Piazza Umberto I from 1900 until 1943, when it took the name of the fascist Ettore Muti, and then, after 1945, it became Piazza Matteotti, a place that would become famous in 1960 for the antifascist movement. For many, the first name that came to mind as fascism fell in July 1943 was that of Matteotti. Socialist-inspired partisan groups called themselves the Brigate Matteotti. Mussolini, it seems, was haunted by the Matteotti murder all his life, and it is said that he was carrying papers relating to the case when he was captured by partisans in 1945. Mussolini's death was directly linked to Matteotti's twenty-one years earlier. A rumor spread quickly on Lake Como in April 1945 that Matteotti's son himself had participated in the execution of *Il Duce*. This story was obviously untrue, but it shows us that "the memory of the socialist deputy was so alive as to promote the legend that his son himself had avenged him."[27]

Matteotti's death marked the beginning of the fascist dictatorship, while Mussolini's signaled its end. Both men became martyrs, both men's bodies lived on well after their death, and both were destined to inspire endless controversy. It was perhaps a quirk of fate, or a cruel coincidence, which led Mussolini to announce the ill-fated (for him, and for the country) entry of Italy into the war on June 10, 1940. That day was the sixteenth anniversary of Matteotti's kidnapping, and its significance would not have been lost on those people who still believed in the power of the dead socialist to inspire and create anger.

The year 1947 saw a new and more serious "Matteotti trial" after the farce of 1926, but Matteotti's fate in the postwar period was not a happy one. He was destined to remain a victim of the numerous splits in the Socialist Party, with each faction making claims to the "Matteotti legacy" (e.g., see Figure 3.1). Moreover, while Matteotti had worked well as a martyr, he inspired few serious studies and little research, and his memorialization became tired and ritualized, rather like that linked to the Risorgimento. Occasionally, the shadow of Matteotti was evoked, as when Togliatti was shot outside parliament in July 1948, but generally his influence over the postwar period was far less significant than it had been under fascism. Many big monuments were built—at Riano, in Rome, and all over Italy, but the Matteotti myth failed to win over a new generation of Italians.

Some fascist massacres were remembered after the war in terms of public memorialization, as with the 1922 Turin massacre, and a few trials were held in the most infamous cases. Yet the vast majority of fascism's crimes (especially those from the *biennio nero*) not only went unpunished, they also went unremembered. Public and official memory only covered a tiny proportion of the victims from the post-1918 civil war. After 1945, squadrism and fascist violence took second stage. For the left, the memory of the Resistance became the priority, and many of the victims of fascism were assimilated to the resistance myth. Much historical work was carried out around the origins of fascism, but the violence of the right rarely played a major role in this research. This was in part due to the overall attempt to play down the civil war aspects of the Resistance. Left analyses of fascism often underlined the need not to repeat the mistakes of 1919 and 1920. In this sense, it was not helpful to remind people of the bitter violence of that period, or that the Resistance had also been a struggle between Italians. Political considerations—as so often in Italy—tended to shape historical research and forms of commemoration.

The First Fall: Memory and July 25, 1943

It was advisable to keep one's eyes well open in the streets of Italy on the days after July 25, 1943, as a lot of material was falling from the sky. This

GIACOMO MATTEOTTI

Il suo sacrificio e la sua dedizione alla causa del socialismo, rimarranno i simboli delle nostre battaglie per la libertà e la giustizia.

PARTITO SOCIALISTA ITALIANO

Figure 3.1 Matteotti portrait: "His sacrifice and his dedication to the cause of socialism will remain a symbol of socialism and of our battle for liberty and justice." 1980s, Italian Socialist Party symbol.

was a strange kind of debris—statues, *fasci*, plaques. It is said that a man in Milan was killed on July 26 by a flying fascist symbol. There was suddenly a lot of demand for sculptors and stonemasons, but this wasn't paid labor: "These were days of hard work for artisans, sculptors and blacksmiths."[28] At Prato Sesia, a bar owner came down the stairs on hearing the news, in his socks. He took down the portrait of Mussolini from the wall and went out on his bike into town describing it as "the best day of his life." News of Mussolini's arrest had came through on the radio at10:45 PM on July 25, but most people remember hearing "the sensational news" much earlier.[29] For nearly everyone, the events that followed that announcement were moved back in time, to the 25th itself. "July 25" became the catch-all moment as people gathered all over Italy to celebrate the end of the regime.

On July 25–26, 1943, the fall of Mussolini and fascism created a new set of divided narratives about the past. Everywhere, Italians took to the streets in a joyous celebration of the end of the regime. Their main targets were the symbols of that dictatorship, not the fascists themselves (who wisely stayed behind the scenes), although in some places there was a "hunt for fascists."[30] *Fasci* were knocked off the walls of buildings, statues of Mussolini were torn down and smashed apart, fascist slogans were wiped out or altered, and new words turned up in their place. Forbidden items were dusted off or created anew—red flags, party symbols, hammers, and sickles. Previously forbidden actions were carried out, in public. Fists were clenched, subversive songs were sung (*Viva Stalin* banners turned up in the crowd) as well as the national anthem. The atmosphere was one of a carnival. In one place, Mussolini's portrait was put on trial and "condemned to death"; in others his effigy was burnt.[31]

The "July 25" created a wealth of private memories. Nobody who lived through it could forget that moment. Everybody had a story to tell. *Il Duce* had been dethroned, shocking fascists and antifascists alike. For some, it felt like a revolution (but they soon realized that they were wrong), for others, like the end of the world. Manlio Morgagni, senator and director of the Stefani Press Agency, committed suicide on hearing the news. Prisoners were released overnight, power changed hands, forbidden gestures, words, and colors were seen on the streets. The streets were crowded, but not with the "oceanic" crowds of the past twenty years. It was a short, liberating moment, but also a time of illusions. The joy and liberation of July 25 was short-lived, as it soon became clear that not only was the war to continue (albeit, before long, against a previous ally) but that the ex-fascist state would not tolerate open political protest. The arrival of the Nazi army en masse brought in a new regime, with its own set of rules and violent ways of imposing them.

As a result of these features (its brevity, its context, its confusion), July 25 produced very little public memory. There are a small number of July 25 squares or roads in Italy. It was not the beginning of the Resistance, although it was the beginning of *a* resistance. July 25 led to the removal of fascist public memory—it showed how important public memory was, or was thought to be. First and foremost, the demonstrators attacked the hated public symbols of the fascist regime. In Franzinelli's words, "The crowds were crushed around buildings egging on those brave souls who . . . knocked down plaques and hacked off fasci."[32]

In Milan, Giansiro Ferrata, antifascist, remembered that people were "anxious to cancel fascism and its symbols."[33] At first, the reactions were largely negative, but there were also spontaneous renamings of streets and squares and the name of Matteotti was everywhere. For Tobia, "in short, the Italy which awoke suddenly after twenty years of dictatorship wasn't interested so much in destruction, but in re-naming."[34] There were few clear ideas among the crowds on the streets. Chants ranged from *Viva l'esercito* and *Viva Il Re* but there were also more subversive moments, such as the speech by communist Pietro Ingrao in Piazza del Duomo in Milan on July 26. In some ways, this was the wide alliance that was to come together in the Resistance, with all its contradictions.

There may well have been a certain amount of overoptimism about the power of monuments and symbols. For over twenty years, fascism had invested time, energy, and propaganda in promoting memory and memorialization. Many may have been under the illusion that fascism could be removed through the destruction of a few *fasci*. This attribution of power to monuments and symbols showed how deeply fascism had been internalized, even among its enemies. For Isnenghi these acts were "forms of self-liberation and social counteracting with respect to the rites of the regime."[35] But people were soon to realize that the regime had much deeper roots in society.

July 25 created new divisions in the present that had an impact on the ways of understanding the past. Many followers of Mussolini became republicans overnight, after the "betrayal" of the king. This changed position had a number of consequences. For one thing, the monarchy and the regime had been entwined for over twenty years, and it was not easy to disentangle them. Italy was covered with monuments to various kings. The republican shift transformed these statues into an uncomfortable reminder of the events of July 25. The reaction of many local fascists was to pull them down. In Novara, on September 28, 1944, monuments to Ferdinando di Savoia, Umberto I, and Vittorio Emanuele were knocked down. Only the latter was ever reconstructed (and in a new place), under the new republic, in 1953. Just as the new antifascists took time out to remove and attack the symbols of the regime, so these new republican-fascists were anxious about stamping their authority in the squares, the streets, and the cemeteries of Italy. Memory remained important, even in defeat.

Memories of Fascism, Fascist Memories: After 1945

> Where the repression of the Nazi-fascists was strongest, so there were the strongholds of the post-liberation revenge. In many cases recent and older memories came together, and accounts which had opened up in 1920–1922 were settled.
>
> —Storchi, "Ordine pubblico e violenza politica nel Modenese e nel Reggiano"

> Many stories and conflicts which had started in the first post-war period (and sometimes before) came to a head in 1945–46.
>
> —Crainz, "La giustizia sommaria in Italia dopo la seconda guerra mondiale"

With liberation, antifascist memories were freed to express themselves. The *resa dei conti* saw thousands of summary executions all over Italy (but in particular in the north and center of the country) in the wake of the end of the war. Many of these killings were in revenge for specific acts carried out during the rise of fascism and under the regime. Memories—*long* memories—played an important part in who was killed, and how. Memory of fascism thus played a key part in the *resa dei conti*, whether it was to do with memories of 1921 to 1922, of the death of Matteotti or of the role of fascism in the 1920s, 1930s, and during the war.

Thus, the *resa dei conti* during and after 1945 was not only in relation to the activities during the Republic of Salò, but also a "long revenge" for the events of the first postwar period.[36] As Dondi has written, "For more than twenty years the fascist beatings . . . went unpunished and unavenged."[37] One incident during the *resa dei conti*—studied by Crainz—saw the murder of an entire family of landowners (five people) in the Ravenna countryside in July, 1945. The reasons behind this massacre included revenge for local events during the *biennio nero*, more than twenty years earlier, as well as those of World War II allied to elements of class hatred.[38] Many of those who took part in the Resistance were the "children of the anti-fascists of the 1920s, those who had experienced the pain of witnessing a relative beaten or humiliated when they were younger."[39] Often the older generation were asked to identify local fascists who were to be "eliminated."

A further layer to the consolidation of antifascist public memory was added by the return of the bodies of socialists who had died abroad, some at the hands of fascists. Turati was reburied in Milan's Cimitero Monumentale after the war, at a ceremony that also saw the presence of many European antifascists. The Rosselli brothers, murdered by fascist agents in France in 1937, were reburied in the Trespiano cemetery (Florence) in 1951. Calamandrei wrote the epigraph on their tomb: "Carlo and Nello Rosselli: Justice and Liberty. They died for this, they lived for this." The new funeral of the Rosselli brothers followed a ceremony in Palazzo Vecchio with the president of Italy, Einaudi, which was addressed by the distinguished antifascist intellectual, Gaetano Salvemini.

De-Fascistization and Its Limits

After the first "spontaneous" wave of antifascism in July 1943, many fascist monuments were removed by local authorities soon after the arrival of full democracy. There was little debate over this process, and it happened in an irregular way across the country. No national policy or law evolved on the de-fascistization of Italy, although the republic and the constitution imposed its own rules on the institutions of the state (such as with the words that were to appear in courtrooms across Italy). Moreover, there is no systematic history available of the "defascistization" of Italy. As Gentile writes, there was a ritual aspect to these processes: "As in every religious war, even between lay religions, the winning religions cancel the symbols of the rival who has been defeated."[40] Fascist monuments were knocked down, removed, or altered in various phases. A first wave of removal took place on or after July 25, there was a second series of deletions after September 8, 1943, and a third phase followed the liberation of various areas by the Allies or partisans and then in the postwar period. Individual decisions over many fascist monuments, murals, and buildings were taken at a local level over a long period of time, often in line with chance events such as the need for restoration.

Some cities—such as Rome—retained strong signs of the fascist past. Some of this nondestruction was a sign of necessity. Why destroy buildings that were important public institutions (post offices, sports stadiums, town halls, train stations)? Often, it was enough to simply remove the most obvious fascist symbols—*fasci*, slogans dedicated to Mussolini, murals. But even here, many were left in place, such as the huge obelisk with *Mussolini* written down the side that can still be seen close to the Olympic Stadium in the capital. Of course, many "new towns" all over Italy were intrinsically fascist in themselves, and a simple change of name (from Littoria to Latina in 1946; Mussolinia to Arborea) made little real difference. Sometimes the names were not changed at all.

While many murals were painted over, some were restored, and can still be seen today while traces of fading fascist propaganda can be found everywhere in Italy. Sometimes, the removal of a fascist monument was transformed into a political event. In Bologna, a bronze statue of Mussolini on a horse was melted down and partly recast as a monument to the partisans in 1947. Mussolini's head had been knocked off by demonstrators on July 26, 1943. This massive head is still conserved in a palazzo in the same city. Other surviving fascist monuments became the focus of ongoing celebrations by those nostalgic for the regime, such as certain tombs in Rome's Verano cemetery. Fascism left its mark in every city, and often in the city center, and these buildings are usually still in use today, perhaps stripped of their more political symbols, mosaics, statues, and messages (but not in every case). The very nature of architecture in the 1930s meant that the "fascist" nature of many of these buildings was deeply ambiguous. Many "fascist" buildings are important examples of modernism—despite being constructed under the regime. It is sufficient to cite two celebrated examples here: Michellucci's station in Florence and Terragni's *Casa del Fascio* in Como.

The 1990s saw a series of debates over fascist symbols, street names, and buildings, as the neofascist right came back into the mainstream political fold, and looked to impose its own memories of the past in various cities. Mussolini's residence in Rome until 1943, Villa Torlonia, was restored and opened to the public. A proposal by the Mayor of Rome in the 1990s, Francesco Rutelli (elected as head of a center-left coalition), to name a road in honor of the fascist Giuseppe Bottai met with a storm of protest, and Rutelli backed down.[41] In 2008, with the election of a mayor in Rome whose background was in the neofascist tradition, there were proposals to name a street after the former secretary of the MSI, Giorgio Almirante. Some argued that fascist monuments and symbols should be left in place as a warning to future generations, as part of Italy's history. These events itself are not only about public memory but also center on the ways that the memory of the regime survived in people's minds, and in their own narratives about the past.

4

Italian Wartime Camps, Italians in Wartime Camps

Traces, Memories, Silences, 1940–2008

Wooden shacks in a field and a monument close to the Reggio Calabria-Salerno motorway; a plaque on a church in Holborn in London and a cross near a remote beach on a Scottish island; a debate over a plan to build a furniture store near Visco (Udine); walls and assorted buildings in a wood in the Province of Arezzo, near the banks of the Tiber.

* * *

All of these constructions, traces of buildings and signs mark the presence—during World War II—of camps where people were held against their will at various times in Italy and where Italians were held outside of the peninsula. Many were used for different kinds of people over time—civilians, prisoners of war, political prisoners, foreigners interned for various reasons, criminals (however defined), Jews and other religious and ethnic minorities, and refugees. Camps and the sites of camps frequently changed, their use and their intake shifting in line with changing fortunes in war and peacetime, moving borders, different governments, patterns of occupation and debates over who was in charge.

When discussing various forms of camps (in Italy, and abroad) in this period, we need to be very careful to avoid confusion, and emotive language. The words "concentration camps" (and *Lager* in Italian usage) tend to invoke—for many, today—Auschwitz and the extermination of European Jews. But most wartime camps were not "death camps," and many Nazi camps were not extermination camps. One "death camp" (with ovens to burn the bodies) operated during the war on what had been Italian soil, in Trieste.

Italy under fascism was crisscrossed with a network of prisons and camps. But the vast majority of these places of confinement, especially before 1943, were created to contain, to imprison. Civilians could be interned or imprisoned after 1940 in Italy for a variety of reasons and in a wide range of places. With the wartime regime, the network of places of confinement took on proportions never seen in the past, but the legacy of these places was quickly forgotten, and most historians showed little interest in this subject until the 1990s.

Let us start with a set of questions: Where were these camps, who was held there, and what happened when they closed? How should "memory" of these camps be transmitted, if at all, and to whom? Was it possible in the chaos of postwar Italy and Yugoslavia to preserve the memory of these places? Should there be museums, plaques, sign-posts? Had simple forgetting taken place, or something more sinister? Was there a desire to destroy signs of this past? Had there been a "general desire to forget the fascist period and the war, and its often painful consequences"?[1] How important was the "myth of the good Italian"? In what sense were the sites of these camps "non-places of memory"?[2]

*   *   *

These issues of history and memory will be at the heart of our journey into this past, and the present, a journey that begins in 1940.

With the outbreak of World War II, all belligerent countries began to round up (and expel, or both) foreign nationals present within their territories, especially from those nations with which they were at war. In most cases, plans were in place for these internments well before the conflict began. Hence, the United Kingdom arrested Germans (from 1939) and Italian men of "fighting age" (from June 1940), while Japanese, Germans and Italian-Americans were interned in the United States.

In Italy, the first round-ups began in 1940, and involved three separate groups. Those nationals in Italian territory against whom Italy was at war (often after Italy had invaded their territory)—at different times included the French, Slovenes, Croats, Montenegrins, English (and later Americans), Albanians, Greeks, Russians. "Dangerous" Italian civilians were also taken to these camps. A second category of people were arrested and interned on religious and racial grounds beyond those to do with nationality: foreign Jews, who were taken in even if Italy was not at war with their country of origin. Finally, camps were also used for prisoners captured during Italy's occupations of Greece, France, Albania, and Yugoslavia—as well as from other places—Allied soldiers, and others from the colonies. POW camps were run by the military, while internment camps were administered by the civil authorities. However, these distinctions were not always so clear-cut in reality, as with so many things in wartime. The definition of who and who wasn't a soldier became fuzzy. Boundaries were blurred.

A galaxy of camps covered most regions in Italy, what Collotti has called "an Italian concentration camp system"[3]—and this system changed in relation to the war itself. Most of these places (and what had happened within them) were entirely ignored (or forgotten) by historians and the local population in the years after the end of the conflict. Some historians felt that they were working in a void when they began to carry out research into these sites. They had to "start from nothing."[4] In some regions, such as Tuscany, the memory of the camps had been more or less wiped out. For Galimi, "None of these buildings is a place of memory: there is no plaque or sign which describes the use made of these places during the war."[5]

This "forgetting" was for a number of reasons. First, people had more immediate worries in the postwar period. Italy needed to be reconstructed and lives rebuilt after the horrors of the conflict. Sometimes—in a bizarre twist of fate—the former camps were used for this reconstruction effort, as temporary housing for refugees or those who had lost their houses in wartime bombing. The last thing on most people's minds was the need to remember the war itself. Second, the people kept in the camps were often there for short periods and many were foreigners, with no natural links with the places where they were kept. Third, the desire to move on from fascism naturally marginalized the idea that thousands of people had been kept in camps all over Italy under the regime. Moreover, the continuity of the state and its institutions meant that many of those who had been actively involved in running the camps, or had made money from their presence, were still around and in positions of power, and very happy to let memories fade. For Italians, these camps were uncomfortable (and complicated) reminders of the past, of the gray zone. It was much easier to pretend that nothing had happened at all. Dominant resistance narratives pushed other stories to the margins. In general, these camps seemed a poor fit with the powerful myth of the "good Italian," which pervaded the nation after the war. Yet, as we will see, some of the camps (for those who had been in them) also *reinforced* the "good Italian" myth in other ways.

Rediscovering the Camps: The Historian and the Writer

In the 1980s, historian Carlo Spartaco Capogreco made trips to many of the sites of these various kinds of wartime camps across Italy. He was followed by writer Fabio Galluccio in the 1990s. As Galluccio in some ways retraced Capogreco's steps, he found out about the historian's work. The story of these journeys (largely in search of nothing, of ruins, of emptiness) is told in Galluccio's subsequent book and, in a more scientific way, in Capogreco's studies of the camps.[6] Both discovered a variety of forms of forgetting and absences, and in fact, this is the very subject of Galluccio's book. Many local studies had been carried out on the history of these sites, but nothing at a national level.

There seemed to be enormous indifference or ignorance about the very presence of many of these places. Local people were reluctant to talk about the camps, or simply overlooked their (past) existence. Some ex-camps had become schools; others were abandoned or had been knocked down. None were intact. Only one ex-civilian camp had become a museum (opened in 2004). Occasionally the place itself was almost impossible to track down, having become something else in the meantime. At times there were signs of official memory, often there was nothing at all. At one site, Galluccio discovered a wedding party in course on the site of a former camp.

These sites had thus not become—with a few exceptions—places of memory. But this was not always true. An attempt had been made to mark some camps with classic forms of public memory—plaques, monuments, signs of what had been there. Occasionally, there were local disputes over this memory. Often, local historians had carried out research into the activities of each camp. In recent years, some of this local work is now getting a national airing, as a sign of a more general reawakening of interest in camps.[7] Some camps were more remembered than others. Part of the explanation for this resurgence of attention about fascism's dark past was political. With ex- or postfascists in power, there had been a number of attempts to rehabilitate the regime by ministers and leading politicians in the 1990s and 2000s. Silvio Berlusconi himself had allegedly described internal confinement sites as similar to "holiday-camps." In reaction to this shift, which was a powerful signal of the break-up of an antifascist consensus issues such as the camps became more fashionable. New areas of historical research were opening up, but the reasons for these new branches of research were often (at least under the surface) political rather than "scientific." The "day of memory" also encouraged more work and interest in the early stages of anti-Semitic persecution in Italy, and in the camp system in general.

Ferramonti: Calabria, 1940–2008

Jews, in themselves, are a danger to public order.

—Arturo Bocchini, head of the Italian police force
(circular to Italian Prefects, November 15, 1938)

Ferramonti's camp was one of the largest in Italy for interned civilians, and specialized in the imprisonment of foreign Jews (as well as Jews in Italy who had been stripped of Italian citizenship thanks to the anti-Semitic laws) from 1940 until the Allied landings in Calabria in September 1943. The place looked like a concentration camp (with barbed wire and fences) and was situated close to the railway lines at about 35 kilometers from Cosenza. It consisted of ninety-two cabins or shacks and something like 2,000 foreigners were held there after 1940, including Yugoslav Jews deported after the Italian invasion. Conditions were poor, and a number of inmates died during their stay. After 1943, it seems that a number of internees joined up with the partisans, some remained in the area while others tried to make it back home.

For various reasons, the camp was destroyed after the war, and only about ten percent remains today. In 1988—thanks in part to Capogreco himself—a Ferramonti Foundation was set up to preserve the memory of this place and promote research and educational activities. Eleven years later, the area received official protection from a government decree. Ferramonti is thus a strong example of memory promotion and discussion linked to an Italian internment camp. Most of the other ex-camps have only been studied locally, or are just beginning to be understood and recognized.

Thanks to the Fondazione Ferramonti, conferences were held and ex-inmates visited the site (as they had done spontaneously throughout the postwar period). The foundation organizes guided tours, and has also tried to preserve what remains of the camp from further damage from the motorway expansion. School groups regularly visit the camp and the Jewish section of the local cemetery, where those who died in the camp are buried.[8] During the 1990s and afterwards, the Fondazione promoted public memory initiatives linked to other camp sites, such as this plaque on the island of Arbe in Croatia, with its short but powerful message (in Italian, and Croatian): "In memory of those who, in 1942–1943, were interned, suffered or died here at the hands of fascist Italy."[9]

When the camp was "rediscovered" by historians and others in the 1980s and 1990s, there were still items left there after the area was abandoned in 1943.[10] The notorious Salerno-Reggio Calabria motorway cut right through the area of the camp in the 1960s, destroying a large section. Thanks to the work of local historians and politicians, however, Ferramonti became the focus of memory creation around the history of the Jews in Italy after 1940, and the whole camp system. In any case, it wasn't just the physical destruction of these places that led to their being forgotten, as Capogreco points out, "Ferramonti . . . was destroyed by forgetting, before the bulldozers and the building sites arrived."[11] Memory and forgetting could not be read directly from the physical state of the sites. Physical sites of memory are important for the transmission of the past—especially with fewer and fewer living witnesses—but they are not everything.

One thorny issue for historians studying these camps was that many ex-inmates had "good" memories of their stay there. There are a number of ways of explaining "happy" or positive memories of these civilian camps (that have not emerged from other camps where Slovenians and Croatians, for example, were interned). Many of those interned in 1940 were in some way "saved" by this measure (and by chance) from a worse fate. Naturally, looking back, these camps seemed (and were) a good alternative to death camps in Germany, Poland, and Austria. By being sent to Ferramonti, some avoided Auschwitz. In comparison with what they went through afterwards, the experience in the camp was often seen in relatively positive terms, even by Italian Jews after the war.

While there is some truth to this assertion, it is also true that a number of those interned in civilian camps were eventually sent to death camps. Some 141 Jews interned in Ferramonti were eventually deported elsewhere during the war. Only eleven of these survived. The dead could not transmit any "happy" memories of the past. Moreover, the very practice of internment and registration provided the Nazis with information that they were to use to round up Jews after September 8, 1943. Oral history, by definition, only captures the memory of those who survived. Finally, the "good memories" of these civilian camps should be seen in the context of the rest of the war, with the powerful myth of the "good Italian," and the dangers of the ever-present and "fatal" comparison with Nazi Germany. The moral stain remains.

As Capogreco has argued, "If it is true that in the fascist camps for the Jews the dignity of the inmates was not offended, it is also true that the dignity of man was offended by the very facts that these camps existed—as an extreme consequence of the 1938 racial laws—which denied many thousand innocent people of their liberty."[12] Thousands of people were arrested and kept in camps in Italy purely thanks to their "religious" affiliations, as well as for political or ethnic reasons. Despite this fact, many ex-internees seemed to support the myth of the "good Italian." These private memories cannot simply be dismissed. They need to be seen within a complicated set of relationships with the realms of historical research, that of politics and the role of official or public memory.[13] Memory of these camps was once again divided.

Sometimes the "good Italian" myth was also translated into public memory, as with this plaque at Urbisaglia close to Macerata:

> *In the gray and dark hours of Auschwitz we always had in front of us, like a mirage, the luminous garden of Fiastra Abbey, in Italy, a country of sun and good people.*

Paul Pollak, 8 September '43–1993.

Yet Pollak was the only inmate to survive of the 100 or so Jews who had been held in the camp, who were later sent to Fossoli and on to Auschwitz. On September 30, 1943, all those interned had been picked up by trucks and taken away by the Nazis. In this sense, this plaque is a strange way to remind people of an internment that led directly, for all but one of its number (Pollak), to the gas chamber.

Renicci: Tuscany, 1942–2008

> The discovery of the existence of a concentration camp close to Anghiari was almost like the unearthing of an archaeological treasure.
>
> —Daniele Finzi, "La vita quotidiana di un campo di concentramento fascista"

Italy's wars created the need for camps to hold so-called opponents of fascism. Slovenians, Croatians, and Serb civilians arrested under occupation were transferred to these camps in the 1940s. "Undesirable aliens"—such as gypsies—were also interned. Conditions were notably worse for "Slav" inmates than in other camps, such as those set up for foreign Jews.

Renicci, a wooded area on the banks of the Tiber in the Province of Arezzo, was one such camp. Internees began to arrive here in October 1942 and the camp eventually held thousands of Croatian, Montenegrin, and Slovenian civilians (alongside Italian political internees). As at Ferramonti, barbed wire surrounded the camp, but memories of Renicci (unlike those linked to Ferramonti) were not happy ones. Death rates here—thanks in large part to poor nutrition and the cold—were high and over 100 people perished. After September 8, the prisoners escaped—en masse—and many joined (or formed) local partisan bands. October 1943 saw the camp reopen under the control of local fascist militia.

After the war, the area was used as an arms dump, until a fatal explosion in July 1946. Since then, locals have built houses close to the former camp. For Galluccio, at Renicci, "nothing has been done in order to remember,"[14] while Capogreco points out that there is "no plaque, no sign."[15] Some traces of the camp remain—the morgue, the house of the colonel who ran the camp, and part of the barracks. None of the exterior fence survived, and apart from these buildings and ruins, "the structure of the camp has been entirely wiped out, just like the events of sixty years ago."[16] Yet locals—in oral history interviews—did recall the presence of the camp and events linked to its history. Some remember prisoners being marched to Renicci from the station, and a local historian has worked extensively on the camp's history, which has become better known thanks to the work of a few isolated but tenacious researchers.

Some local attempts have been made to remember Renicci. In 1973, a collective grave was created for 446 Yugoslav partisans who died during the Resistance in this area and in 1977 a museum was opened in nearby Sansepolcro. Ex-prisoners returned to the camps, often without any kind of official blessing. Yugoslavia's civil war in the 1990s and the creation of Croatia, Slovenia, Serbia, and Montenegro did not help in terms of the issue of memory and commemoration of the victims from these countries in Italy, and in Italian camps. For one thing, it wasn't clear anymore just whose memory was to be remembered. From one reference-point, there were now at least four, all with different agendas, and none of whom were necessarily in line with the way memory was organized, or promoted, under Tito.

Other Camps: Memory and Legacy

How many camps were there? Nobody seems to know for sure. Capogreco has estimated that there were at least 130 in the whole of Italy, and has produced detailed lists of the civilian camps. But "Italy" was an elastic concept from 1940–1943, as it included all the territories that had been occupied by the Italian army – in Albania, Greece, Yugoslavia, France, and the colonies.

Chronology was also a problem. When did camps stop becoming camps? Can clear lines be drawn between 1940–1943 or 1943–1945 and even with after 1945? Should we not link fascist confinement policies with those of war and then with the Republic of Salò and under the Nazis? Many camps were also reused as *camps* for prisoners of war or Istrian refugees. This was true, for example, in Trieste, Bolzano, and at Fossoli (three of the most important camps).

The least remembered groups of prisoners (in Italy) were probably the Yugoslavs, who were also the biggest group of internees beyond prisoners of war. Gypsies and other religious minorities were also written out of history, and were branded as "nonpeople" in prison and confinement. After Italy invaded in 1941, 100,000 Yugoslavs were interned, as a large part of that country was annexed, and the ethnic cleansing policies that had been applied throughout the period of the regime were exacerbated.[17] In May 1941, Italy took over the Province of Lubiana, and created camps for opponents of various kinds on the island of Arbe and elsewhere. These sites were in addition to camps for Yugoslavs inside Italy's former borders, such as at Gonars near Udine and at Renicci.

Very few Italians are aware of the existence of such camps, and even fewer are well-informed about the history of these places. An oft-reproduced photograph of a skeletal man from Arbe was passed off as a photo from a Nazi camp on a number of occasions after the war. One reason for this silence and ignorance was the absence of judicial proceedings against Italians after the war. Not one Italian official, general, or soldier ever stood trial for any of these war crimes. Twenty percent of the inmates at Arbe died, an extremely high figure that is close to that of some Nazi camps. Yet, until recently, there was not a single book about Arbe or Gonars published in Italy.[18]

The myth of the "good Italian"—and the related myths of Italians as victims and Italy as having "won the war"—were reinforced by (and also contributed to) the impunity of the entire Italian army for its crimes abroad. International politics did the rest. This failure to take responsibility for the occupations of and crimes in Africa, Yugoslavia, Greece, France, and Albania was also part of an international pact of forgetting, where Nazi Germany was the universally acknowledged bad guy. Italy was not alone in this collective failure to remember or acknowledge its recent past. It would take time to acknowledge "what had really happened during the war" and for a long time there was "an overwhelming desire to block the memory or else recast it in a useable way that would not corrode the fragile bonds of post-war society." [19] In Italy's case, this pact came at a high cost, as investigations of Nazi crimes were shelved in the "cupboard of shame." Justice was not done, and many conflicts remained open.

Italians Abroad: The Tragedy of the Arandora Star

On June 10, 1940, Mussolini declared war on Great Britain, a country with thousands of Italian immigrants. The British-Italian community was a social and cultural mix, including factory workers, chefs, waiters, tailors, intellectuals, knife-grinders, shopkeepers, and ice-cream salesmen. Politically, the Italians were divided, with well-organized fascist sympathizers and a number of antifascists. There were even Italian Jews who had thought they could escape persecution in the United Kingdom.[20] That night, the British police began to round up hundreds of men of Italian origin largely between the ages of seventeen and sixty. At a stroke, these men were branded as "enemy aliens." Overnight, it became obvious to them that they were still Italian, even if they had been born in England, or had been working there for years. Winston Churchill summed up this policy with a pithy and oft-quoted phrase: "collar the lot."[21]

Most of these men were kept in camps, with a large number on the Isle of Man, in the North of England and in Scotland. Many were deported in large groups, within days of being arrested and without being accused of any crime. On the night of June 30, 1940, a ship—the Arandora Star—set sail for Canada with about 1,200 Italians and Germans on board (plus 370 or so members of the crew and guards). The ship had no protection, but there were guns visible on deck.

Some of the Italians on board were antifascists who had emigrated to escape from the regime. A few had sons in the British army. The next morning, a German submarine sunk the liner close to the Irish coast; 446 Italians died. Many of the survivors were packed onto another ship on July 11. This time, the deportees were bound for Australia. Luckily, this ship arrived at its destination.

The response to this tragedy since then has been a long silence, at least in terms of official, national memory, both in Italy and in the UK. But local memories of the disaster (and of the "injustice" of internment, as well as the anti-Italian riots of 1940) were strong. As Bernabei wrote in 1997, "For the Italians in the UK this memory was very strong and in the following decades the sinking of the Arandora Star never lost its immediacy."[22] Italians in London and elsewhere tried to obtain justice and kept the memory of their loss alive. Twenty years after the tragedy (but on the anniversary of Vittorio Veneto—November 4—not that of the sinking) a plaque was unveiled on the front of the Italian church in Holborn:

> *In Memory of those who died in the sinking of the Arandora Star*
> *2 July 1940 . . . the memory is still alive in the hearts of the relatives, the*
> *survivors and the Italian community*
> *4 November 1960*

London's Italians thus combined the memory of World War I with that of World War II, and the monuments for both events were located in the same place. After 1960, the anniversary and the commemoration for both events became that of November 4. Memory was also created and carried forward by the Italian community in Scotland. Silences and "forgetting" of this tragedy were neither straightforward, nor total. There was no blanket forgetting of the Arandora Star, but a set of memories and silences that varied in time and space, and were patterned by politics, local factors, and myths, as well as by the activities of individuals (historians, journalists, relatives of the victims). Initial silences (in part due to the climate of the war, and the very nature of the disaster, or as ways of creating "a protective cover by those affected"[23]) were often followed by "rememoration" and it was on this basis that there were a flourishing of local initiatives in Italy and the UK since the late 1960s and 1970s.[24]

None of this, however, became part of the national memory of Italy or the UK. There was no national audience for this story, and it jars with prevailing narratives of resistance. Attempts to raise the issue at a political level also fell on deaf ears. For Umberto Sereni, historian and Mayor of Barga, the tragedy had been "forgotten twice: by fascist Italy because the ship was sunk, in an act of war, by the German Allies, and by post-war Italy, because the English were no longer our enemies and the new Allies had defeated the Nazi-Fascists."[25]

In the 1980s, Bernabei—an Italian journalist and playwright based in London—produced an excellent television documentary about the Arandora Star, but found few who were willing to listen to this story back in Italy. But over time, and in part thanks to research of Bernabei and that of Maria Serena Balestracci, taboos have also fallen away, as with so many other "difficult" areas relating to World War II.[26] There has been a proliferation of monuments, commemorations, and events linked to the Arandora Star over the last decade, which has created a series of sites and places of memory that are no longer merely local or linked to the private memories of relatives of the victims.

Forty-six of the victims were from the small town of Bardi, near Parma. Most had been arrested in Wales. In Bardi, a small chapel is dedicated (to all the victims) of the sinking of the Arandora Star, with photos added by relatives of some of the victims from other parts of Italy. A committee had been set up to remember the victims from Bardi in 1968. Over time, Bardi has developed into the center of ceremonies for all the Italian victims of the tragedy. Barga in Tuscany now also has its own plaque and memorial. A commemorative plaque was put up in 2004 in Lucca. A further eighteen of those who died were from Picinisco, a tiny hill town in the Lazio mountains. A plaque there is dedicated to the local victims of the tragedy, and the inscription on the stone (put up in 1988) is a call for "peace" and reconciliation, which makes reference to the liberation of Italy by the British army. In other places, names from the Arandora Star were added to local war memorials.

Other memorials were more unusual. Bodies of Italians and Germans washed up on the Scottish and Irish coasts, where various local monuments remember this shocking event. Many were never identified. Giuseppe Delgrosso's skeletal remains reached the remote island of Colonsay in the Hebrides, forty-five days after the ship had gone down. A 61-year-old ice-cream salesman, Delgrosso (who was originally from Borgo Val di Taro, near Parma) had been in the UK since 1913. He was identified via a piece of paper in his pocket. A simple wooden cross marked the place where Delgrosso was found, and since 2005, a monument stands at the same spot, with this inscription (although his body was moved to his family plot in Glasgow):[27]

Sacred to the memory of
Giuseppe Delgrosso and of more than 800 others who perished with
"Arandora Star"
July 2nd 1940
fo sgàil do sgiathan falaich mi
Psalm 17, v. 8

Until now, the British government has never apologized for this war crime, which remains something of an open wound in Italian communities in Great Britain and in some towns in Italy. The memory of the Arandora Star was for many years a local and marginalized memory, but it was not a case of divided memory. Local memories met with a wall of indifference and official silence.[28]

But in recent years, books and documentaries have been produced. Journalists have taken up the story in the national press. Songs have been written, streets have been renamed, plays and musicals have been performed, and exhibitions staged. There has been a flourishing of memory.[29] The Arandora Star has become part of Italian and British memories of that conflict, with all its contradictions. A clear sign of this change was the joint memorial opened in Liverpool in 2008—to all the victims (and not just the Italians). A memorial garden is also planned for Glasgow. It is significant that Balestracci's book about the disaster was republished in Italian and English in 2008 (thus confirming the increasing interest in the case in both countries, and not just among Italian communities) and with a new title: *Arandora Star: Dall'oblio alla memoria* (From forgetting to memory).

The Camps, Walls, Monuments, and Divided Memory: Bolzano, Mauthausen, Gusen

I was blocked, I couldn't speak. I saw everything as it was then and I was struck dumb. By closing my eyes I can still see those things even today.

—Roberto Banassi, remembering his first
return trip to Mauthausen in 1975

It looks like a normal wall: nondescript, anonymous. It stands on the outskirts of Bolzano, near the edge of Italy, in a neighborhood called Gries. Behind the wall, which measures 91 x 146 meters, there are some standard blocks of flats.[30] People sit on balconies, they hang out their washing, they take in the view of the mountains around the city.

This is no ordinary wall, however, and the houses are in no ordinary place. Here—where the blocks of flats now stand—once stood one of the biggest Nazi transit and work camps in operation during World War II in this area. At least 11,000 people passed through this camp on their way to other camps in the rest of occupied Europe between the summer of 1944 and May 3, 1945.[31] Bolzano had been incorporated under direct Nazi rule into the Third Reich after September 8, 1943, ceasing to be part of Italy.

Many of those held in the Fossoli camp near Carpi were moved to Bolzano in 1944 when the camp in Emilia was wound down in that year. Many also died in the Bolzano camp, although nobody knows exactly how many (the "official" figure is forty-eight, but this is almost certainly an underestimate). Thousands were used as slave labor. Most were political prisoners, although there were also Jews and Gypsies, as well as some gay men and lesbians. Prisoners were assigned different colored triangles—red (political), green (family members), or yellow (Jews).[32]

The camp was built by prisoners on the site of a barracks used for military transport vehicles, and opened around July 1944. It consisted of four large buildings, a series of some fifty tiny cells, as well as a roll-call space. Bolzano's camp was therefore constructed on a large scale, and was also a place of death as well as a site of torture and murder (although it wasn't a death camp as such; it wasn't built to exterminate people). The punishment block was largely under the control of two Ukrainians, Michel Seifert and Otto Sein.

When the camp was in operation, there were from three to four thousand prisoners here at any one time. Many of the women were forced to work in a local factory producing spherical cushions, while the men were employed in various war-related jobs, such as the maintenance of those same railway lines that would transport many of them to death camps outside of Italy. Bolzano-Gries was closed at the end of April 1945, and its prisoners released.

After the war, for a short time (as with many other camps) the area held German prisoners. It was then utilized for children's games and as a summer camp, and then as temporary refuge for those made homeless by wartime bombings. Much later (between 1962 and 1968), what remained of the camp was razed to the ground, and then private housing went up. Only one side wall was left standing. People moved in to their new homes. At this point, it seemed, the camp itself would be forgotten forever. At about the same time, the ex-Nazi camp known as the Risiera di San Sabba in Trieste became a national monument.

Divided Memories or Silence?

Public opinion repressed for a long time the very existence of the Bolzano camp.

—Pfeifer, "Il Polizeiliche Durchgangslager Bozen 1944–1945"

The legacy of this camp was an extremely uncomfortable one in a city with deep social, political, and ethnic divisions. Memory in postwar Bolzano was highly contested, and it was extremely difficult to construct shared ideas about the past. Few tried to do so, and the past was exploited for political gain. It was not easy to use the camp's history in direct political terms, and this "nontranslatable" nature of the site contributed to its absence as a place of memory. For this camp, there was a kind of shared silence—*a pact of forgetting*. In postwar Bolzano, it was easiest, and quite simple, to ignore this place. The ex-camp thus represented a case of silence. Divisions over memory were kept hidden, almost like the location of the ex-camp itself. If the "Monument to Victory" was over prominent—too visible—then the camp site was invisible.[33]

There were (and are) monuments dedicated both to the resistance and to the memory of the camp in Bolzano, but they have tended to be peripheral (physically, and politically), more or less ignored (in many cases), moved around, objects of attack, or simply not part of the official series of ceremonies linked to the liberation. Bolzano's camp was also a place of organized resistance, but this history was little told, and rarely listened to, in the city.

There were a number of explanations for this state of affairs. For one thing, Bolzano citizens had profited from the camp and the exploitation of prisoners as slave labor. Some historians also claim that in the city, "public opinion was behind the political system which had created the camp."[34] Moreover, the prisoners in the camp usually hailed from elsewhere. Many, for example, came from prisons in Milan, Genoa, and Verona. In addition, memories emerging from the camp cut across the ethnic divisions that laid down the political fault lines in the city. Nazis had run the camp, after all, with the help of Ukrainians, German-speakers, and Italians.

It was only in the 1990s that this situation began to change, and Bolzano's "memoryscapes" finally began to include Gries.

Individual Memory: The Camps

Memories of these camps remained strong in the postwar period for the individuals who had experienced these places, and many wrote down their accounts in the form of autobiographies or diaries. Aldo Pantozzi, the son of a station manager in Bolzano, was twenty-five years old in 1944. He worked as a teacher in Trento and was active in the (small) resistance movement. As a result, he was arrested by the Gestapo in November 1944. Imprisoned in Trento, he was transferred as a political prisoner to the Bolzano camp in January 1945, where his hair was shaved off, he was assigned number 8,078 and given a red triangle. Deported to Mauthausen in February, he was there issued with a new number, 126,520. Mauthausen was a living hell, as is clear from the many studies now available of that particular camp. Liberated in May 1945 along with other survivors, he was able to return to Bolzano in June 1945. Pantozzi always carried a photo in his wallet: of a pile of naked bodies from Mauthausen. For many, Bolzano was the last stop before Mauthausen.

Stories like Pantozzi's did not find much of an audience in postwar Italy. His autobiographical account first came out in 1946, but most of the copies were lost, and it was only republished, finally, in the 1990s.[35] Witness accounts of the horrors of deportation failed to become part of national, local, or political memory in the years following the conflict. A minority of activists, and a number of combative organizations, carried out extensive memory work, but in general it took decades for these these private and group memories to become part of a national public discourse about the past. Ex-deportees frequently kept artifacts from the camps, triangles they had been forced to wear, work clothes, letters, and photographs. Often, this material did not emerge from the private sphere until various institutions, such as the Archivio Storico in Bolzano, began to actively look for and collect such relics in the 1990s. This is not to overlook the crucial role of the various deportees and associations, particularly at a local level.

Many Bolzano deportees had barely spoken about their experiences until they formed part of a massive and unique research project involving at least 200 filmed interviews—carried out by two organizations in different parts of Italy—the Biblioteca Civica Popolare of the Comune di Nova Milanese and the Archivio Storico in Bolzano. These interviews have provided a wealth of material, and created an extraordinary set of sources for those interested in the private memories of the deportees.[36] Other research managed to trace and document the names of nearly 8,000 people who passed through Bolzano.[37]

Judicial Memory: The Seifert Trial

Michel Seifert arrived in Italy in 2008, on a military plane from Canada. He was eighty-four-years-old, and had probably thought that he would never be arrested, let alone brought to trial, for his activities in Bolzano during the war. But Seifert was wrong. The wheels of justice had moved very, very slowly. And yet, in the end, they had got their man, who was described at his trial in bureaucratic language, as born in Landau (Ukraine) on March 16, 1924, and resident in Vancouver (Canada) at 5471, Commercial Street. A (military) trial was held, a culprit had been found, and that same man is now serving time in a military prison in the south of Italy (in Santa Maria Capua Vetere). Michel "Misha" Seifert had lived a quiet life in Vancouver in Canada for more than fifty years after the end of the war. And then his past came back to haunt him. Seifert was arrested for the first time in May 2002, but it was to take almost six more years for extradition proceedings to finally come to an end.

The first Italian judicial inquiries into the events linked to the Bolzano camp date back to 1946. Detailed lists of the torturers and murderers who worked in the camp were produced in 1945 and sent to the legal authorities. Legal investigations were opened in after the war, and eight local ex-guards stood trial in 1945–1947 in Bolzano. These men were, however, soon released. A number of witnesses were interrogated and information was collected with regard to Nazi crimes in the camp, but this long-running inquiry was finally shelved by a military tribunal in 1960. In that decade, further judicial investigations were opened in Dortmund in West Germany with relation to the Bolzano camp. In Italy, there was total silence on the judicial front for more than thirty years, until the 1990s.[38]

As with the Trieste and Risiera trial in the 1970s, the trial of Seifert proved to be a useful exercise from the point of view of justice for the victims and historical research. Unlike with Trieste, the Bolzano trial actually saw the arrest and imprisonment of a living protagonist of violence in the camp. Seifert had been responsible for murder and torture in Bolzano, and his sadistic behavior was remembered by many. Twenty witnesses were heard during the trial. Accused of fifteen specific murders (and torture), Seifert was given a life sentence in November 2000 (confirmed in 2001 and 2002 by the higher courts) for eleven specific cases.[39] It was only thanks to material found in the "archive of shame" in the 1990s, information that had been deliberately covered-up by the Italian state, that the trial against Seifert was able to take place.[40]

Seifert was a murderer, and had taken part in torture during the war. But his arrest, trial and imprisonment was also a question of chance—above all the fact that he was still alive. Justice here was as important; above all on a symbolic level. Seifert's trial had little impact, however, with relation to the political and state-run system responsible for construction and organization of the camp system and deportations under the Nazi empire. One "bad apple" had been prosecuted, but Bolzano had been part of an operation where thousands of people were systematically exploited, starved, beaten, and eliminated. This system was left untouched by the Seifert trial.

Public Memory

Public memory of the Bolzano camp was minimal in the city until the 1990s, when renewed interest in deportations as well as in the holocaust, and the extraordinary work of Carla Giacomozzi, responsible for the local historical archive, began to create places and routes of memory across the city.[41] After a long battle, the surviving camp wall was renovated and saved by law (in 2003) as a historic monument. Plaques and information boards, as well as a statue-monument, were put up there, as well as signs indicating the route to the wall. Other monuments to the deportees were placed all over the city. In 2000, further institutional support and space was created by the law on the day of memory for the Shoah, which also contributed to changes with regard to the commemorative activities linked to the Bolzano camp. With the day of memory law, local authorities and politicians were obliged to organize—or simply take part in—events linked to the memory of the Shoah. As a result, these events gained publicity, funding, and were accompanied by activities in schools and within local communities. Some of this was perfunctory, and purely ceremonial, but it also provided space for important research, and for a recognition of the importance of the holocaust.

Annual ceremonies are now held on both January 27 and April 25 (at the Monumento ai Caduti per la Libertà in Piazza Adriano). Exhibitions have used some of the material gathered by Giacomozzi, including drawings and items preserved by camp survivors and their families.[42] Interviews were gathered with hundreds of survivors and witnesses. It was no longer so easy to ignore what had happened in the city during the war. Bolzano's memoryscapes had been enriched. The city's pact of silence, or forgetting, had broken down.

In recent years, three monuments by the same artist have been placed at different points in the city, and are thus united in terms of style and subject matter, as a reminder of three different, yet linked, aspects of the Nazi camp system—forced labor, the prison camps themselves, and the transport of people to camps elsewhere. Thirteen wagon-trains full of prisoners left Bolzano for various camps between August 8, 1944, and March 22, 1945, and their destinations included Mauthausen (five trains) and Auschwitz (one). Christine Tschager from Bolzano won the competition, and the monument close to the train lines is particularly effective, with its abandoned luggage and clothes sculpted in white stone (Figure 4.1).

After years of silence, there has been a serious attempt to sustain and create places of memory across the city, through a complicated set of commemorative and informative and artistic sites. Before all this memory production, there were a few monuments to the victims of the Nazis and the

Figure 4.1 Bolzano: Public artwork dedicated to wartime deportations.
Christine Tschager (artist).

deportations, but they were often contested, marginalized in terms of their
visibility and their positioning, and not sponsored by state institutions.

The first monument to appear in Bolzano in connection with the camp
was put up in 1955, thanks to the initiative of a priest who had taken part
in the resistance. Today this monument stands not far from the ex-camp,
in the garden of a church. Nearby, there is another monument from 1965,
which was the first official attempt to commemorate the Gries camp. Initially, this monument, which also carried a simple map of the camp, was
much closer to Via Resia itself. The inscription on the 1965 plaque was as
follows: "Here men of different nationalities suffered and died for the cause
of liberty in the struggle against Nazi-fascism [with the same message in
German]. 1945–1965."[43]

In 1985, however, the map was removed (nobody knows why) and
replaced with an official dedication for the fortieth anniversary of the liberation. At the same time, this monument was moved from its position
in a small garden near the ex-camp site to the garden of a church nearby.
It was, in this way, both re- (and) de-faced and de-localized. Thus, while
the official blessing was a step forward, the marginalization in a physical
sense of the monument represented two steps backward. Discussions have

continued about the inscription itself ("men" but not "women" are mentioned, nationalities but not religions). In 1999, a petition asked for the plaque to be put back in its original setting, but the previous site is not public property and nothing has changed since then.

1943–1945
Men of different nationalities suffered and died for the cause of liberty in the struggle against Nazi-fascism [with the same message in German].

The City of Bolzano on the fortieth anniversary of the Liberation (for these monuments, see Figure 4.2)

Figure 4.2   Bolzano: Plaques dedicated to the memory of the wartime Nazi camp, 2008.

In the same year, a statue nearby was also erected for the same reason. In 2008, Italy's president visited both this site and the wall in Via Resia. Memory of the camp had finally achieved official blessing at a national level.

Over the years since 1945, many war-linked monuments in Bolzano—and not just the Monument to Victory—have been attacked at different times, such as the *Monument ai caduti per la libertà* in 1957 (only two years after its unveiling). Monuments and plaques in Bolzano (and the rest of the region) were a key part of an ongoing and violent "memory war," which was linked to the overall "question" of Alto Adige, and which rumbled on throughout the postwar period.

Today the ex-camp, as we have seen, has become part of a "route of memory" through the town, and numerous studies have been produced detailing what happened there.[44] Bolzano's camp is no longer forgotten or silenced. Its memory has—to some extent—become both official and "shared" and its surviving wall has become a place of memory. Meanwhile, behind the wall, where the camp used to be, people sit on their balconies, hang out their washing and water their plants.

BBPR: Architecture, Resistance, and Memory

Suffering filled every space, like something solid. You could feel it in the slow rustling of those who moved around [the camp], you could recognise it in voices and gestures, it was transmitted to objects, places, landscapes.

—Lodovico Barbiano di Belgiojoso

Two young architects were held briefly in the Bolzano camp. Lodovico Barbiano di Belgiojoso (born in 1909) was arrested in Milan in March 1944 as a result of antifascist activities. After San Vittore and Fossoli, he was transported to Bolzano in August 1944, and then to Mauthausen and then to the subcamp of Gusen, where he managed to survive. Gian Luigi Banfi was less fortunate. Arrested on the same day as Belgiojoso, he reached Gusen in the same transport group. On the day before he was taken to Austria, Banfi had a letter smuggled out to his wife. This is part of what he wrote: "This experience is difficult, bitter: my distance from you breaks my heart, but my morale is high and I am not complaining about this deep experience . . . this descent into the abyss." Banfi was gassed in the camp just two weeks before the liberation. He was thirty-four years old.

Both these architects had already set up a practice in Milan—known as BBPR thanks to a combination of surnames—with Ernesto Rogers and Enrico Peressutti. After the war, BBPR maintained its full name and the well-known "abstract" monument to the deported—in Milan's Cimitero

Monumentale—was in part a tribute to the memory of the two Bs, Banfi and Belgiojoso, who had suffered deportation.[45] Rogers's father Romeo had also died in Auschwitz. Belgiojoso's drawings of the camps were to form part of a powerful recent traveling exhibition that has been shown in Italian cities, alongside the sketches and material collected by his friend and fellow prisoner Germano Facetti.

Belgiojoso dedicated an important part of his postwar architectural work to the memory of the deportations and the Shoah. He went on to design—with others—a series of monuments dedicated to the deportees: the memorial at Gusen (Mauthausen), where Banfi was killed, the remarkable Italian pavilion at Auschwitz, the Deportees Monument-Museum at Carpi and the powerful Monument for the Deported in the Parco Nord (1998) in Milan.[46] This body of work represents a unique attempt to create a network of permanent memorials for the deported from Italy, as original forms of "land art" and, in the case of Gusen, the only permanent memorial on that site (although there is now also a visitor center). For Belgiojoso, "Memory was both a torment and a duty."

Belgiojoso once said that he had "a deep desire . . . for silence," but he continued to work intensely around the memory of the deportations after the war. The project that was closest to his own experience was the Gusen memorial at the subcamp of Mauthausen where he had been held, and where his friend Banfi had been killed. This site had an extremely complicated and problematic history following its liberation in 1945.

After the area had been under U.S., and then Soviet occupation, it came under Austrian sovereignty in 1955. A plaque and stone had been placed near the furnace in that year. Here there had once been "the oven in which from 1941 onwards the incurably ill, the disabled and those with infectious diseases were killed."[47] Money was raised in Italy in the early 1960s (as well as in France and Belgium) to finance a monument on the spot where the crematorium stood, and a decision was taken to build a permanent monument in 1961 and 1962. There had been plans to remove the crematorium altogether and move it to the Mauthausen museum. Housing was also constructed on the site of the former camp. Austria wanted to forget what had happened there. A reassuring narrative of Austrians-as-victims dominated public narratives around the war and there had been arguments over the cost of creating museums or memorials.[48]

But other groups and individuals were determined to remember Gusen. An Italian whose brother had died there, Ermete Sordo, provided much of the money to buy this large piece of land and laid the first stone for the monument in 1963. Gusen's memorial was officially opened on May 8, 1965. A kind of museum was therefore created with money from the survivors and their families, and is now covered with plaques, photos, and other memorials.[49] The BBPR Gusen project is simple but very moving. It creates—as with the Auschwitz spiral and the museum at Carpi—a journey through the monument itself, making architectural references to the stone crusher in the infamous quarry and "the material used and the location are an illusion to the closed world and the labyrinth of death of the camps."[50] A maze of rooms surround the central memorial space, with its windows and a large cross on the side. Normal houses surround and even overlook the memorial. As Elisabeth Höltz has written, "There are barely any visible traces left of one of the worst and biggest sub-camps linked to Mauthausen."[51] Without the BBPR memorial and the preservation of the oven, Gusen's past would have been rendered invisible. The memorial itself was frequently contested and physically attacked, with numerous examples of graffiti and vandalism over the years.[52] Inside the memorial, a wall is covered with individual and collective plaques, photos, and flowers. As with many other monuments, people interact with the Gusen memorial, leaving physical objects as a sign of their presence.

In 1997, the Austrian government took over management of the site (for years, the key to the memorial had been left at a restaurant nearby from where visitors could pick it up). A new visitor center was opened in 2004. Elsewhere, however, housing was built on the site of the former camp, and the entrance to Gusen has now been transformed into a beautiful villa.[53] As in Bolzano, postwar Austrian reaction to many of these camps (which, in the case of Gusen, were death camps) was to pretend that they had never existed. Mauthausen, to the dismay of many ex-inmates, was cleaned up and made easier to visit, and many signs of the past were removed.

An art project called Audiowalk Gusen (2007) attempted to address the problem of the disappearance, or "normalization" of large sectors of the former area of the camp. An audio guide led visitors on a walk through the town and, with the use of testimonies and other information, recreated audioscapes of what is no longer there. According to those who created this project, "The Gusen Audiowalk seeks out the concealed memory of an area that contained the concentration camps Gusen I and II during the Nazi dictatorship. While following the Audiowalk Gusen, a voice over the headphones will lead you through a pleasant residential and recreational landscape whose surface reveals no traces what happened here in the past . . . You will hear what no longer is visible. You will see what there is at present."[54]

After 1945, therefore, the BBPR group created a series of monuments and nonmonuments that mapped out a new way of understanding both the form and content of commemoration and memorialization. These were also memorials that referred directly to the subjective experiences of members of the BBPR group and families, a way of keeping the memory of their dead partner alive (as with the retention of the Banfi "B" in their firm's name), as well as referring to their own deportation and trauma, and transmitting those memories to others.

Belgiojoso died in 2004. One his last projects (designed in 1998 with his son Alberico) was also linked to the memory of the deportations, and is now to be found in the Parco Nord on the edge of Milan. It consists of a large metal pole carrying stones, with containers of ashes from the camps held below. Long lists of the names of those deported from the industrial areas of nearby Sesto San Giovanni surround the monument. Some of the stones come from Gusen and Mauthausen, as a direct reminder of the quarries where so many prisoners died, and this description made this link clear: "The blood of the deported was washed onto these stones in the quarries of Gusen and Mauthausen." The monument, located up on a hill in the park, is open to the public at all hours, and perhaps it was lucky that Belgiojoso did not live to see what happened on the night of June 13–14, 2008. That morning, park keepers discovered that the monument had been splashed with red paint and partly burnt. The glass of five of the six containers of ashes had been damaged. A demonstration was held at the end of June and the physical damage was quickly repaired, but the moral stain remained.

Italy's Auschwitz "Memorial" is to be found in block 21 of the site, and was inaugurated on April 13, 1980. The initiative for the memorial (or mausoleum as it is sometimes called) came from the *Associazione Nazionale Ex Deportati* (ANED), the national deportees' association, who obtained permission from the Polish government to build the monument at the end of the 1970s. The film director Nelo Risi was involved in (the very long) discussions about the memorial, as was Primo Levi, who wrote the text for the monument (but in the end, only one paragraph of his was actually used). In the words of the organizing committee, the memorial was not intended to be "a copy of the many existing exhibitions about the deportations, but a place of quiet thought and memory." Music was composed for the site by Luigi Nono.

For Auschwitz—and the Italian memorial there—Belgiojoso came up with an abstract form, a spiral walkway. The interior of the memorial was painted with murals in bright colors by Mario Samonà, who wrote that the spiral "presented itself to me like an obsessive vortex which destroyed all the positive propulsions of human life." For Belgiojoso, the spiral was intended to "create and allusion to a nightmarish atmosphere, the nightmare of the deportee torn between the near-certainty of death and the tenuous hope of survival . . . it is an idea of an obsessive and unitary space, created with a rhythm of zones of light and shade which alternate between themselves, allowing for a view, through the window, of the other 'blocks' of the camp, a vision which is just as obsessive."

However, in recent years, and less than thirty years after its inauguration, problems began to emerge with the Italian "block." According to some, "The Memorial seemed abandoned and in a poor state of repair."[55] Moreover, there were issues not just about the practicalities of the monument, but also around its very form. Historian Giovanni De Luna, writing in *La Stampa*, was critical of the memorial, arguing that it was "old, so old that it is almost incomprehensible for the visitor" and that it provided "a vision which is close to the spirit of the 1970s, but has little to do with Auschwitz."[56] A debate followed between ANED president Gianfranco Maris, De Luna, and others at a conference in Turin.[57] In 2008, government plans were revealed to restore the monument, which led to a series of protests and debates, and suspicions were aired that the real plan was to remove the spiral and its contents.

This was a debate not only about how Auschwitz, the Shoah, and the history of the deportations should be remembered (the appearance of the memorial, the possibility of using audiovisual material, the experience of visitors there) but also about what should be remembered (the specific experience of the Jews, the role of antifascists).[58] These debates mirrored those over the day of memory itself, and over commemoration of the deportations. Which camp was more important for Italian memory? Mauthausen or Auschwitz? And which deportee memory was to be remembered?[59] Above all, the debate (although not explicitly) was about the Jewish nature of the Holocaust in Italy and in the camps, and about the political legacy of the war. In this case, a specific place within Auschwitz itself had become the touchstone for these debates, and was thus particularly significant and sensitive. Levi's text for the monument, as Robert Gordon has argued, had been a "political tightrope-act" and "an effort to render Auschwitz integral to a shared national history and national trauma."[60]

The memorial was, in fact, titled "*Memorial in onore degli italiani caduti nei campi di sterminio nazisti*" (Memorial in honor of the Italians who fell in the Nazi extermination camps) and was not specific to Auschwitz (apart, of course, from its location), or the experience of that camp.[61] For the ANED, the memorial was a work of art, and needed to be conserved as such. The defense of the memorial was also a defense of their own history, and of the people associated with the monument's construction. But the ANED seemed to take on board some of the points made by De Luna with regard to the ways in which the memorial should be visited, especially by school groups. They "intend to create the possibility of a dialogue between past and present, and the basis for an interaction between the testimony created by the memorial and the survivors and the next generation." In the summer of 2008, a group of thirty-two young art students from Milan, accompanied by their professors, historians, and representatives of various associations, spent a week in Auschwitz. A project was organized to renovate and rethink the spiral, while maintaining its original form and remaining true to the original idea of the memorial-as-experience. It seemed possible that a compromise would be reached, which would preserve the artistic qualities of the memorial while creating different possibilities for visitors to understand the place they were in, and its relationship with the history and memory of the deportations.

5

1940–1943

Victory, Occupation, Defeat, Collapse, Memory

No historical event is like war, which forces each and every individual to
come to terms with "big" history.

—Gabriella Gribaudi, *Guerra totale*

World War II was presented to the Italians as a heroic moment, and
opposition to Italy's entry into war was muted, not least because the
country had been under a dictatorship for the previous twenty years.[1] Yet,
after an initial sense of "victory," as France surrendered two weeks after
Italy's entry into war, defeat came rapidly, first in Greece and Albania, then
in Africa, then in Russia, and then in Italy itself, in Sicily. This was no ordinary defeat, as its consequences led to the collapse of fascism (on July 25)
and then the break-up of the entire Italian state, with the disintegration of
the army after September 8, 1943.

The Retreat from Russia

The disastrous Soviet campaign (1941–43), involving over 230,000 men,
has been the subject of pioneering historical work and literature by "lay"
historians such as Nuto Revelli and writers like Rigoni Stern.[2] Thousands
of Italian troops were more or less abandoned (and surrounded) on the
freezing banks of the Don river without backup or proper equipment, subject to constant bombardment from Soviet tanks and planes.[3] More soldiers died from the cold than in actual combat. Nuto Revelli's work reveals
his own personal odyssey from convinced fascist to antifascist via the terrible experience of the retreat from Russia, on foot. "And my country?" he
writes, "the only country I believed in was that of the poor beasts who paid

with their lives the mistakes of the 'others' . . . the 8th September moved me, and my choice was immediate, instinctive. As soon as the Germans arrived in Cuneo I ran home, gathered up my three automatic weapons . . . and put them in a rucksack. Then I went to my first partisan base."[4]

The Soviet campaign continued to divide Italians after the war, with arguments with the USSR over prisoners of war and the vast numbers of those who were defined as "missing in action" and "neither dead nor alive."[5] Some Italians were still waiting for final news of their relatives in the 1990s. Human remains continued to arrive, periodically, in zinc coffins. Names were added to many World War I monuments, such as at Redipuglia and a special monument was created for those who died abroad, in Bari. These debates became part of the cold war, with the Italians often being painted as the victims of Russian aggression. As with Yugoslavia, the invasion itself was forgotten. The Russian campaign inspired a number of popular accounts, novels, and works of history in the 1950s and 1960s.[6] As with the Ortigara battles during World War I, the retreat from Russia strengthened the myth of the alpini.

War rapidly became unpopular at home as news filtered back of death, imprisonment, and defeat abroad, and the economic and social effects of the conflict began to hit the home front. Military hubris led to the desperate decision by the King and the Fascist Grand Council to arrest Mussolini, replace his administration, and dissolve the Fascist party. Wartime defeats brought down the regime, just as Caporetto indirectly led to the collapse of Liberal Italy. The forty-five days that followed have been analyzed and reanalyzed by historians, politicians, and others ever since. Italy veered between its allies and the Allies, as the pact of steel came apart at the seams.

World War II, Italy, and Divided Memories

World War II was a turning point in the lives of everyone who experienced it. Ever since the end of that conflict, controversies over the events of wartime have taken two main forms. There have been endless debates over events themselves—what happened?—and connected disputes over the interpretation of those events: why? Both types of controversy had an effect on memory and forms of commemoration. It might then be argued that what has been called divided memory is not only the result of a dispute over memories of the past, but of a debate over why those events happened at all—over their explanation, their origins. Thus, these were debates over history, which have had an impact on memory.

Memories and Total War

On the 10 September these planes arrived and we were children, and naturally we were happy to see these planes because they were the Allies. We were
at the Central Bar waving at these planes, they were the liberators, the liberators . . . because we didn't think anything else would happen.

—Michele Malatesta, Cassino, in Gribaudi, *Guerra totale*

World War II crashed through the lives of Italians like an apocalypse. They
were bombarded from the air, attacked on the ground, rounded up and
deported, arrested and tortured, called up to various kinds of armies,
raped and beaten, deprived of shelter, food, and economic well-being. The
experience was one of *total war*, where civilians were as much of a target
as soldiers—and often more so. During World War I, only Trentino, Alto
Adige, Friuli, and parts of the Veneto had gone through this kind of total-
izing conflict. Between 1940 and 1945, the experience of total war was to
affect large swathes of the peninsula. Few towns escaped bombing, and few
areas were not—at one time or another—used as battlefields. Cyclists and
journalists following the 1946 Giro d'Italia (Tour of Italy) were faced with
a country on its knees. In his report on the course, Armando Cougnet,
the Giro organizer, wrote of "rubble, ruins, destruction and white crosses
everywhere on the route, reminding those who might have already forgotten that a hard partisan war has just taken place."[7]

Some towns were virtually wiped out, such as Cassino, Ortona,
Benevento, Capua, Salerno, Avellino, and Foggia. Big cities suffered carpet bombing—Rome, Milan, Turin, Naples. Nazi massacres of Italians
took place in places as distant as Cefalonia in Greece, Boves in Piedmont,
and as far south as Castiglione di Sicilia. Jews were rounded up en masse,
or simply taken out and shot. Mass rapes of Italian women—by their
"liberators"—traumatized an entire subregion. And this is not even to
mention the experiences within the army, such as the retreat from Russia. Even the end of the war did not bring relief, as the after-effects of
trauma, loss, and reconstruction continued. Rape-produced babies were
born throughout 1945, a malaria epidemic—deliberately started by the
Germans—swept through Lazio[8], soldiers took months, and sometimes
years to return home.

For decades, this experience of *total war* was downplayed in the history books and in public memory linked to the war. The war from 1940
to 1943 was largely ignored, and the resistance was acknowledged as the
only "real" war that had been fought. Bombings, which played (and play)
such a strong role in private memory of the war, were all but removed

from public memory. Mass rape found space in fiction, and in cinema, but not in political narratives about the war. Much of this simply did not fit. Why remember the bombings when those who were doing the bombing had since become Italy's allies? Why study the rapes when the rapists were in the French army, which fascist Italy had "stabbed in the back" in 1940? A cleansed version of the war was passed down, with the partisans as the (only) heroes, as well as a few sacrificial victims (priests, Salvo d'Acquisto) and largely without that sense of "civil resistance" that has recently become so important to the history of the war. Gaps were often created between private memory and public memory, between family-based recollections and narratives and those coming from above, or inscribed in the memoryscapes of cities, towns, and villages. This chapter will attempt to analyze these gaps, to study "the ways in which episode are remembered or forgotten in terms of public narratives."[9]

Rapes and Memory

> They stayed for 9–10 days and in those long days they did what the Germans hadn't done in six months.
>
> —Maria, in Gribaudi, *Guerra totale*

The mass rape of women in Campania and Lazio, largely at the hands of Moroccan soldiers, is fairly well-known thanks to recent historical work and above all—culturally—to Moravia's 1957 novel, *La Ciociara*, and the subsequent film directed by De Sica. However, little serious historical work has been done in this area. The subject was taboo, for many reasons. As Gribaudi puts it, "A discussion of the mass violence used by the Moroccan troops would have meant shedding light on the contradictions of the war . . . it would have signified criticising the way the Allies operated, and a denial of a dualistic view of the war—with good on one side, evil on the other."[10]

Gribaudi dedicates a long section of her book, *Guerra totale*, to the rapes, showing how the women often suffered from the humiliation of rape well after the war was over, and were largely ignored in their lonely quest for compensation or help. In some villages there were no doctors left. The shameful role of military command in this whole episode has never properly been explained, until now. Most of the women, meanwhile, were destined to remain in silence. The ambiguous and unique position of Italy in 1940 to 1945, as she moved from aggressor to "semi-ally" left the civil population vulnerable to revenge and violence from all sides. The Nazis saw the Italians as traitors, and treated them as such. The French army were "liberating" a country that had invaded France in 1940, and had little pity for the locals. The raped women certainly did not recognize what had happened to them as something that could be called "liberation."

Civil Resistance and Total War

The real heroes of World War Two were not recognised by either side.

—Gabriella Gribaudi, *Guerra totale*

With the acceptance of total war came the idea—almost naturally—of a *civil resistance*. If the war itself was no longer confined to a battle between armed combatants, then the whole idea of the resistance needed to be rethought. How did civilians resist occupation and survive the war? This concept also took the resistance out of its traditional heartlands—the mountains of the north and center of the country—into cities across Italy and especially in the south. The resistance lost its capital letter. It became a series of individual and collective acts of defiance. As a result, the memory of the war and resistances to that war also changed. No longer was this to be a memory confined to soldiers or partisans, and mainly to men. Memories of civil resistance were very different, and often linked to women. This was a resistance—frequently—without arms and "nonviolent." But it was also heavily linked with the armed Resistance. Without the support networks that sprung up spontaneously all over Italy, the partisans would have been unable to fight at all.[11]

The very term "civil resistance" is an umbrella definition for a series of isolated or collective acts that "cover a series of different forms of behaviour, whose only common denominator is that they were carried out without arms and by people who had shared very little apart from the fact that they came from the same country."[12] After September 8, 1943, women were in the front line in taking in, hiding, and protecting the hundreds of thousand of soldiers (Italians and non-Italians) on the run from the regular army. For Bravo this was "a huge operation aimed at saving people's lives, perhaps the biggest in our history . . . which represents one of the more specifically feminine moments of the Italian civil resistance."[13] But civil resistance also included the hiding of Jews, the refusal to join the army, or simply a kind of "passive" hostility toward the occupiers. After the war, it was cinema that was to provide the most potent symbols of this form of resistance—the unarmed Anna Magnani shot in the back in *Roma, Città aperta*, for example. Resistance was also, at its most basic level, an act of survival, a refusal to accept the apocalypse that had arrived with the weapons of total war, an ability to carry on when all seemed hopeless.

Clearly, memories of these forms of resistance did not translate well into public memory, or even collective, social memory. It is hard to think of a monument to the civil resistance, although there are now sites dedicated to those who helped Jews during the war. The Resistance itself (and the military aspects of the war) was far easier to understand and memorialize. It had martyrs, it was politicized, it had fought real battles. Other forms of resistance survived in private and family memories, but did not lend themselves either to commemoration, or to official memorialization.

For a whole series of other reasons, many of them to do with the persistence of gender-based stereotypes, women were excluded (apart from in a "supporting role") from the history and memory of the Resistance. Moreover, when women were discussed, it was usually in terms of a series of positive and negative clichés. On the one hand, there were the staffette (message carriers for the partisans) or "generous" peasant women. On the other, there were spies or women who "went with" the Germans, as depicted (again) in Roma, Città aperta. These women were often heavily punished during the resa dei conti—usually by being shorn of their hair and marched through public spaces.[14]

In the 1970s, thanks to feminism and the "new women's history," these historical commonplaces began to change. A series of works appeared concerning the role of women in the war and the resistance (while in terms of numbers, the most important Italian protagonists of the civil resistance were the Internati militari italiani, nearly all of whom were men).[15] Moreover, the way in which the war was fought in Italy (and through Italy) afforded particular importance to women both as victims of the conflict and as those in charge of protecting their families (with the men away, or in hiding). The work of Bravo and Gribaudi has reinterpreted the war through this kind of lens. So important is this work that it is now impossible to understand—and therefore depict—the resistance as purely a matter for armed men in the mountains of the center-north. The whole experience of total war needs to be included in the picture, not as a footnote, but at the heart of that history, and therefore also of its memory.

Finally, the idea of civil resistance was also linked to territory. Southern forms of resistance did not fit into categories of Resistance in the north; "the memories of individuals, families and southern communities were deprived of a general narrative structure."[16] This also applies to the "non si parte" (we won't leave) protests in the south in 1945, which were often dismissed as "fascist" or "politically disengaged."[17]

The Problem of Memory and the Bombings

Innocent Victims
Of the Liberating Guns
6 June 1944
Proietti Cleofe
Proietti Maddalena

—Plaque, Via Casilini, Rome

Bombing does not lend itself naturally to the creation of public memory. Often entire places were destroyed, making the construction of a "place of memory" difficult. Ruins or damage can be left as a warning or a sign of damage, but this needs to be put in context to create public memory. There is also a natural desire to reconstruct, to clear up, to rebuild all activities that destroy evidence of what had been wiped out. Occasionally, a decision was taken to leave a damaged building (or to repair it as damaged) as a sign of what had happened, as with Coventry Cathedral in the UK, but more often this "legacy" was left to chance. In San Lorenzo in Rome, gaps where bombs had hit were left unfilled for years. When bomb-damaged buildings were not repaired, this was not a positive choice to remind people of the horrors of war (as with the Kaiser Wilhelm Gedächtniskirche in Berlin), but a sign of inefficiency that was often interpreted as symptomatic of bad government, especially in the south. Palermo's wartime ruins were seen as symbolic of its backwardness after 1945.

Aerial bombings created chaos and dispersal. The event itself was part of its own forgetting process. These various silences "provoked resentments, dissatisfactions and deep divisions in terms of public narratives."[18] Bombers were invisible: only the sounds of their engines, and the screaming cries of the bombs, could be heard. "Death that comes from the sky" was sometimes placed within an apocalyptic, almost prepolitical vision of the world that almost removed it from the war experience. In the aftermath of the carpet bombing of San Lorenzo, in Rome, people remembered dead horses and the smell of smoking flesh.[19]

All over Italy, plaques were erected to bomb victims, but not in any systematic way. Moreover, these stories were uncomfortable. After all, it was the Allies, the liberators, who were doing the bombing. Silence was the easiest way out, or displacement of responsibility toward the Germans, or the Italian fascists. For Gribaudi, "Those who brought death from the sky is never named, they had no face. In the rhetoric of the time the Germans were the only ones held responsible."[20] Responsibility was shifted away from the bombers, who disappeared from accounts of these events. Research into the heavy bombing of Pistoia in October 1943 found that the event was almost entirely blamed on the Germans and the Italian fascists.[21] Portelli's study of San Lorenzo shows how survivors and witnesses not only held the Germans responsible in a generic sense, but also often attributed the bombings directly to Hitler's army. These contradictions emerged within private and public memories of the war. They were part of the contradictions of war itself—as in the plaque in Rome analyzed by Portelli.[22] Many private and public memories of the bombings did express anger toward the Allies. Fascist propaganda, after all, had immediately attempted to exploit the bombings for their own ends. To cite Gribaudi again, "A slogan was placed, before September 1943, on the ruins under which there were unburied bodies: it read 'they died for the Fatherland.' And those whose relatives had died wore a badge with a number."[23]

This changed after September 1943, above all in battle zones where the Allies had already taken control. Once again, Gribaudi provides us with the most pertinent analysis: "Those who died in the bombings became a nonsense of war, something which was there but not explained, a 'natural' tragedy of war about which it was better not to dwell too much. This process blocked . . . the memory of cities and villages."[24] Often, symbolic destruction created more memory than human suffering. The bombing of Cassino's abbey is one of the most famous (and controversial) images of the war in Italy. Yet the savage battle to take Cassino, and the carpet bombing of the town itself in March 1944, is far less well known, even in Cassino itself. As Gribaudi points out, "The city celebrates the monument, but not itself."[25] It was only in 2001 that the first (poorly attended) commemoration of that event was held in Cassino. Meanwhile, annual commemorations at the abbey remain an important moment of official memory. Private and family memories kept the past alive—including that of the bombings—but with great difficulty. And here—again—there was often the impossibility to mourn, the lack of a body, or—worse even—a mass of unnamed bodies to bury.

Bombings not only left victims in their wake but led to major population movements. Many people escaped from the cities to the hills, or sent their children away. It is one of the ironies of history that a number of those killed in the massacres at Sant'Anna in 1944, or by an explosion in San Miniato in the same year, were *sfollati* (evacuees) from Livorno, Pisa, and other cities that had suffered heavy bombing. The experience of sirens, fear, and the dark bomb shelters was something most people would never forget. Bomb damage remained in the cities for years, a material and constant memory of the war. In Palermo, Luchino Visconti shot the war scenes for *Il Gattopardo* in 1963 amid buildings never reconstructed after Allied bombings. Bomb damage altered many cities forever, as systematic rebuilding was not carried out. Some places became national symbols of the damage caused by the war—above all Monte Cassino.

In other cases, the repair of bomb damage symbolized urban and political rebirth. An Allied bomb crashed through the roof of the La Scala opera house in Milan on August 15, 1943, destroying large sections of the theater. No reconstruction was possible during the war. With the conflict over, Antonio Ghiringhelli supervised the rapid rebuilding of the theatre. In May 1946, in record time, the theatre reopened with a concert directed by Toscanini (on his return from exile) interrupted on numerous occasions by wild applause.

While bombings rarely led to important examples of official memory, they were often followed by small-scale examples of local commemoration. Sometimes, names of those who died in bombings were added to war memorials, while on other occasions special monuments or plaques were created. Often, the memory of the bombings was carried forward at a private or neighborhood level. Only the far right tried to exploit the bombings for political ends. Under the surface, controversy and bitterness over the bombings rumbled on throughout the postwar period. When the writer Giovanni Guareschi (in 1954) accused De Gasperi of having supported the bombing of Rome in 1944, he ended up in prison after losing a libel case.

Cities, Bombs, and Memory: Naples, Milan, Rome, and the Historians

If they are coming to free us, why are they killing us?

—Antonello Branca, a seven-year-old child, San Lorenzo,
July 19, 1943, in Portelli, "Roma tra guerra"

Napoli was the most bombed city in Italy during World War II. There were twelve nighttime raids in November 1942 alone, and things would soon get worse. The nightly experience in makeshift shelters (where people often died in the crush and panic) marked many young Neapolitans for years. Anyone who has been to Naples can only imagine the effects of a bomb, for example, in the area of the Quartieri Spagnoli. Yet these events, and the private memories linked to them, "have not created public narratives and have remained closed within individual, family and community memories, or simply consigned to silence."[26]

On July 19, 1943, Allied bombs rained down on Rome for three hours, dropped from 662 U.S. planes. It was the first time that the capital city had suffered such an attack. The neighborhood hit hardest was San Lorenzo, close to the railway station. A "red" and antifascist area, San Lorenzo lost something like 3,000 of its residents in these bombings. Many survivors were traumatized by the experience, which had numerous apocalyptic aspects (at the time, and in terms of memory afterward). A major monument was only created for these victims in 2003, sixty years later, although the zone and the city were marked by numerous older and smaller monuments, plaques, and signs of the bombings.[27] Gaps were left where some bombs had fallen, and the visit of the Pope to the neighborhood in the aftermath of the bombings was remembered with a special monument. Some of these bomb-gaps were indicated by political graffiti that described them as "an inheritance of fascism," although this has now been removed.

Milan was heavily bombed on a number of occasions, especially in 1942 and 1943.[28] Dozens of factories, monuments, and private houses were hit, as well as monuments such as that dedicated to World War I. As in Rome, the 1943 bombings in Milan created a sense of a turning point, in people's lives, and for Italy as a whole. Cristina Seyssel (born 1922), who experienced the bombings that year in Milan, later remembered her own vision of the city after the sirens had stopped. Her words are cited by Boneschi: "I was getting to used to all kinds of things, but I will never forget that bombardment. As well as my house which burnt down some time later, as the men who threw away their uniforms after the 8 September 1943, that bombardment was for me the end of an epoch."[29]

Yet, despite their scope and the damage and suffering they caused, the "memories" and history of these bombings were largely ignored by contemporary historians after 1945, and certainly did not receive the weight they deserved in terms of the war experience. Serious historical research on the bombings of Italian cities only really began in the 1980s. In turn, these events created little in the way of public memory. Bombing deaths fit very awkwardly with discourses around the resistance. Who were the victims, after all? Martyrs? Heroes? Or just people who happened to be in the wrong place at the wrong time? Indeed, these were victims of Italy's *allies* (after September 8) and thus historical narratives became more and more complicated. It was much easier to ignore these events altogether, or blame them on the fascists (for having started the war in the first place). It is perhaps not surprising that private memories often attribute the bombings directly to the Germans. Once again, a shift in the scapegoat had taken place.

Politically, as well, the bombings created serious problems for memory. As in the plaque in Rome studied by Portelli (cited above), the victims of the bombings had died thanks to "liberating guns." Mass bombings killed "innocent" victims, but they also brought the end of the war closer, and were often interpreted in this way. They inspired "political ambivalence."[30] The "cheering" for the bombing was also a sign of defeatism—or active defeatism, the idea that the conquering of Italy would bring down fascism. Many monuments dedicated to the bombings, as Portelli has shown, "express the tensions of history—just as individual memories were in themselves divided . . . within the unreconciled double consciousness of individuals and social groups."[31]

Furthermore, the meaning of the "U.S.," and of "U.S. bombs," changed over time, and is still changing. The idea of U.S. troops as liberators, as "exporters of democracy," was increasingly hard to sell—even historically—after Korea, Vietnam, and Iraq. Sometimes this political ambivalence—the Allies as liberators, the United States as an enemy—was expressed in private and public memories. These contradictions were particularly acute during the cold war, and are evident in another small plaque at San Lorenzo that reads, "Paolo Morganti / who died on 19 July 1943 / also for you / no to the Atlantic Pact."[32] Often, a generic antiwar message appeared in these memorials, an expression of the postwar pacifism so prevalent in Italian society, but this was also another way of avoiding the issue of who had actually dropped the bombs.

In the absence—for so many years—of adequate forms of public memory, people created their own (part private, part public) memorial sites. San Lorenzo's barber became a self-appointed custodian of the memory of the bombings, and his shop was covered with photos of victims and articles about July 19, 1943. Local figures told and retold their stories on numerous occasions, as with the owner of Il Pommidoro restaurant in San Lorenzo, who lost his mother that day. The bombing of Rome was also reproduced in popular fiction (such as Else Morante's *La Storia*, 1974) and cinema, as in Federico Fellini's *Roma* (1972). As with so many other areas, this all changed in the 1990s.

A further part of the memory of the San Lorenzo bombings was linked to the visit of Pope Pius XII on the afternoon after the bombings, and in particular a powerful photo depicting the Pope his arms spread wide, in pain, or pity, in front of a crowd of onlookers. This photograph was reproduced as a statue in Piazzale Verano in 1967 and is also part of public and Catholic memory. Francesco De Gregori's song *San Lorenzo* included these lines: "E il Papa la domenica mattina da San Pietro, uscì tutto da solo tra la gente, e in mezzo a San Lorenzo, spalancò le ali, sembrava proprio un angelo con gli occhiali" [And the Pope that Sunday morning at San Pietro, went out alone among the people, and in the middle of San Lorenzo, he spread his wings, he seemed like an angel with glasses] (1982). It is often said that the Pope handed out cash to the faithful crowd and that his white tunic was stained with the blood of some of those who had been injured. Pope Benedict XVI visited this statue in November 2008. But the memory of the Pope's visit is a divided one, with some claiming that Pius XII stayed on the edge of the neighborhood because of its "red" reputation, while others—particularly from within the church—have outlined the support his visit provided for the local population.[33] Through careful analysis of the well-known photograph of the Pope, researchers have since been able to show that it had not been taken in San Lorenzo at all, but outside another church in Rome, and on a different date, August 13, 1943.[34]

On October 20, 1944, a U.S. plane unloaded a set of bombs on the northern periphery of Milan. The sirens had sounded, and the schoolchildren and teachers in Gorla's Francesco Crispi Elementary School were either rushing down to the shelters, or already below. A bomb hit the stairway where many of the children were and destroyed the shelter itself, killing 184 children and 19 adults as well as other by-standers. There were over 600 victims in the neighborhood as a whole. Since then, these children have been known as the "martyrs of Gorla." The Gorla bomb formed a potent part of the memory of the war among the Milanese, as in the words of Adriana Centurelli, "their death was the death of us all."[35] But the "Gorla massacre" had been used by the right as a propaganda weapon, both during and after the war.[36]

Under the surface, it was clear that the bombings had opened up problematic divisions over the memory and history of the past. It is said that at the Toscanini concert that relaunched La Scala (and Milan itself) in 1946, some flowers were allegedly sent to the director with the message "I morti di Gorla" (The dead of Gorla). Toscanini had been in the United States during the war. It is also said that somebody removed the message before the director saw it. After the war, it seems, there were arguments between the families of the victims and the local administration over how to remember the "martyrs of Gorla." It is also said that the U.S. authorities were opposed to a specific memorial. In 1952 an abstract monument was inaugurated with this simple message, on the spot where the school had once stood. There is no mention of the "origins" of the bomb itself:

> **THIS IS WAR**
> **20-X-1944**
> **THE PEOPLE**
> **CRY FOR 200 CHILDREN**
> **KILLED BY THE WAR**
> **HERE IN THEIR SCHOOL**
> **WITH THEIR TEACHERS**

Agreement over the memory of bombings could be reached via the phrase inserted in the Italian constitution "Italy repudiates war." Generic antiwar or pacifist sentiments created common ground, which went some way to overcoming the in-built contradictions created by the bombings. This type of sentiment can be found at the monument at Gorla, with its phrase "THIS IS WAR" followed by the names of the victims.

The same generic idea of the horror of war can also be seen in this plaque in Milan, which refers to the same set of bombs as those of the school:

ON 20 OCTOBER 1944
THE DEVESTATING FURY OF THE WAR
ATTACKED THESE HOUSES

In recent years, many monuments have been set up to the victims of wartime bombings. As with so many other areas, taboos and silences have fallen away since the end of the cold war. Often these new monuments or plaques were created by left or center-left administrations (Grossetto in 2003, Empoli in 2004). These monuments are a way of remembering the entire experience of "total war." Where there were no actual monuments to use as a focus for commemorations, other forms of ceremony were adopted, as with the "Percorso della memoria" (A memory route) in Livorno in June 2008, which linked a series of memory sites and small plaques. Livorno was one of the most heavily bombed cities in Italy, with over 1,300 victims from 116 raids between 1940 and 1944.

There has clearly been a flourishing of research in recent years into the bombings, their history and their memory, and this has been accompanied by public initiatives.[37] This is true not just in Italy, but also in relation to the Allied bombings of Germany and Japan.[38] In 2004 a large-scale exhibition was organized in Milan about the bombings of that particular city, attracting thousands of visitors. The Gorla school bomb was evoked through photos and names of the victims in a special room.

Memory, however, is not always linked to the telling of stories, and events do not always create coherent forms of memory. As Forgacs has written (with reference to the bombing of San Lorenzo):

> After a traumatic collective event such as this, in which many people are killed and the life of a community is suddenly and severely disrupted, it is not uncommon for survivors not to wish to speak about it at all. When they do speak of it, their account may either be stereotyped, pieced together from accounts given by others, or evasive or incomplete, marked by silences and repressions, omissions and ellipses. In other words, an event may affect memory without being openly narrated or commemorated. Memories do not always find a place; they may be repressed or "removed" (*rimosse* in Italian), displaced into repeated and stereotyped recollections or subsumed into formal rituals and monuments of commemoration.[39]

The "revival of memory" of the bombings is not just a political issue, then, and can also be explained as the power of the trauma linked to these events that has faded in recent years, with the death of many of the witnesses and the passing of time.

A Fascist War of Occupation: Memory and Silence, 1940–1943

In 1943, foreign troops marched into a small village in an occupied country, following an attack by a group of partisans, which had left nine of their soldiers dead. The town was razed to the ground, and more than 150 men were taken out and executed. For the general in charge of the operation, the reprisal had been a "salutary lesson for all the inhabitants of the zone." This massacre did not take place in Italy, or in France, but in Greece in a village called Domenikon, and its perpetrators were not the Nazis. The general's name was General Benelli from the Pinerolo division of the Italian army and this war crime was carried out by the occupying Italian army on February 16, 1943. It is—like many other similar massacres—more or less unknown in Italy, and only recently has historical research begun to analyze the brutal tactics of the Italians in Greece and elsewhere. Yet local memory has not forgotten this shocking event. As Santarelli has written, "The traveller who journeys all the way to the little village of Domenikon in Thessaly will discover, in the middle of town . . . a stone monument that commemorates the 'victims of the occupation slaughtered 16 February 1943 by the Italian army of occupation.'"[40] Italy's fascist army was responsible for numerous war crimes between 1940 and 1943 but, unlike almost all the other armies and countries involved in the conflict (and especially those on the side of the Nazis), not one single Italian general, politician, or soldier ever stood trial for those crimes, committed outside Italy.

September 8, 1943

As the army was dissolving before his eyes, and the situation was becoming ungovernable on the home front, Pietro Badoglio, the Italian prime minister marshal, was forced to sign an armistice with the Allies. This was made public on September 8, 1943—a date overloaded with meaning that has pivotal importance for the history of modern Italy. How was this defeat to be remembered?

The dramatic events of September 8 produced deep divisions over the facts themselves and their interpretation—debates that continue to this day. Moreover, the very history of September 8 was extremely messy and open to different interpretations, as was Badoglio's announcement itself, even as it was happening. It was thus not particularly surprising that September 8 produced a fractured memory and interpretations from historians that were totally counterposed.

Remembering Defeat

It would be very strange if France celebrated the defeat at Sedan in 1870 or if in the USA they did the same for Pearl Harbour. Yet this is what happens in Italy with the 8 September.

—Giovanni Belardelli, September 13, 2005

It is not up to us to calculate how many Italians experienced the 8 September as a "death" or how many saw it as a birth. We need to recognise that those who saw it as a birth, or a rebirth, were the best Italians. Perhaps this is enough to consider the 8 September—in its own, tragic way—as something like a celebration.

—Sergio Luzzatto, September 17, 2005

How can defeats be remembered? One way is to represent them *as victories*. Another is to pretend that they didn't happen. History is full of "glorious defeats" that have been reinvented or used as ways of cementing national identity, as myths of heroism and courage, as examples of the ultimate sacrifice for the fatherland. Think of General Custer or the Alamo in the United States, or Garibaldi's retreat from Rome in 1849, or the doomed landings at Sapri, or Dogali.[41] The Charge of the Light Brigade—when 600 British soldiers rode to their death in the Crimean war in 1854—was reinvented as a heroic defeat by journalists and the poet Tennyson.

But September 8 was not just a military disaster. It was a capitulation after a long series of military defeats. It did not even take place on the battlefield, but in a tent in Sicily. As such, the September 8 peace agreement and surrender could not be presented as a heroic defeat apart from in a few isolated cases (above all Cefalonia). Defeatism—in the sense of hoping that your own nation would lose a war—was widespread in Italy by the autumn of 1943. Increasingly, since 1940, many Italians had hoped, wished, and even prayed for the defeat of an army and a war with which they could not identify. This group of "defeatists" included moderates like Croce and Calamandrei, as well as hundreds of thousands of ordinary soldiers. Croce, for example, wrote this in his diary from the war years: "Even though I tried hard in my soul to pretend that I wanted my country to win, in the end I had to obey the voice of my conscience and hope for the defeat of Italy."[42] For Salvatore Satta, "the dominant note of the war is that the Italian people, the immense majority, wanted their own defeat."[43]

Thus, the *acknowledgement* of defeat, which occurred on September 8— was also applauded by many. It was seen as the end of the *fascist* fatherland, of a war inspired by twenty years of fascism, of the whole fascist project.

As Rochat has argued, "On the 8 September it was the Fascist Fatherland which died."[44] Many Italians were thus relieved, happy even, when they heard of the armistice. Others began to "see the light," to change their minds about fascism. Most were faced with some sort of choice (for the first time in years).[45]

Seen in this way, from these points of view, celebration of September 8 after 1945 is not such a strange idea. Any such celebration was destined, however, to divide Italians (or reproduce some of the divisions of the war itself). September 8 *in itself* was quite difficult to celebrate—so other events have often been linked to that date or celebrated at other moments. Often, on April 25, commemorations are held to remember the "beginning of the Resistance" in Rome (after September 8).

Similar commemorations of the "beginnings of the resistance" can be seen in this plaque near Carrara:

HERE
ON THE 8 SEPTEMBER 1943
THE PEOPLE AND THE ARMY
JOINED TOGETHER TO BEGIN
THE LIBERATION STRUGGLE
THIS STONE REMEMBERS
THE GLORIOUS FALLEN
13 SEPTEMBER 1953

The events in Cefalonia provided the best and most malleable event in terms of postwar memory of September 8 and led to the production of a vast range of public and private memorials.

Army, Nation, Defeat

The main effect of September 8 on the official Italian army was one of collapse. Fenoglio wrote that "there will never be an Italian army again."[46] The dominant experience was one of disorientation and of a desire for *Tutti a casa* (Comencini 1960), the title of a popular and poignant film based around the period of the armistice. Alberto Sordi's confusion in that film later became emblematic of the farcical elements of September 8: "Colonel, an incredible thing has happened: the Germans have allied with the Americans." Some 82 generals, 13,000 officers and 402,000 soldiers were disarmed by the German army in Italy itself.[47]

Certainly, the uniqueness of the Italian experience should not be exaggerated, and it is surprising how little historical work compares the French and Italian cases. France also experienced defeat and invasion and set up a collaborative puppet government. Much more research is needed into the reactions and debates across these two national moments of defeat. Italy did not produce a reflection of the quality of that of Marc Bloch, French historian and a soldier in both world wars. Bloch's *The Strange Defeat*, published in 1940, is an incisive account of the collapse of the French army in the face of German advance, ranging from social to cultural to psychological history. It was, as with September 8, a moment "when everything collapsed"[48] and Bloch delves deep into French history, as well as into the wartime tactics of the army, in his "disposition of a defeated man." "It will not be easy to remove," Bloch predicted, "the shadow of the great disaster of 1940."[49] The continuing debates in the 1990s over the Pétain government and France's wartime record were testimony to the prescience of Bloch's comments.

September 8 has inspired considerable discussion as a singular moment in Italian history. Galli della Loggia interpreted the armistice and the dissolution of the Italian army as the *death of the nation*. The whole idea of the nation, argues Galli della Loggia, collapsed with the disintegration of the Italian army (and State). While Galli della Loggia's intelligent polemic carries a certain force in its depiction of the extremity of the events of 1943, his argument is based on an extremely specific idea of "the nation." Galli della Loggia has used his analysis of September 8 essentially as a spring-board for a wider political critique of the Resistance, the so-called myth of the Resistance after 1945 and the postwar politics of the republic and the Communist Party.

Others have traditionally viewed September 8 in positive terms, as a moment when Italy (and the Nation) was reborn through armed resistance to the Germans and the fascists, despite the break-up of an entire army and even the "collapse of an entire history."[50] Thus September 8 is presented in ways that cannot be reconciled—as death and birth at the same time—as "a symbol of collapse and at the same time prelude to a revival."[51] The fascists themselves also saw September 8 as a moment of possible renewal, with the origins of the Repubblica sociale italiana (RSI), and the decision to fight on with the Germans against the Americans and the "Italian" army.[52]

For nearly every Italian (at home and abroad), September 8 was a complicated and confused moment, a time of defeat, of new allies and of momentous choices that were to have life-changing consequences.[53] No reconciliation is (or was) possible among these versions. For the communists, the choice between the Red Army and Mussolini's (or Badoglio's) Italian army was no choice at all. Communist Party leader Palmiro Togliatti was still in Russia when the country was invaded by the Italians. Many Italian nationals simply did not identify with the Italian army. As Pavone noted, "even today, to look on September 8 as a tragedy or the beginning of a liberation process is a line which separates interpretations by opposing schools."[54] The controversies over the responsibility of Badoglio and the Italian state in this collapse continued to rage on in the postwar period, and even in the 1960s there were attempts to block the important historical work of Zangrandi dealing with September 8. Other (long-running) debates concern the size and importance of that "gray zone" of Italians who neither supported the Resistance nor the Republic of Salò.[55] Some of the first Italians to be faced with stark choices about their immediate, and long-term futures were those in the army. Suddenly, overnight, an army of occupation and conquest (but also of defeat) had become something else—something undefined. These choices had an impact on the rest of the war, as well as in the countries where the Italians were stationed. One of the places affected most dramatically by the imposition of these choices was Greece.

Cefalonia 1943

Everywhere there were memories and reminders of a massacre that not even the earthquake had been able to blot out.

—Marcello Venturi, *The White Flag*

In September 1943, the Greek Island of Cefalonia hosted an uncommon series of events. Two countries that, days earlier, had been military allies in the occupation of the island, turned on each other. Over 1,500 soldiers were killed in the subsequent battle. On September 22, the Italian troops surrendered to the Germans. As the Wehrmacht took control of the island, thousands of Italian soldiers and officers were systematically executed as "traitors," including their commanding officer, General Antonio Gandin. This was the biggest single massacre of Italians by Germans in the whole period of the war. In the decades since that battle and massacre, witnesses, locals, priests, politicians, soldiers, judges, journalists, historians, and others have argued over what happened on the island, and over how to remember, or forget Cefalonia.

We know—thanks to the importance of the events there—more about Cefalonia on and after September 8, 1943, than in most other places around that crucial date. The Italians had occupied the island in May 1941 (at least 11,000 troops from the *Divisione Acqui* were stationed in Corfu and Cefalonia, alongside 2,000 Germans) and had been there for over two years before Badoglio's ambiguous orders filtered through concerning the "armistice." Rusconi's account is the most convincing in analysing what happened next.[56] The Italian troops on Cefalonia (and their generals) had one priority: to return to Italy, safely, with dignity and with their weapons. Yet—and they did not know this at the time—this option was not available to them. In no case did the Germans allow Italian troops to keep their arms, or return to Italy after the armistice. There were also no resources available for an alternative route home.

Moreover, the Italians were isolated, which gave them time to negotiate and debate their strategy, but also created space for a rebellion to develop against the military hierarchies on the island. Most other Italian soldiers did not have this "luxury," which, in Cefalonia, was to lead to tragedy. Unlike in many other areas, there was a strong feeling among the Italian troops at Cefalonia that they should not simply hand over their arms to the Germans. This sentiment has often been interpreted by historians and others as "anti-German." Cefalonia revealed a stark transformation in one key choice for Italians still at war: who was now the enemy?

The Italians were faced with two "unacceptable" choices: they could either fight the Germans, or face deportation—unarmed—to internment camps. The Italians were thus dependent on their ex-allies if they were to leave the island peacefully, and the latter were not willing to accept any solution that did not begin with disarmament. Given this situation General Gandin first negotiated, and played for time. Then, and under pressure from below (and his hand may have been forced by the actions of some of his officers) decided that his troops would fight and defend an island that they had occupied against their ex-allies, perhaps in the vain hope that similar resistance was taking place elsewhere. It wasn't. It is often claimed that a form of "referendum" was held to consult the troops about this decision on September 13 (organized by Gandin), at which a vast majority of the soldiers (or "100 percent" in many accounts) allegedly "voted" to resist the German attacks. This refusal to surrender led to an attack by the Germans (with heavy air support—127 German planes were used in the battle).[57]

There was only one possible outcome of such a battle.[58] After seven days of fighting, Gandin surrendered on September 22. Over 1,300 Italians were killed in the fighting itself, while at least 2,500 solders and officers were shot after hostilities had ceased.[59] Thousands of Italian prisoners were taken, however, and hundreds of deported troops died when transport ships were sunk. We have no precise figures as to the numbers of dead, nor of the survivors. Just over a thousand Italians returned to Italy in 1944, while others were interned in Germany or Russia. More than a thousand Italians remained in Greece and joined the antifascist resistance there (on both sides of its political divide). In November 1944, 1,256 of these soldiers managed to return to Italy, with their arms (an extremely rare event—again unique to Cefalonia). These soldiers had achieved the original aim for which Gandin had negotiated, but the costs of their "victory" were extremely high.

Thousands of Italian prisoners were thus executed by the Wehrmacht (although here, as well, the accounts as to "who was responsible" differ widely). These were soldiers in uniform who had surrendered. As such, this was a war crime and it was necessary—in Germany—that a veil was drawn over these events, especially as the perpetrators were not the SS, but the Wehrmacht.[60] Special treatment was reserved by the Germans for the Italian officers, guilty of leading what they saw as a "betrayal." The events at Cefalonia became part of the accusations levelled at the German army during the Nuremberg trials.

Ever since September 1943, events at Cefalonia have been the subject of historical and political debate. There have always been those—historians and nonhistorians—who have criticized certain Italian soldiers in Cefalonia for a "rebellion against military authority." Cefalonia—as with so many other events on and around September 8—produced divided memories and interpretations, and these divergent memories were translated into different forms of public memory, in Cefalonia itself and all over Italy. Cefalonia was a complicated event—open to multiple interpretations and exposed to what Rusconi calls the "political use of history"—which is, as he writes, an "attempt to depict historical choices as politically clear (and claim them politically) when they were neither clear not straightforward."[61]

The Nation: Dead or Reborn?

> They decided not to give up their arms. They preferred to fight and die for the Fatherland. They kept faith with their pledge. This is the essence of what happened in Cefalonia in September 1943.
>
> —Carlo Azeglio Ciampi

Italy's President Ciampi visited Cefalonia in 2001. There he made an oft-cited speech where he claimed that Cefalonia was the beginning of the Italian resistance. This was in direct opposition to interpretations by historians who have argued in recent years that September 8 represented the "death of the nation."[62] For Ciampi, Cefalonia was a moment of rebirth, not death. In his words it was an event that "demonstrated that the fatherland was not dead . . . Italy was reborn on this basis . . . their conscious choice . . . was the first act of the Resistance, of an Italy free from fascism."[63] The timing of Ciampi's speech was important. Sandro Pertini had already made the same "pilgrimage" as Ciampi (as president) and delivered more or less the same speech, but Ciampi's words had far more impact. This was because they intervened directly in a debate over history and the past—"the death of the nation"—while Pertini's visit took place while there was still a consensus over the Resistance and September 8.

However, as we have seen, it would be a mistake to generalize from Cefalonia. The vast majority of Italian soldiers reacted to September 8 as if the war was over. Hundreds of thousands refused to carry on fighting when asked to do so, and were interned in Germany or Poland. Many were taken prisoner by the Allies (in Africa, in the South of Italy), while others deserted and tried to return home. Even in Greece itself, Cefalonia was the exception, not the rule. As Mario Cervi has written, "I was in Greece on the 8 September and I can assure you that the climate was one of 'everyone home.'" A small minority joined the armed resistance, while another minority later carried on the war on the side of the Germans and Mussolini.

After September 8, the Italian state fractured into parts, and lost sovereignty in the north and the south. One section moved south with the Royal Family and set up the "Kingdom of the South," leaving authority in the hands of the Allies. Another part was integrated into the semipuppet RSI in the North. The Italian army ceased to exist in its previous form, as did the nation. No Italians—north or south—were under the exclusive jurisdiction of their own governments either in terms of territory or military strategy.

Memory and Rhetoric

The heroism of the Acqui has been ignored by public narratives around the Resistance.

—Galli della Loggia, in *I traditi di Cefalonia*

Cefalonia has not been forgotten.

—Giorgio Rochat, "Ancora su Cefalonia, settembre 1943"

Considerable rhetoric surrounds the event known as "Cefalonia 1943." There are two sides to this rhetoric. The first is the constant claim that the events of Cefalonia have "been forgotten."[64] This is a frequent and usually uncontested statement. Don Ghilardini wrote in the 1950s about "a page of history which has been willingly hidden away," while Luciano Violante claimed in 1998 that "for many years the extraordinary military and civil achievements of the Acqui Division has remained at the margins of our collective memory."[65] In 2005, Vito Gallotta described what he saw as a "long oblivion" with relation to Cefalonia.[66] This rhetorical statement crosses political lines, and it used by different factions as a political weapon. It is also untrue. Cefalonia has not been forgotten.

There are probably more books dedicated to Cefalonia than there are to the rest of September 8.[67] It could be argued that the bulk of public memory linked to the events of September 8 is connected directly to Cefalonia. Numerous memorials have been dedicated to the massacre, anniversaries celebrated, exhibitions organized and conferences held. This "remembering" is also in part thanks to the recent popularity of the Corelli novel but above all is linked to the size (of the massacre) and its symbolic importance. As Santomassimo has written, "The constant presence of ceremonies dedicated to the martyrs of Cefalonia on the 8 September, the 4 November and the 25 April across a long arc of national history shows that the routine statement that this memory had been 'hidden' is incorrect."[68] In fact, Cefalonia worked well with moderate ideas of the Resistance as "loyalty" to the crown and the flag, and as such was often cited and celebrated after 1945.[69] But it could also be molded to more radical interpretations of the Resistance, with its "democratic" referendum and the sacrifice of the "partisan-soldiers."[70]

Moreover, this constant remembering has been a feature of the entire postwar period. A number of books were published immediately after the war. Venturi's *Bandiera Bianca a Cefalonia* (1963, 1972, 1997, 2001) won an important literary prize in 1963, and went through a number of editions. Important research has been carried out by leading historians. We know a lot more about Cefalonia than we do about many aspects of the Italian occupation of Greece (especially the negative parts linked to the occupation, which certainly have been forgotten until very recently).[71]

In no sense, therefore, can Cefalonia be seen as having 'been forgotten', and certainly not by the left. Public memorials were constructed throughout the postwar period—and were opened by politicians of national importance. Parliamentary commemorations have been held on various occasions, such as in 1963, 1968, and 1998 (when the proceedings were published in a special book). Often, communist deputies went out of their way to praise "the heroes of Cefalonia," as Pietro Secchia called them in 1963.[72] A plaque was put up in Modena in 1947 and there is a plaque in Piazza Maggiore in Bologna (see Figure 5.1). Leading participants in the Resistance—from Pertini to Ciampi—took time to commemorate and remember the events at Cefalonia.

Official memory has been plentiful. A mission visited Cefalonia in 1948 (the original plan had been to build a *sacrario* on the island, but the civil war made this impossible) and thousands of bodies were brought back in 1953, and buried in Bari with full military honors.[73] Bari now has 2,000 victims of the massacre in a special *sacrario* for the victims of wars abroad (1967) and there are Cefalonia monuments in Padua, Pisa, Calcinana, Rome, Pontedera, Faenza, San Remo, Torino, Palermo, Mantua, Genoa, and Massa among other places. Rome has a *Viale degli Eroi di Coo* (Heroes of Coo Avenue), and Rodi, Cefalonia, and many other parts of Italy have

Figure 5.1 Bologna: Plaque commemorating the events of Cefalonia and Corfu. "Bologna. Gold medal for its contribution to the Resistance, remembers the sacrifice of the Acqui Mountain infantry division. The fallen of Cefalonia, The fallen of Corfu. September 1943–November 1944."

roads or squares dedicated to the "martyrs" or heroes of Cefalonia. Gandin and many others were awarded medals by the state. Eighteen gold medals were given to those who died, and four to the flags of the various regiments. Aldo Moro, speaking at the inauguration of a massive monument dedicated to the victims of Cefalonia in Verona in 1966, claimed that "a country is alive if it is connected to its traditions and its history."[74] In that same year, that city created a *Via Cefalonia*. A huge monument was opened in Parma in 1970 (with the inscription *Parma ricorda i suoi eroi* [Parma remembers its heroes]), another in Cesena in 1985 and yet another in Rome in 1988. Leading Christian Democrat (DC) Paolo Emilio Taviani wrote a rhetorical preface to a book about Cefalonia in the early 1980s.[75] A special and important memorial was built in Argostoli itself in 1978 (a large cross had been there since 1966), and has been the focus for a number of commemorations in recent years, as well as hosting the visits of three Italian presidents since 1980.[76]

In Acqui Terme, where many of the men came from (and where the division was based) there is a complicated memoryscape linked to the massacre. Many of the most important contemporary historians in Italy (and others in Germany) have studied and reflected upon Cefalonia. There is also a rich bibliography of diaries, biographies, and other accounts of Cefalonia. Songs, poems, and even an opera have been dedicated to the events at Cefalonia. So, rather than "being forgotten," Cefalonia has, if anything, been "over-remembered" in comparison with September 8 as a whole.[77] Remembering Cefalonia has been a way of forgetting September 8.[78]

Given the fact that Cefalonia has been in no sense, and at no time since 1943, "forgotten," why have there been constant claims and statements that argue that either a selective or political forgetting has taken place? One reason is a simple failure to examine the memorial production arising from Cefalonia. However, the second reason for this "rhetoric of forgetting" is much more powerful. Different groups have tried at various times to "claim" Cefalonia for themselves—politically or in terms of the historical importance of that event. By stating that Cefalonia has been forgotten, commentators or historians are trying to claim back Cefalonia as part of their own analysis of 1943, and at the same time take "Cefalonia" away from those others who are also trying to use that event for their own ends. Moreover, the idea that Cefalonia "has been forgotten" is rather strange, as "the event" fits well with the double-myth of the "good Italian" and "Italian-as-victim" that have dominated both left- and right-wing interpretations of World War II for many years. It is difficult to imagine what "remembering properly" might mean within the context of the constant rhetoric that claims that Cefalonia, or other moments in Italian history such as the Moro Case (see Chapter 8), for example, have "been forgotten." How much memory creates a situation where an event has "been remembered"?

Cefalonia, far from being forgotten was often remembered in its "canonical" form—as a sacrifice, in line with World War I and the Risorgimento. Moreover, by remembering Cefalonia in this way, many uncomfortable areas of the past could be forgotten, or silenced—the role of the military command on and after September 8, the "running away" of the head of state (the king), and the behavior of the vast majority of soldiers. And remembering one form of "Cefalonia" was also a way of forgetting its more problematic aspects—the revolt of some of the troops and officers, the overall desire to return home, the abandonment of the troops by the high command. Klinkhammer's sophisticated account sets up a link between forms of memory that also work as forms of forgetting. For Klinkhammer, "In the 1950s and 1960s, the 'Cefalonia' case was 'buried' through official commemorations."[79] In some ways, then, agreements over Cefalonia have been "based around the silence and the covering-up of the more problematic and critical aspects of its history."[80]

For example, the "remembering" of Cefalonia overlooks the entire period of the Italian occupation of Greece, from the attack in 1941 onward. Attempts to talk about this period of history have been systematically avoided, or silenced, since 1943. Moreover, the "remembering" of Cefalonia avoided too much emphasis on the Germans themselves, in order not to rock the boat in postwar Europe. In the 1950s, attempts to make a film about Cefalonia were blocked. Moreover, attempts to bring the Germans to justice for the massacres at Cefalonia were blocked by postwar Italian politicians. Cefalonia presented the Italian army as victims. The occupation of Greece itself was in this way forgotten.

Versions: Interpreting Cefalonia

The Acqui represent a continuity between the period of World War I and that of the actual war of liberation.

—Minutes of the Council of Ministers (Cabinet), September 13, 1945

Different versions of Cefalonia were carried through the postwar period. Some drew lines of continuity with the Risorgimento and World War I. This line was first laid down by the Parri government in 1945 and was that taken up by Ciampi in 2001. Rusconi calls this the "canonical" version of Cefalonia (the Badoglio government, before Parri, had tried to push an idea of widespread resistance to the Germans after September 8, in part to cover up its own responsibilities). The "canonical" interpretation also contained religious elements and used religious and patriotic language. For Don Ghilardini, Cefalonia had been "a page of the purest glory."[81]

President Saragat, speaking at the inauguration of the sacrario for the victims of Cefalonia in Bari in 1967 called the victims "heroes of the purest kind." There is no doubt that, within the army, a conscious decision was taken—right from the start—to push a specific version of the Cefalonia events and play down the controversial aspects linked to the "case." As a 1948 official report argued, "Cefalonia has already become a myth."[82] Continuities were drawn with other national myths, as in a 1958 official commemoration that described the victims of Cefalonia and "their brothers on the Grappa and the Piave."[83]

A second, more radical interpretation underlined the new aspects of Cefalonia, with an accent on the idea of the Resistance, the "partisan-soldier" and the democratic revolution represented by the "referendum" among the troops. An attempt has often been made to generalize the Cefalonia events there as part of an ongoing Resistance myth. In the way they died, the victims of Cefalonia could be compared to executed partisans back in Italy in 1943 to 1945, or the civilian victims of massacres in the same period. Some of this rhetoric was similar to that used under fascism, as the "martyrs" of Cefalonia "hanno saputo morire" (they knew how to die).[84] But Cefalonia was a rare (and almost unique) example of the Italian army fighting as an army. For both of these narratives, the heart of the Cefalonia events was an idea of sacrifice, and this element is present in many monuments and plaques dedicated to the massacre. For example, the monument in Verona (1966) depicts four dead or dying naked figures (in an abstract, not a realist style) surrounded with barbed wire. As with all myths, those linked to Cefalonia were ways of simplifying the past, and of pushing political and ideological points of view.

Also with Cefalonia, a divided memory emerged that was linked to the families of the victims, who brought court cases and published books that pushed alternative versions of and explanations for the tragedy. This was a particular kind of antipartisan memory, which blamed specific officers for having provoked the massacre.[85] There are also revisionist accounts of Cefalonia that attack the "military model" of democracy that was supposed to have been put into practice in 1943. But these represent different historical interpretations of an event, and are not linked necessarily to questions of memory.[86]

Captain Corelli and His Mandolin:
Tourism, History, and *Italiani, Brava Gente*

The garrison and the island's people lived peacefully, even happily, together
until the Armistice.

—Marcello Venturi, *The White Flag*

Captain Corelli's Mandolin was a bestseller in almost every country in the
world—apart from Italy. It is a novel that has sold over two and half million copies, and is set in Cefalonia during the Italian occupation in World
War II. Its form, content, and reception tells us a lot about the role of Italy
and Italians during that war and the ways in which history has been represented through fiction, cinema, and popular myth.

The Captain Corelli phenomenon makes a neat link between war and
tourism. Guides to Cefalonia now contain references to the film and the book
and this reinvented "event" is now part of the "tourist experience." As for the
"novel" itself, it was based largely on English-language sources, including the
translation of Venturi's *The White Flag*, which is a fairly accurate account of
events at Cefalonia in 1943.[87] De Bernières adds in his own magical realist
style, turns the Greek communists into monsters, and plays up a series of
Italian stereotypes. In the film, the Italians spend most of their time singing
and keep apologizing for their occupation of such a "beautiful island." There
are Corelli tours of Cefalonia and Corelli bars. All this is based on a comfort-
able silence, which wipes out any memory of 1941 to 1943 and has history
beginning—once again—with September 8, 1943.

This is yet another indication that the "good Italian" myth is an international one, not produced entirely from within, but also from without.
Good Italian and peaceful Italian stereotypes (despite Italy's almost con-
tinual wars before 1945) are international ones that also cut across political
boundaries. Corelli also reproduces other stereotypes and tropes, such as
that of the "Good German" (or the fiery and proud Greeks), which often
turn up in private memories. Italians are music-lovers, peaceniks, roman-
tics, and uninterested in war.

What *Captain Corelli* (the film) can't do is explain the real history of
September 8, 1943 to a Hollywood audience. So it doesn't even try. In a five-
minute sequence we hear that (at the same time), "Mussolini has fallen, the
war is over." Of course, Mussolini did fall, but the war was certainly not
over, not for the Greeks, nor for the Italians, nor for the Germans. Then we
are told that it is September and that "Mussolini has been arrested." Finally
we are informed that "Mussolini has surrendered to England and the USA."

This, of course, never happened. The film conflates July 25 and September 8, 1943, with 1945.

Similar historical confusion emerges in texts based in some way on the film or the book. A special issue of the *Rough Guide to Cephallonia* is somewhat bemused about September 8, 1943. This is what is to be found in the introduction to the guide: "When Captain Corelli and his unit of Puccini-loving men arrive on Cefalonia, they see their stay as a prolonged Grecian holiday. Pelagia and the other villagers resent these uninvited guests, but the Italians' charm and passion for music and life begin to blur the divisions of nationality and imposed circumstances." The introduction continues in this way: "The war arrives on these idyllic shores and the invading German army disarm the Italians. Later, a savage ambush of the Italian unit leaves only Corelli alive." Of course, the war had arrived in 1941, with the Italian invasion. The "invading" German army had been the allies of the Italians and they only managed to "disarm" the Italians after killing large numbers of them during and after a vicious battle. Finally, there was no "savage ambush."

Sadly, many tourists would have seen and been fed this—false—version of history. This might seem like an easy target. But accounts like these are pernicious and popular. The book and the film make no attempt to deal with the stereotype, and perpetrate an incomplete and damaging version of the past. Hollywood's Cefalonia is a pastiche that adds another layer to a story that has been much remembered but still divides and confuses.

6

Nazi Massacres and Divided Memory

Stories, Causes, Scapegoats, Memoryscapes*

Unfortunately, the Resistance was not entirely made up of well organised, well studied, well carried out actions. That attack was a mistake.

—Edoardo Succhielli, partisan leader, Civitella in Val di Chiana

The Search for a Scapegoat

On thousands of occasions between 1943 and 1945, Italian villages and cities were forced to mourn their victims, after massacres carried out by the German army. The *modus operandi* was often the same. German soldiers would arrive early in the morning, round up all the men they could find, and shoot them. The bodies were often burnt. Massacres took different forms—some were clearly reprisals for partisan attack (with the choice of a specific number of victims), others were intimidatory massacres of entire populations (and not just men, but also women and children), while there were also brutal round-ups of partisans followed by summary executions. Some massacres had straightforward military objectives—partisans. Others—the majority—looked to intimidate and terrify the entire population, and were part of a war against civilians. Italy's decision to break the alliance with Germany in September 1943 also had an impact, as the idea that the Italians were traitors held sway in the German army.

In many cases, the immediate cause of the massacre was not always clear, and in almost every case, psychologically, a scapegoat was needed—in order for those who had survived the horror to understand what had taken place. As Contini has written, after massacres, "a process began which is well known to medieval historians . . . the search for, or rather the construction of, a scapegoat."[1]

As anthropologists and historians have shown, this scapegoat or scapegoats—the person or group who took the blame—were usually local or "internal" figures.[2] One of the most important conclusions from the series of studies of the memories of wartime massacres lies precisely here. In the vast majority of cases, the immediate blame, and the way in which this story was carried down through time, was not linked to the perpetrators, the Germans, the Nazis. No. The scapegoat was often identified in local partisans. The precise nature of this mechanism, however, varied from place to place and has changed radically over time. Nonetheless, the "discovery" of these divided local memories in the 1990s by a group of historians was a central moment for postwar Italian historiography, and for the left "born from the resistance." These memories were a jarring note for one of the key features of the resistance myth. They could not coexist with the widespread idea of harmony, solidarity, and alliances between local populations and the partisans. Moreover, these divisions were also written in stone. Public memory reflected these diverse narratives over time, creating complicated local memoryscapes. Partisans were well-suited to the role of scapegoat; "they are from within the local community, but also outside of it, they are on the edges, but well defined and visible, known to all by name."[3]

The study of these divided memories blew resistance myths apart. In many different areas, right across Italy, local fissures had opened up between those who had lost their families in Nazi massacres, and the protagonists of the antifascist resistance. These tensions divided families, villages, and neighborhoods, and in some cases these arguments lasted for decades. For these historians—nearly all of whom came from the left—it was a delicate experience.[4] These memories were "shocking" and scandalous.[5] They undermined the basis of the resistance itself, for what kind of resistance failed even to gain the support of those who had seen their own fathers, husbands, wives, and children massacred by the Nazis and the Fascists? The massacres—and the way they were interpreted—also revealed a division between forms of civil resistance and the organized, armed Resistance.

These narratives forced historians to touch deep wounds and look into the dark corners of the resistance, areas that could no longer be avoided, just as it is impossible now to avoid the voices from Civitella, Gubbio, Guardistallo, of both the partisans and the families of the victims. Thus, the resistance legacy began to be analyzed for the first time, warts and all—with its errors (that were not without consequence), its internal divisions, and its creation of myths and legends. These were also debates over the question of responsibility, over ideology and over politics.[6]

But these studies also show how important memory is for an understanding of postwar Italy, something that had been more or less ignored for so very long. Studies of the development of memory narratives, debates, and commemorations in Sant'Anna di Stazzema, Rome and Civitella are absolutely central not just to an understanding of memory issues, but to the whole postwar experience. Rome's complicated relationship with the memory and commemoration of the Fosse Ardeatine massacre is key to many of the issues of subjectivity and identity that have marked the capital since 1944. And the same is even more true for the small towns where massacres patterned the whole postwar period. Without these memories, without these experiences, the postwar history of these places makes little sense. But for years, these memories were hidden, "overlooked," minimalized.

Of course, there were also places where the blame was aimed primarily at the perpetrators of the massacres, the Nazis, and to a lesser extent the Italian fascists. But these places were in the minority. They are hard to find (and not without their problems when you do find them, as with San Miniato). Even in the case of the most "nationalized," horrific, and well-known series of massacres, those that are usually categorized generically as "Marzabotto," elements of divided memory, were seen after the war.

Time and again, divided memories turn up after massacres—from Gubbio, to Guardistallo, to Sant'Anna di Stazzema. If you scratched the surface a bit, and dug underneath the rhetoric, the story was more often one of division than agreement. But the form of division depended on local factors as well as politics, rumors, propaganda, the public use of history, geography, and the specific role of the Resistance. Divisions also changed over time, and were often overturned, or reawakened. History and historians mattered, as did books, films, poems and even town planning. Justice—or the lack of it—was also extremely important.

This chapter will examine some of the most important cases of divided memory arising from Nazi massacres. We will visit the hill-towns of Civitella Val di Chiana and Guardistallo and the tiny hamlet of Sant'Anna di Stazzema in Tuscany and also Italy's capital, Rome.

* * *

In June of 1969 in Civitella Val di Chiana, Tuscany, the annual ceremony was held to commemorate the massacre in this tiny hill-town, some twenty-five years earlier. A monument was unveiled and leading Christian Democrat politician Amintore Fanfani was present, as were partisan leaders and relatives of the victims. Previous commemorations had been marked by tension between these two groups. Many of the widows and children of the victims held specific local partisans responsible for having first provoked the 1944 massacre, and for having failed to protect the town. During the ceremony, a speaker made reference to the Vietnam War. This was the spark for an open protest on behalf of the families. Fanfani vowed never to attend this particular ceremony again. But he did not keep his promise, returning in 1984 (a date seen by many locals as the first "real" commemoration of the massacre).[7]

The bitter divisions over the past in Civitella, which had also led to an unpleasant court case, thus exploded into the open in 1969.[8] Earlier, in 1964, there had been a dispute over a possible medal for "military valor" for the town, which was transformed into a medal for "civil value" because, for the widows, "their husbands were not heroes."[9] Over time, after 1944, Civitella constructed complicated memoryscapes that reflected the divisions over memory in the town. Public memory was as dynamic and multilayered as private memories. Monuments in different places referred to different groups, and their memories, and were used in different ways by the various sections linked to these divergent narratives. The most recent monument is an official plaque (in two languages) dedicated to British soldiers for the help they offered people after the massacre. It could be argued that this plaque represents new forms of shared memory that have developed in Civitella since the 1990s.

In other areas, on the sites of the various massacres that took place that day, there are simple monuments, which hold a neutral line between the various commemorative factions, such as this example:

Civitella's Local Council
On the 25th anniversary
Of the killings in Cornia
1944 1969 (names of the victims)

In Civitella itself, much of the public memory is linked to the church, both physically and ideologically. This plaque's language is religious, not political, and there is no mention of the resistance, or of the perpetrators. The "killing" was "tragic" and the victims were both "innocent" and "glorious":

Most of the innocent victims died here
With their priest
During the tragic killings in this town
On the 29 June 1944
To the glorious dead
Memories and Prayers for eternity

A special chapel in the cemetery (built in 1962) is dedicated to the massacre and carries a series of plaques and epigraphs on its walls. Inside, there are a number of small plaques with the names of the victims (and their ages). Civitella's geography of memory also includes straightforward resistance plaques, as with this one (marginalized in terms of space) in the town's cemetery.

On the 30th Anniversary of the resistance and the liberation
The town council of Civitella di Val di Chiana
Remembers its own sons
Who fell in the fight for freedom
(names)
29 June 1944–29 June 1974

This plaque is a dramatic example of divisions over the past, as the "liberation" of Civitella coincided with the 1944 massacre. The town's central monument, not directly linked to the church, erected in 1969, carries an epigraph by antifascist poet Franco Antonicelli with numerous religious references. This text both tells the story of the massacre (and includes a reference to the perpetrators) and makes reference to the relatives—"the women who remained alone"—and to memory itself. The accompanying art work depicts the town on fire, while women try to escape, clutching babies to their breasts.

Civitella had thus seen the contestation of public commemorations as a result of divisions within private memory. With time, these divisions were mapped onto divided (and complicated) forms of public memory.[10] These publicly acknowledged divisions helped create—over time—a kind of uneasy truce in some places. Each side had their own memorials, monuments, ceremonies, their own dead to mourn, their own past to remember. Tensions exploded when there were attempts to remember that single event by all sides, together, in the same place.

In many cases the partisans were (and sometimes are still) seen as not only provoking massacres, but also as having "failed" to defend the victims of massacres or of not having given themselves up in place of those who were killed (even if such an act was impossible). This is the case with the Fosse Ardeatine massacre in Rome (March 24, 1944) studied by Portelli. Ever since those killings, there have been claims that the partisans involved in the attack that led to the reprisal should have "handed themselves in" to save the others. Despite the fact that it is relatively easy to show that such a choice was not available, this myth has continued to be repeated and believed by many, on both the left and right of the political spectrum. Even

Portelli's book has not proved capable of extinguishing this false vision of the past, which continues to turn up at regular intervals.[11]

One of the other great "crimes" of the partisans was that they were still alive, while those who had died in the massacres—obviously—were not. Trauma and mourning turned quickly into anger, but anger itself was also part of the healing process. Families felt humiliated by ceremonies and monuments that failed to reflect their views, as well as medals awarded to individual partisans and to entire towns. These arguments were exploited by the right—and those opposed to the resistance—but not invented by them.

Communities of survivors looked for some sign from the State of the price they had paid. Sometimes, this was something as simple as a road, which was conceded in Sant'Anna but never built in Vinca. But the idea of recognition was a delicate issue, especially when partisans were involved. Medals created further conflict in Civitella (where locals rejected one kind of medal), and the reasons given for medal awards by the state were also controversial. Meanwhile, the medal awarded to Sant'Anna was welcomed by the local community, leading to subtle changes in narratives around the past, which also impacted upon the political and social identity of the town.

Public and private memories clashed in towns and villages that had suffered wartime massacres. State-based and public speeches and monuments often jarred with local memories and versions of events. Far from helping with mourning processes by creating a means of closure, they were often the source of further and bitter division. The state failed to acknowledge different narratives while local people contested the versions of history presented down to them in their town squares and in history books. The cold war provided the context for many of these debates, and it was no accident that alternative memoryscapes often had a key setting, the local church.

The representation of many massacres after the war seems to follow a similar pattern. For much of the postwar period there was a phase of consensus, or apparent consensus. An official version was laid down and codified through public ceremonies, anniversaries, medals, plaques, monuments, books, and often in films, songs, and poems. No matter if many people locally either silently (as in most cases) or noisily (as at Civitella, for example) refuse to accept this official version, and hence its memory production. These other versions were also (usually) ignored by most historians. A mixture of political censorship and self-censorship kept most of these conflicts under control, and out of the public eye.

In the 1980s, things began to change and official versions of events started to come under fire. Other accounts appeared in print and were given public airings, often through the work of journalists or unofficial historians. Acknowledged truths were publicly challenged. One of the remarkable features of the shifts in the memory of the massacres is the importance of texts—history books, photographs, films—in the development of positions and debates. Often, the contestation of the official version led to a crisis of public memory, with a collapse of the legitimation afforded to the usual ceremonies. There were calls for plaques to be altered, for new monuments to be erected, for changes to the public memory linked to these events. Divisions that were latent (or simply ignored) become open, and began to be studied and taken seriously by historians.

Historians were sometimes called upon to "resolve" disputes, but they usually failed to do so, and nor could they have done so. Memory itself, after all, was the subject of many studies. Trials also played a part in this history of memory, especially after the opening up of the "cupboard of shame" in the 1990s. The identification of specific Nazi perpetrators and their codification through a judicial process allowed a public and official airing for memories of the massacres themselves (and not just the reasons behind the massacres). A series of trials thus played a part in bringing together postwar divided memories. The perpetrators, the Nazis, came back into the picture.

Stories: Sant'Anna di Stazzema, 1944–2008

Those of us who are still here talk about it all the time—it has always been on our minds.

—Survivor of Sant'Anna di Stazzema massacre, in Cappelletto,
"Public Memories and Personal Stories"

As you drive along the two-lane coastal motorway that runs from La Spezia past the fashionable resorts of Forte dei Marmi and toward Viareggio, you come across an unusual roadside sign. Amid the tourist attractions of the zone, there is suddenly a picture of a woman whose hair seems on fire, in striking red and black. The words are simple, but intriguing: *Sant'Anna di Stazzema. L'eccidio* (the killing).[12] On the left of the motorway, high in the hills, lies the tiny town of Sant'Anna. In 1944, on August 12, this was the site of one of the most horrific Nazi massacres of the war.

This tiny series of hamlets had a normal population of about 400, but this had been swelled—like many mountain towns in Tuscany—by those looking to escape from the war and bombings in coastal towns. It was seen as a safe place. This was a terrible mistake. Many children had taken refuge in Sant'Anna during the war, and the most celebrated premassacre photograph shows a group of them dancing in a circle—and this later formed the basis for an art work to be found in the village. Many men in Sant'Anna had been exempted from military service thanks to their work as miners. There was no road to the village. It could only be reached on foot.

Arriving in the morning, in the hamlets and isolated farmhouses on the outskirts of this remote village, four columns of SS soldiers killed everyone they came across—men, women, and children—in an orgy of destruction. A hundred or so people were closed in a barn and killed, with bombs being thrown for good measure. Another 100 or so people were machine-gunned in the church square and burnt in a huge fire using the pews. A pregnant woman was torn open, and her fetus shot. On their way down the mountain, the Germans rounded up hundreds of men who were deported or summarily killed.[13] Accounts of the numbers of those killed range from 362 to 560, although the "official" figure (that used for many years after the massacre, and recorded in documents and on monuments) is the higher one. Only 430 victims have since been identified, despite the fact that "those who were about to be burnt took out photographs of themselves in a last heart-rending hope of being recognised afterwards," something that was "rendered futile by the flames."[14] Many people were buried immediately, and no proper inquiry into the massacre was carried out until the trials in the early twenty-first century.[15]

The whole Tucci family from Livorno—nine in all—were killed, apart from the father. Two priests were among the victims. Something like 130 children perished.[16] One child survived by hiding in an oven; others ran into the woods or slept in caves, and "for days those who survived lived like wild animals, suffering from a collective trauma which was impossible to cope with."[17] In its form, the massacre was closer perhaps to some of the round-ups from this period, such as that at Monte Grappa in September 1944, where whoever the Germans (and Italian fascists) captured was simply eliminated.[18]

Initially, the massacre simply would not go away. The smell from the bodies continued to pervade the area for a long time after the event, and bodies kept emerging from the ground. As Contini has pointed out, "In Sant'Anna di Stazzema after a few days the bodies buried in the tiny town square began to decompose and disturb the soil which covered them."[19] The town was haunted, unable to move on from the horror it had experienced. Sant'Anna itself was identified with the massacre. The problem of those buried in front of the destroyed church was not resolved until 1948. In that year, the proper burial of the dead—so important to mourning processes—"began with its opposite," with the exhumation of remains and their transferal to the charnel-house. "Since then," as Cappelletto argues, "the annual commemoration has been marked by an intensity of emotions that makes it seem like a true funeral rite. These are also the times when the members of the community gather together and recount 'their story."[20] A "cult of death" took hold in the village.[21] Many of the destroyed houses were left in ruins for years, as silent witnesses to the 1944 tragedy. The same process took place around Marzabotto in Emilia, in the wake of the massacres there.

The reasons for the massacre have never been fully explained, beyond the generic tactic of "war against the civilians" adopted by the German army in Italy, and elsewhere, during World War II.[22] Nonetheless historians (and the judges who looked at the case) now agree that the massacre was not a "reprisal, but an act of preventative terrorism aimed at the civil population"[23] For many years, this version of events did not tally with that put forward by the witnesses and survivors of the massacre.

Sant'Anna di Stazzema: Changing Memories

Memories linked to the Sant'Anna massacre went through a series of phases. The first set of memory narratives to prevail were those that blamed partisans for the massacre. This "blame" was linked to a specific story. It was said that partisans had taken down a printed German order to evacuate the area and replaced it with their own leaflet that was a call to resist. Many survivors (and those to whom the story has been passed down) still adhere to this version of events but, unlike with Civitella, "a closed and impermeable memory of the events of 1944 did not develop."[24] As with so many other massacres, the survivors were "obsessed with causality," with finding a meaning for an event that, in reality, had no meaning outside of the horrific logic of total war. This was true of all the massacres: local debates after massacres returned time and again to the same questions: who fired first? Why did they attack? Who pinned up that leaflet? Why didn't they defend us?

The very first commemorations had seen protests against the partisans. This antipartisan memory did not last (at least publicly) in Sant'Anna, in part because there were few local partisans to blame. What was at stake after the war was the very survival of the town itself, as a place, and thus this battle became central. For years there were just a few widows and widowers there, and even today just twenty to thirty people live in the area all the year round. A committee was formed that managed to bring electricity to the area (in 1955) and then, crucially, a proper road was constructed in the 1960s.

The award of a gold medal "for military valor" in 1971 was a crucial moment in the solidifying of a different kind of memory at Sant'Anna. The award was the result of a long legal and political battle. In other areas, medals had solidified divisions, for Sant'Anna, the medal seemed to create the possibility for new, unified narratives about the past. This moment—according to the work of Rovatti—represented a turning-point in the way the town saw itself, and its own past.[25] The strange thing was that the medal had been awarded for military valor, when the massacre was clearly a case of a massacre of unarmed civilians. In other places, a medal had led to further divisions. In Sant'Anna it created a new, more united memory. The village became the symbol for the history of the resistance in Tuscany. Official recognition of and knowledge about the massacre began to increase. A series of Italian Heads of State visited Stazzema over the years: Pertini in 1982, Scalfaro in 1991 and Ciampi in 2000. A museum was opened in 1991 and a new structure in 2007. A "peace park" had been created in 2000.[26]

Until the award of the medal, at least in terms of what Rovatti calls "internal memory," "the narrative heart of the stories of the massacres of Civitella and Stazzema—one might almost say the structure that sustained them—was the theme of the partisans' guilt."[27] A shift then took place from stories about why the massacre took place to those that concentrated on the event in itself, its survivors, and its witnesses. There was a decision, conscious or otherwise, to "tone down accusations against the communists, the partisans,"[28] although, beneath the surface, there remained an "undercurrent of anger" toward the partisans.

Thus, as Rovatti has pointed out, there were many contradictory aspects of Sant'Anna's memory: "From the very beginning, Sant'Anna has been a town which carried forward an anti-partisan memory, as well as a place which looked to renew itself through the idea of anti-fascism, and which was ashamed of that very set of memories."[29] Narratives changed over time. The past was molded to the needs of the present. Forms of victimhood changed. From a massacre of civilians, designed to terrify the local population and cut off any possible links to the partisans, this event became one where the victims were specifically chosen, or at least did not die by chance. The victims, according to the reasons behind the 1971 medal, had been killed thanks to a premeditated act of war.

Nonetheless, these "shifts" in memory did not lead to a complete acceptance of resistance narratives (especially in private). People in the town continued to organize their own alternative, silent, "nonpolitical" torch-lit ceremony, held annually on the night before the anniversary, on August 11. As one participant put it in August 1988, "There is silence; they go there just with their torches and their candles up to the ossuary, because the day afterwards there are too many people and the sun is beating down."[30] Antipartisan narratives continued to exist under the surface, as if the "real truth" lay elsewhere. These narratives were constructed around a number of stories and legends, in the obsessive search for a motive for the massacre. Many, in private, continued to tell oft-repeated stories about the causes of the massacre (above all that linked to an infamous "leaflet" that had sup-posedly been pinned in the Church Square in July 1944).[31]

In line with the series of trials that followed the discovery of the "cup-board of shame," a judicial investigation was opened into the 1944 mas-sacre in the 1990s. This later led to a full trial, during which many personal testimonies were heard in court. In June 2005, life sentences by the Military Tribunal in La Spezia were handed down to ten ex-SS soldiers, all of whom were in their eighties at the time. As with other trials with regard to war-time massacres, the hearings were an opportunity for witnesses to have their stories heard officially (sometimes for the first time) and to "obtain justice." As elsewhere, these trials also reopened old arguments and debates. In 2007, these sentences were finally confirmed by the Cassation Court in Rome. For the court, the massacre was not a reprisal, but a premeditated act of terrorism.

Resistance to the Germans was symbolized by one key story from the massacre, where a young woman, Genny Bibolotti Marsili, had thrown her clog at the troops before being shot dead (and in doing so, she saved her son's life). This symbol of struggle, with its echoes of Enrico Toti, was picked up in many narratives. It was also a strong visual image, a picture of a brave and spontaneous sacrifice. A drawing of this event was widely distributed—as romanticized by an artist in a popular magazine—and was used on the cover of the first history book dedicated to Sant'Anna.[32] For Calamandrei, Marsili was a "symbol of a people's resistance."[33]

This was also a clear example of civil, unarmed resistance, a case of female defiance against a powerful and heartless enemy. Marsili was awarded a posthumous Gold Medal for Civil Valour by President Ciampi in 2003 (on April 25, thus cementing her position as a resistance martyr). In that same year, the photographer Oliviero Toscani staged an exhibition of photographs of survivors of the massacre in the Resistance museum.

Silence and the "Curse" of Sant'Anna di Stazzema

For years, Sant'Anna (and its massacre) was largely forgotten and ignored at a national level. The event was difficult to place within the wider story of the Resistance, and was thus often left out of these narratives. But the state did not ignore Sant'Anna completely. Giovanni Gronchi (at the time Presi-dent of the Camera) was present at the inauguration of the monument dedicated to the massacre in 1948. The idea that the town was in some way cursed became linked to moments of commemoration around this time. This "curse" myth was created by two specific events. In 1947, two workers employed on the construction of the monument were killed after being struck by lightning. This fact is now also commemorated by a small plaque on the monument itself, which was quickly developing into a palimpsest. Sixteen years later, on August 12, 1963, a helicopter hit the church at the end of the celebrations and three people were killed. The remains of the helicopter were left as a monument to those who died (and a further small monument was created in 1964). Part of the local silence over the massacre also seems to have been dictated by fear. Italians certainly took part in the massacre, and there seemed to be the possibility of meeting the very perpetrators of the massacre on a daily basis.

Public Memoryscapes

The history of Sant'Anna's public memoryscapes—and their use—is a story in itself, and tells us much about the ways in which memories of the massacre have been passed down through time. A first competition was held for a monument in 1945, but the memorial was not opened until 1948. The final statue was not added until 1971 (the money had run out, it was said). There had been some debate about the position of this main monument, but a decision was made to place it up the hill, and therefore away from the actual sites of the massacre.[34] In this way a *via crucis* was created. The names of the victims on this monument tell their own stories. Many of the surnames are the same and entire families were wiped out. The list also brings home the high number of victims who were children and the high numbers of women.

Sant'Anna's church is covered and surrounded with plaques and monuments. One makes a specific comparison with the Fosse Ardeatine and Marzabotto. Others refer to the priests and other victims of the massacre. Today, the car park in the village is dedicated to the youngest victim of the massacre: Anna Pardini, twenty days old when she was killed in 1944. Today's memory routes take in the museum, the church, the cemetery, and the *via crucis* that leads up to the monument. Outside the museum, there is a plaque with an inscription by Calamandrei, which deals precisely with the question of memory. Visitors to Sant'Anna today are faced with a rich patchwork of public memory sites. The whole town is now organized as a massacre memoryscape.

Who Fired First? Guardistallo, June 28–29, 1944

We must stop glowering at each other once and for all and forget forever those arguments which have created friction amongst us, because if we continue in this way we will only repeat the tragedy of the war which left millions of people dead.

—Angiolino Benci, Mayor of Guardistallo,
June 29, 1948, commemoration speech

Citizens! We must be careful because experience shows that when hatred and evil thoughts take control, men, and nations, lose their sense of reason and war can break out whose consequences are unknown.

—Benci, Mayor of Guardistallo, June 29, 1950, commemoration speech

On June 29, 1944, at dawn, a skirmish took place between a large group of partisans on the march toward the coast and the retreating German army, close to the small hill-town of Guardistallo. Just after the exchange of fire began, German troops went on the rampage, killing forty-seven locals in nearby farm houses. Eleven partisans were shot dead, either during the conflict or after being taken prisoner. The nonpartisan victims were aged between seventeen and seventy-six. Some were women. The Germans left the area that evening, and on the 30th, the Allies arrived. Ever since, as in Civitella and many other places, the population of the small hill town of Guardistallo has been divided over what happened, who was responsible, and how to remember the massacre.[35] That same day, 130 kilometers to the east, the massacre at Civitella was also taking place.

Most locals had no doubts that the partisans were to blame. In 1944, a British army report found that "a lot of hatred is directed at the partisans . . . in some cases the witnesses are more interested in denouncing the partisans than the enemy."[36] As with many other cases, there were clashes between partisans and the families of the victims at the first commemoration of the massacre (in 1945). On many occasions since the end of the war the partisans "couldn't attend" these commemorations.[37] As in other cases, the partisans were also accused of not defending the victims from the Germans.

Ever since June 29, 1944, in Guardistallo, there has been a "battle over memory."[38] In the 1990s, Pezzino, one of the leading experts on the massacres in Italy, was asked by the Guardistallo town council to carry out research into the history (and the memory) of that single event. He accepted, and structured his subsequent book (following Todorov) in the form of a legal judgment. During the writing of the book, Pezzino found himself immersed in conflicts that had embedded themselves in the town's very identity. He was faced with different versions of the past, and was forced to choose between these versions. The disputes, as in other cases, were in part about "what had really happened," but they also went deeper than that—taking in questions of resistance, the gray zone, and were patterned by local versions of the cold war. Who shot first and why? These questions mattered—and were the subject of endless debate—but the history of postwar Guardistallo was shaped by what people believed had happened, which was also subject to the power of the imaginary.

Pezzino shows in his book how some participants in the clash with the Germans on the morning of the 29th falsified the importance and content of this "battle" in a series of publications: "They changed a banal and accidental clash—which only by chance led to tragedy—into a victorious battle."[39] Local people, especially those who had lost loved ones in the massacre, refused to identify with this myth. Moreover, they created a powerful countermyth linked to the figure of Don Mazzetto Rafanelli, whose brave negotiations with the Germans saved a number of other civilians (who had already been captured) from execution. Rafanelli became the physical representative of this countermemory in the town (despite being transferred to Volterra in 1950). He spoke at commemorations, was awarded a gold medal by the town in 1964 and locals insisted that he be buried in Guardistallo in the 1980s.[40]

Angry divisions over the past had a profound effect over how that past was remembered. Commemorations, anniversaries, and concrete forms of memory were highly sensitive moments, where bitter recriminations often surfaced. Already on the first anniversary of the massacre, on the June 29, 1945, there were reports of open tension between some of the widows and the partisans. Angiolino Benci, the postwar socialist mayor, made frequent calls in the early years for reconciliation. But clearly these appeals fell on deaf ears, because in 1952, the mayor refused to make a speech at all.

The families of the victims often complained about the tone of speeches in later years, or the presence of partisans, or if Don Rafanelli was not mentioned as a key actor in the story of the massacre. As with Sant'Anna, or Pedescala, alternative ceremonies were developed, or people stopped going to the official ceremonies altogether. A medal was also awarded to Guardistallo after a long political struggle. The official reasons for the award of a bronze medal for "military valor" (in 1996) used traditional resistance language. Far from uniting the town, as Pezzino argues, a medal of this kind "represented the fixing . . . of the separation between private and public memory."[41]

There is no doubt that, during the Resistance, partisans did sometimes act irresponsibly and "politically." That is, at times their actions were intended to show that they had the power to act, as in the idea of taking control before the

Allies arrived. This was clearly the case in Guardistallo, where the partisans who clashed with the Germans near the town "were on their way to Casale Marittimo so as to arrive there before the Allies, and in line with the orders of the Livorno resistance leadership, [and so the decision to march in this way was] a political and strategic decision rather than a military one."[42] Partisans did not always act within a the strictly military logic of other kinds of armies, nor did they always discuss or take into account the possible consequences of their acts for the local population. But this analysis cannot allow us to conclude that the whole Resistance in itself was an error. People obviously would have preferred not to have been the subject of massacres and violence. But if every Italian had decided to "not disturb" the German army, then the Resistance would not have existed at all.

Women, as in Civitella, were the main "accusers" of the partisans. These women, described by Paggi as "the isolated community of widows dressed in black," were largely excluded from resistance narratives. As Gribaudi has argued, partisans tended to use a "national political language, which lacked the words which could have created a link with women's pain and mourning."[43] For Paggi, writing about Civitella, "the massacre created a society . . . which was drastically simplified from the point of view of gender, with the physical elimination of the great majority of the men."[44] In Guardistallo, the widows were—for many years—the main "carriers" of grief. It remains to be seen if, with the passing of that generation, the divided memories with which they identified will also disappear with them.

In Guardistallo, divisions over the past are also written in marble and etched in stone (see Figure 6.1). On the front of the town hall, there are two plaques: one dedicated (a year after the killings) to the victims of the massacre of June 1944 (but only to those who were from Guardistallo, twenty-seven names in all) and one to those from "outside the comune" (twenty-four names), with a separate section for "partisans" (eleven names). The division between partisans and other "victims" underlines the splits that have riven the town ever since that massacre. One of the strange things about this division is the presence of the name of the partisan Mario Tarchi among those "not resident in the comune." Tarchi was from Guardistallo, and was only twenty-one when he was killed. It is as if the very fact that he was a partisan excluded him from the community.[45]

In the local church (dedicated to Santi Lorenzo e Agata) there is a special side-chapel dedicated to the massacre (created in 1989). Inside are frescoes depicting peasant life, the massacre, the monument, a book of photos of the victims and various other memorial objects. Finally, close to the place of the massacre (on the outskirts of the town), stands a small set of monuments that are the focus of annual commemorations. The main monument, a simple obelisk in a field, is reached via a gate and a path lined

Figure 6.1   Guardistallo: Plaque dedicated to the massacre of 1944. "In memory of our fellow citizens who fell as victims during the German killings of the 29 June 1944."

with cypresses. Erected a year after the tragedy, it is still the main site for annual commemorations. Here, unlike in the town, no distinction is made between partisan and "civilian" victims:

> Here where
> On the 29 June 1944
> The ferocity of the Nazis
> Killed and Tortured
> Many victims
> Guardistallo
> Erects
> In affectionate memory
> Of those who died
> And as a snub and warning
> For the butchers
> 29 June 1945
> the living to the dead: rest in peace in glory
> the dead to the living; be free in peace, work, love.

Guardistallo's divided geographies of memory, as in Civitella, San Miniato, and Sant'Anna, thus reflect the different and complicated ways in which the past has been understood and is currently remembered.

The Historians: Books, Research, and Divided Memories

I remember five enormous pools of blood, on white stone, where they had carried out the shootings . . . a terrible smell, of burnt flesh and bodies.

—July 20, 1993, interview with Leonardo Paggi,
born in Civitella June 28, 1941

My husband and I were awakened with a start by very violent knocks on our door and we both realized the Germans were coming into the house. Gastone jumped right out of bed and rushed to the floor below—we were sleeping on the second floor—in the instinctive desire to defend his house and family against the invaders and looters but probably never thinking that he would be assaulted and killed immediately . . . I followed him a moment later and went as far as the stairway from which I saw him on the first floor landing, eight steps away from me, his face overwhelmed with an expression of awful horror. The staircase is made in such a way that I could see Gastone but not the German soldier. A shot rang out hitting my husband in the abdomen. He groaned, gave me one last look without saying a word and, holding his stomach, leaned against the wall. For one brief instant, I stood as though petrified, then I ran onto the stairway to shake him, but hardly had I reached the fourth or fifth step, when a second shot was fired which hit my husband's neck and made him collapse, this time unconscious, in my arms. However his heart was still beating. My father and mother ran in, and the children, too, crying and calling their papa . . . The German soldier, after killing my husband, ran away immediately, and we remained alone by the side of my beloved husband as he took his last breath. My reason for living disappeared with him . . . Barely had my husband died then seven, eight, ten of these ferocious beasts burst into the house and set the beds and furniture on fire shouting: "Outside! Outside! House kaput!" They threw us outside, barefoot and in nightclothes—my four children, my mother and me . . . I had on my nightgown, all splattered with my husband's blood; gathered around myself, who was from now on their only frail means of support, were my mother— her face drawn in misery and horror—and my four children, barefoot, in pyjamas, trembling, and crying.

—Elda Morfini, Widow Paggi, in Menchetti, "The Witnesses of Civitella"

Leonardo Paggi was one of the "four children" in this story. Paggi's father, Gastone, had been advised to return to his hometown of Civitella to join his wife and four children for his own safety, given his active support for the resistance in Florence. On June 29, he was shot in his own house. His father-in-law (seventy-nine-years-old at the time) was killed immediately afterward. This terrifying account of Leonardo's father's death was one of the stories of the massacre published as a collection of interviews

in the periodical *Società* in 1946. Leonardo Paggi was an unnamed protagonist of these testimonies, which he later helped to publish in English
(his wife, Victoria de Grazia, translated them from Italian for the first
time).[46] Romano Bilenchi, a close friend of Gastone Paggi, had collected
interviews with widows in 1945 and Gastone's wife, Elda Morfini Paggi,
was the intermediary for that research.[47]

In these ways Leonardo Paggi was both an actor (a witness, a protagonist in other stories) in the past history of Civitella but also active in the
study of the town's history and memory. By helping to organize the 1994
conference and publishing work on the massacre, he also contributed to
changes in the ways that past was understood, and remembered. This conference in Arezzo/Civitella (*In Memory. Revisiting Nazi Atrocities in World
War II*) was a turning point. Historians influenced these memories as they
studied them, and their studies changed the historians themselves. As we
have seen, on June 29, 1944, a three-year old Paggi had witnessed the massacre. Ever since, his mother had carried forward her own version of that
past. The massacres were and are potent sources of intersubjectivity, but
these connections have rarely been studied. They are not out in the open,
usually remaining in the background, between the lines.[48]

It thus took someone who was both a witness and a historian to open up
the way the memory of the massacres was studied, and understood. This
two-way process was particularly potent for Paggi: "For me . . . the experience of moving, backwards and forward, between these two communities
[Civitella and the 'scientific' community], and the use of historical analysis
for an event which was so close to me and my emotional life, has had thera-
peutic effects." Paggi's work on Civitella reinforced his "identity as a person
and as a historian."[49] His edited book about the massacre was dedicated
"to the memory of my parents"[50] It was also significant that Paggi used the
word "truth" in quotation marks.[51] Paggi discussed the way his mother had
reacted to the massacre, providing details about her life that perhaps only
he and his immediate family could have known (and taken from his own
memories). In this way, Paggi interviews himself, and his own interviews
betray his double role. They are a mixture of analysis and testimony.

Paggi's research on the massacre was also a way of working through his
own trauma. His mother, unlike many of the other widows in Civitella,
had not elaborated an antipartisan memory, and she had also left the town
after the war, for Florence. Nonetheless, Paggi often leaves himself out of
the story (or rather does not always make his own role explicit), writing
of his father as if he was just another victim of the massacre. Was there a
danger of getting "too close" to the witnesses, of becoming part of the community of memory—of being the mouthpiece for certain narratives? Paggi
also suffered from survivor's guilt—"I think I had a terrible sense of guilt,

because I was still alive."[52] For Contini, similar feelings had led some of the survivors—in the years after the massacre—to commit suicide.

By studying the memories of the massacre at Civitella, Paggi was also—and inevitably—studying himself, and his own family. He was also "studied" by other experts on massacres and memory. Contini interviewed Paggi as part of his research on Civitella (as a witness, but also as a historian). The attention paid to Civitella affected the way the past was understood there. Memories themselves changed. The study of memory, and those who studied these memories, as well as the texts they produced (including conferences, articles, debates, and presentations) became part of the story. This relationship was not always a happy one, over time. As Cappelletto argues, "In Civitella and Stazzema, over the course of more than half a century since the massacres, there have been many points of tension and friction between the outside and the inside world with regard to the political representations of the massacre. At the 1994 Arezzo conference, one of the ways in which people dealt with these tensions was by expressing them explicitly, and the result was a network of narrative relations which itself formed a sort of new story there re-lived as performance."[53]

In 1993, with the impending arrival of the fiftieth anniversary of the massacre, the mayor of Guardistallo and a citizen's committee called on Paolo Pezzino to carry out research into the massacre of June 1944 and the events leading up to it, as well as the memories that had emerged in the town since then. Pezzino, who has since become the leading expert on the massacres in Italy, was asked by the Guardistallo town council to "establish the facts." After three years of work, Pezzino's book appeared in 1997, the same year as the publication of the other, fundamental, book-length study of a massacre that happened on the very same day: Contini's *La memoria divisa*.

Pezzino described the task assigned to him as "a delicate one." He soon became aware that his role was complex, and was clearly not just about a "search for truth," the discovery of "who fired first." His own relationship with that particular massacre runs right through both editions of his book.[54] Pezzino wrote of a "strong . . . emotional impact of the encounter with the citizens of Guardistallo."[55] Contini had a similar experience with Civitella, where he was struck by "the orphans of Civitella from an emotional point of view."[56] The survivors told their stories in the 1990s as if the massacre had just happened. Contini's doubts about carrying out the research were overcome by the power of these stories.

During his work on and in Guardistallo, Pezzino often became an outlet for those who wanted to "re-establish" the "truth," and not just about the 1944 massacre. Perhaps in line with the way the book was commissioned, Pezzino organized the book in the form of a trial, with the taking of evidence and a final judgment. By 2007, and after long personal experience of the justice system thanks to his work as a consultant on various real trials, Pezzino was convinced about the deep differences between "judges and historians." He also reflected on his own past, as a historian, and his relationship with the study of Guardistallo. These reflections led Pezzino to conclude that he would not write the same book today as he had in 1997.

Meanwhile, that book itself had become part of Guardistallo's history and the debates over memory. Pezzino's work is seen—by many, in the town—as the "last word" on the Guardistallo case, and is widely quoted on Guardistallo's official Web site. When I visited Guardistallo in the summer of 2008, the local priest asked me if I had read Pezzino's book. Pezzino's assumed role was a difficult one, as Von Boeschoten argued; "by becoming an 'authority' in local history [researchers] might deprive the community of memories it cherished very dearly and of alternative ways of coming to terms with the past."[57] The interaction between historians and the local communities they studied continued long after their research itself was completed.

Portelli first decided to write about Via Rasella and the Fosse Ardeatine for reasons linked to politics, and to public and private memory. As he writes in the English version of his book, on the day Silvio Berlusconi was first elected as prime minister of Italy in 1994, "I discovered a big black swastika painted over the stone, across the street where I live, that commemorates the fourteen men murdered by the Nazis on June 4, 1944 . . . As I watched the neighbourhood artisans discuss the best means to erase the outrage from the monument, I felt that it was my duty, as a citizen, to respond to this outrage with all the means at my disposal—that is, with the tools of my trade."[58] Yet Portelli takes a very different approach to Pezzino. As he states at the start of *L'ordine è già stato eseguito*, "This book does not contain scoops or revelations. In terms of what happens I will accept the conclusions and the uncertainties—of published historical research."[59]

Over time, Portelli's book and Portelli himself were part of the history, and the memory, of both Via Rasella and the Fosse Ardeatine. They also led to other texts, such as Ascanio Celestini's *Radio Clandestina* (2005). It is now difficult to discuss the Fosse Ardeatine massacre without direct reference to Portelli's research. Portelli was appointed as an official consultant on memory by the Rome city council (*Delegato per la Memoria Storica del Comune di Roma*). He was also instrumental in setting up a specific institution in the city dedicated to memory: the *Casa della Memoria* in Trastevere. George Bush and Berlusconi visited the Fosse Ardeatine in June 2004, and—on taking power—the site was one of the first places visited by the new ex-neofascist mayor (Gianni Alemanno) after his election in May 2008.[60]

Historians working outside of academic institutions, journalists, and locals have also dedicated extensive time and research to the study of the massacres. Paolo Paoletti's book on San Miniato was particularly important, and has become crucial to local memories.[61] Paoletti has also written on Pedescala, Cefalonia, Corfu, Sant'Anna di Stazzema, Fossoli, and the murder of Giovanni Gentile. His method is to take established stories or versions of events and to attempt to destroy them through a rereading of the evidence. Often this involves personal attacks on other historians—in particular Pezzino. His books are polemical, but they sometimes have the merit of unearthing new evidence and opening up debates.

Both Contini and Pezzino have homes in Vinca, a tiny town in the Alpi Apuane mountains in Tuscany that was the scene of another particularly horrific massacre in 1944. Contini studied this massacre, and has written about it. Contini "discovered" Vinca through his work on the 1944 massacre there. Another historian, Paul Ginsborg, also has a house in Vinca, and was invited to give a speech at the annual commemoration of the massacre.

Many of those who have written about the massacres have described their personal links to these stories. For anthropologists and oral historians, this is natural: it is an essential part of the research process (and its outcomes). In the Greek village whose memories she was studying, Von Boeschoten was uncomfortable when she was asked to "teach them [the villagers] a certain version of their own past."[62] Cappelletto wrote that "at first, I noticed a certain suspiciousness of the research I was doing. Often the people of Stazzema asked me if it really was 'that' I wanted to know, that is to say 'whose fault it was.' . . . It was a relief to them and to me when I explained that I was interested in something else: I wanted to know how that past history was lived over the years and in the present, and what were the networks of social relations that sustained the narrative."[63] Many of these places are suspicious of outsiders and of attempts to tell their stories by others.

Conclusions: History and Divided Memory

These studies of divided memories emerging from wartime massacres lead to many conclusions. They also tell us about the importance of the geography of war. Contini has argued that the links between partisans and nonpartisans at a local level were different above and below the Gothic Line, where he has mapped out two "models of memory" with regard to massacres and the resistance. Above the Gothic Line, the links with the partisans were far stronger; below they were weak and liable to create lasting forms of divided memory. For Contini, "The different shapes of collective memories below and above the Gothic Line in Tuscany depends on the time which passed between the massacre and the liberation . . . the memory of the massacres underwent a significant transformation with respect to the 'Civitella model,' in the places which remain to the North of the Gothic Line . . . where the massacres followed months of Nazi occupation."[64]

However, divided memories of this kind were not limited to Italy. They also express a general psychological and social response to particular forms of trauma created by World War II massacres. In the village of Drakeia, in Eastern Greece, for example, 116 men were killed by SS troops on December 18, 1943. This massacre, as with many in Italy in 1943 to 1945, was carried out as a reprisal for the deaths of two German soldiers a day earlier. As Dutch ethnographer Von Boeschoten has written, "Conflicting memories and . . . political splits had divided the community ever since," or as one villager put it, "Half of the village hated the other half."[65] In Drakeia, as in Civitella, many (but not all) locals blamed partisan leaders for provoking the reprisal. These narratives include conspiracy theories and the familiar claim of having failed to protect the eventual victims (while supposedly protecting themselves). As in many Italian cases, in Drakeia there was also a sense that the massacre had been "forgotten," as well as a series of attempts to exploit these strong feelings for political gain. In many ways, the divided memories in a very different historical and social context bear a striking resemblance to those in Civitella. This points toward the need for the acceptance of a deeper psychological explanation, which goes beyond specific historical reasoning.

Divided memories are a potent reminder of the fragility of the resistance, which "does not represent a founding myth of a new national identity . . . but rather a factor which divides Italians, and historians would be well advised to begin to look at this contradiction, to investigate these issues without fear, if they really want to understand our national history over the last fifty years" [66] These studies show us the power of memory to shape history, underlining the fact that "telling and remembering are themselves events, not only a description of events" [67] Divided memories also reveal much about the gap between public and private memories. State-based and public speeches, monuments often jarred with local memories and versions of events. Far from helping with mourning processes of creating a process of closure, they were often the source of further and bitter division. The state failed to acknowledge different narratives while local people contested the versions of history handed down to them at official commemorations and in history books. Finally, these stories show how different actors viewed the same events in vastly different ways, and they shift the focus back to the victims (those who died, and those who mourned those who died).

7

The Resistance

Three Wars, Many Memories, Many Silences

> The Resistance epic has, in the end, damaged the memory of the Resistance.
>
> —Sergio Luzzatto, "Sangue d'Italia. Interventi sulla storia del novecento"

Remembering the Resistance

Claudio Pavone, in his *Una guerra civile*, identified the "three wars" that made up the resistance: a war of national liberation, class war, and civil war. These three wars have produced—at least—three different sets of memories. To these wars, moreover, we should now add a fourth kind of struggle: that which has become identified under the term "civil resistance" and which is linked, above all, with the role of women civilians.

This chapter will examine the ways in which public and private memories of the resistance created forms of memory over time, and in space. It will also look at the gaps and silences in this memory, and the disputes over the past that have marked the way the resistance has been understood since 1943.

Public Memory: Monuments, Anniversaries, Commemorations

> It is time to study monuments (one by one, in groups, altogether) with serious and rigorous critical methodologies, as an integral part of the history of the Resistance.
>
> —Marco Francini, "Per non metterci una pietra sopra"

Resistance memories came in all shapes and sizes. In the zones where the armed resistance was active, the landscape is crisscrossed by tiny and simple plaques, testimonies to those who died in battle, or were executed. These simple plaques are similar in form, if not in numbers, to the spontaneous cemeteries of World War I. They had an intimate link with the territory of struggle itself—the battlefields—and were a reminder of the shape of the resistance movement in the hills and mountains of central and northern Italy. These geographies of memory were a constant reminder that the armed resistance had been a guerrilla war, fought by isolated groups of makeshift soldiers, who often died alone, and were buried where they had fallen. Resistance memory is intimately linked to death, to sacrifice and to the places where "martyrdom" occurred. It was often a memory, for Isnenghi, of "who had been killed." Forms of memory reflected debates over what the resistance had been, and who had led it. They were also closely connected to contemporary politics.

In towns and cities, spontaneous monuments appeared after the war, often on the walls of houses of partisans who had been killed in battle, or deported. Simple monuments also marked places where partisans and antifascists had died, often during the final days of the war. Not all partisans were remembered in this way, and the presence or absence of monuments was the result of a variety of factors, chance, family presence, and pressure, politics, the strength and activism of local partisan organizations. These local monuments have been the focus of ritualized ceremonies since 1945, with the annual hanging of wreaths on each and every plaque on April 25 (usually led by ex-partisans) as well as the reading out of potted biographies of each "martyr."

In many cases, the names of those who died between 1940 and 1945 were simply added to World War I monuments, perhaps just with dates, or with simple inscriptions, creating a kind of alliance between those who died fighting with Mussolini's armies between 1940 and 1943 and those who fought in the resistance after September 1943. These names and the palimpsest-like monuments they helped to create reflect a deep ambiguity about how and where to remember the victims of World War II, and which victims should be commemorated.

Alongside the many simple, spontaneous monuments, there were much bigger, city-wide or neighborhood memorials. These monuments were a mixture of the general and the local. They were dedicated to The Resistance as a whole, but also reflected its local forms and patterns. In Bologna, the mothers who gathered in the city center during and after the war, looking for their sons, often carried photos of their children with them.[1] This visual memory became the basis for one of the city's most influential monuments, which consists of a series of photos of young men side-by-side in Piazza Maggiore. Very similar monuments can be found in Modena and Ferrara. Cooke has called these monuments "photographic walls."[2] In this way, specific acts of memory developed into an official monument, which also includes those for whom there is no photo available. Resistance memory was adapted to local needs and patterns and—with a few exceptions, such as the Fosse Ardeatine memorial site in Rome—national places of memory were not created. There is no national resistance museum in Italy, but hundreds of local museums, research institutes, and partisan organizations.[3]

Collective monuments were usually placed at the sites of massacres of partisans, or civilians—as with La Storta in Rome, the Parco Giurati, and Piazzale Loreto in Milan and numerous other urban and rural sites. Waves of monument-creation were created in line with various anniversaries: 1965, 1975, and 1985. By the 1980s, monument creation for the resistance was effectively over. The biggest surge of resistance monument-building (beyond local, personal monuments, which have rarely been studied) took place in the 1960s and 1970s. This was, in part, a political effect. Center-left alliances at national and local level used antifascism as a legitimizing tool. This was also a time when militant fascism was on the rise, and thus an appeal to the past also carried a contemporary message.

Official resistance monuments obviously told one side of the story from World War II. They excluded those who fought for Mussolini's armies between 1940 and 1943, and then for the Republic of Salò (or RSI). For their part, RSI veterans and those who identified with neofascism after 1945 made the attack on the resistance into one of the central features of their propaganda. The idea was to "de-nationalize" the resistance, to separate the idea of the nation from that of the antifascist movement between 1943 and 1945. To this end, neofascists highlighted the civil war aspects of that period, playing down any idea of national liberation.[4] They also attacked—physically—public memory produced by antifascists. In this way, plaques (and larger monuments) were the object of conflict. Memorial sites were smashed up, bombed, or covered in graffiti, and wreaths put up on April 25 would often be burnt. These events often created their own memory as—in reconstructing monuments—a message that would often be left referring to the past destruction, and to who had been responsible. In this way, as in 1919 to 1927, Italy experienced yet another memory war after 1945.

In Carrara, for example, the reconstruction of a bombed monument in 1965 carried a new plaque that reads, "This new stone, [is here] because the bestial insult, of the evil people, will remind the Carraresi of their duty and their scorn, in order to prevent any return to the past, 10 April 1965." The rebuilding of the monument was—in itself—a warning against a possible return of fascism. Readers of the plaque were asked to remember what had happened to the previous version (Figure 7.1). Often, in line with this idea of memory-as-warning, the damage would be left "intact," and referred to by further plaques. This was the case with another monument near Carrara, which was seriously damaged by a bomb. Here, the damage was left as part of a new, two-part monument, with this extra message, which also referred

Figure 7.1   Carrara: Damaged monument to the Resistance. The fourth "wall" from the left was knocked down by a bomb in 1981.

back to fascism's origins: "*1921–1981 The bomb which destroyed part of this monument is the continuation of fascism's criminal design. The Italian Federation of Anarchist Partisans, Carrara Town Council*" (Figure 7.2).

Another example of this can be found in Fiesole, north of Florence. Here an original damaged double-plaque was replaced (one part was for soldiers in the war, another for partisans), with a new inscription. It reads, *Fiesole's Town Council, placed this in 1963 in future memory after vandals had destroyed the previous plaques.* Events of this kind were frequent and took place all over Italy, although no study has yet been carried out of their effects, or of the new monuments that were built, or altered, to reflect this "memory war."

Some monuments were rhetorical—inspired by socialist realism. Others were more abstract. Others were simply lists of names. Their form depended on the artist, the place, the time, and the political context in which the monument was constructed. Some were calls to arms, active depictions of armed partisans, other reproduced the model of the martyr, the saint, the dead hero, the idea of sacrifice. In Imola, it is said that the postwar resistance monument (1946) was a remodeling of a proposed fascist statue. As Dogliani has written, "The young militia-man was rapidly recycled into a young partisan, while still keeping some of its fascist style and features."[5] The figure, with a clenched fist and a gun, nonetheless also

Figure 7.2   Carrara: Plaque relating to the damage to the monument. "1921–1981. The bomb which destroyed part of this monument is a sign of the criminal continuity of fascism. The Italian Federation of Partisan Associations. Carrara Town Council."

reflected a militant model of the resistance. The names below also reflect radical ideas, with the listing of jobs as well as ages to underline the social nature of the movement.[6]

Parma's resistance monument (1956, architect Lusignoli, sculptor Mazzacurati) contains a series of symbols and myths linked to the resistance. A heroic, glamorous partisan, machine-gun in hand, standing proud and high in the air, hair and cape flowing in the wind, dominates the monument. Below, however, lies a dead partisan (*il fucilato*) hands tied behind his back, bare-footed. This site combines all the most familiar elements of the resistance myth. At the back of the monument, a wall "used for executions" is recreated using bricks from a building bombed in 1944. The monument depicts the partisan as both (active) hero and martyr.

Inside Bologna's football stadium, a huge statue of Mussolini on a horse had stood throughout the period of the regime. On July 25, 1943, that statue was partly pulled down, and Mussolini's "head" was paraded through the streets. After the war, the city's partisan association had the metal from the horse melted down and made into two, large partisan statues (a woman and a man, both armed), designed by Luciano Minguzzi. Originally, these were kept close to the ANPI offices but were later moved to Porta Lame, in a highly visible position and on a site of resistance battles. The construction of this monument became an antifascist act in itself, a symbolic and actual moment of destruction and reconstruction. In 1947, the symbolic de-fascistization of the stadium was completed by the organized removal of a series of fascist symbols by young, politicized volunteers.[7]

Sometimes, simple collective war or resistance monuments were put up, with many visual features similar to those erected after World War I, such as the obelisks on Monte Sole, Amole, and Vado di Setta, all built between 1946 and 1953. Many monuments had names and inscriptions added to them. They were complicated examples of a "stratification of signs."[8] In the 1980s, a whole series of abstract monuments were built, in reaction to the overbearing rhetoric of the past. The geography of monuments, plaques, and signs of the resistance—the *memoryscapes* of the resistance—provided ways of drawing political and social maps of various places. In recent years, complicated and detailed guides to these memoryscapes have been produced for many cities, regions and provinces, including Turin, Trentino, and Bolzano.

Anniversaries and commemorations focused on monuments and monumental sites. Yet April 25 struggled to become a day of national unity and other dates were recycled to provide an alternative. After 1945, November 4 developed into a central day for public commemoration. This showed both that the postwar memory wars had been forgotten and that the fascist nature of many war monuments was being ignored. World War I, by 1945, carried none of the divisive elements of April 25, with its echoes of civil war and recent violence. As Nizza puts it, "It was as if the victory at the battle of Vittorio Veneto was celebrated in 1948."[9]

Most cemeteries contained special areas reserved for partisans, and different sections for those who died fighting for the RSI (as well as during the *resa dei conti*). Both sides celebrated their dead on April 25, and municipal cemeteries often saw clashes between ex-fascists and ex-partisans, in a kind of parody of the civil war that had just finished. In Milan, camp 10 was and is that reserved for RSI victims, while the partisan "camp of glory" was in another sector of the city's huge Musocco cemetery. During his time in office, Mayor Gabriele Albertini caused a minor scandal by visiting both ceremonies (but on November 1, the Day of the Dead), one with his mayor's sash, and one without. In 2007, a proposal was put forward to move all the bodies of the partisans and those who had fought for the RSI to the city's main war memorial.

Myths, Heroes, and the Civic Religion of the Resistance

You partisans always shout: "Long Live Moscatelli!" but I am telling you that
it is time to stop using these myths and it is time to cry: "Long Live Italy!"

—Cino Moscatelli, 1946

Myths linked to Resistance leaders were created and spread "to coun-
ter those created and imposed by fascism."[10] Moscatelli, the communist
partisan leader who operated in Piedmont, was well aware of the importance of symbols in maintaining control over his followers. Various stories
were linked to his exploits during the war: a red car he was supposed to
have driven around in, his ability to use disguises, the idea that he was
"everywhere, and nowhere." This myth was spread through popular stories,
poems, books, songs, and images. Part of the mythical nature of Moscatelli
was also that he "did not believe in his own myth." As a politician in postwar Italy, Moscatelli was seen as a man of his time, but the mythical aspects
of his partisan past remained ever-present.

A different kind of local myth was constructed (and self-constructed)
around the figure of another partisan leader who operated (and died) in
the same area as Moscatelli, Filippo Maria Beltrami. As a martyr, Beltrami's
mythical status was particularly powerful, and was constructed around stories and fables. The myth was reinvented over time, and reinforced by an
annual ceremony in Beltrami's honor. Resistance stories in this area were
not fixed, but dynamic. As Colombara has written, "With the passing of the
generations, the resistance community took on new forms of conservation
and transmission of memory."[11]

The most important national myths were also those linked to martyrs,
above all the seven Cervi brothers, shot in 1943 in Reggio Emilia and the
object of a powerful cult, transmitted through their father, throughout the
postwar period.[12] Alcide "Papà" Cervi was "a heroic and positive figure as
well as a peasant patriarch who travelled far and wide, always wearing on
his jacket the seven medals that had been posthumously awarded to his
sons."[13] Books, films, and monuments were dedicated to the Cervi story
and their house became the closest thing Italy had to a national resistance
museum, alongside the Fosse Ardeatine site in Rome.

The meaning of the resistance in terms of public memories, anniversaries, and commemorations changed in line with political developments.
There are now many studies of the patterns of this memory over time.[14]
In the 1940s and 1950s, public memory often ignored the radical aspects
of the resistance, as the cold war took hold. As Taviani said in a speech in
1954, "In celebrating the past we should not open up wounds which are

already too deep."[15] But culture was as important as politics, especially in the regions where the resistance had been strong. As Gundle argues, "The resistance tradition is also made up of symbols, rituals, commemorations, monuments, images and cultural artefacts."[16] A civic religion of the resistance developed over time, which was intimately linked to society, community, and local traditions, as well as the work of intellectuals, artists, film-makers, and cultural activists.

The center-left in the 1960s relaunched the public memory of the resistance, especially after the events of 1960 in Modena, Reggio Emilia, and Genoa. Later, the movements linked to 1968 reacted, often violently, against the conservatism of these forms of commemoration. In 1962, the *Quaderni Piacentini* criticized "professional antifascists" and argued that the radicalism of that period had been forgotten: "The Resistance does not scare anyone anymore, it is dead: and so long live the Resistance." Later, this kind of idea would be translated into slogans like *The Resistance is Red not Demo-Christian*. New songs were created that linked past and present, arguing for continuities with certain features of the resistance.

In the 1970s, some militants called themselves "the new partisans" and rediscovered certain features from 1943 to 1945, especially the activities of the urban *Gappisti*.[17] *Lotta Continua* attacked what it called "celebratatory mummification" of the resistance.[18] Militants claimed that they wanted to fight a *new resistance*, and not consign that period to history. While criticizing the obsession of the "old" resistance with memory, students and "the movement" built their own—and often very similar—monuments for their martyrs. Red terrorists mythologized the violent, underground aspects of the resistance.[19] The "constitutional arc" of parties who formed alliances against terrorism and the rise of neofascism in the 1970s also claimed to be the heirs of the resistance. It was precisely the complicated and often contradictory elements of Italian history between 1943 and 1945 that allowed such a variety of groups to argue that they were the true holders of the resistance legacy. The division of the partisan associations themselves into three separate groups by 1949 was symptomatic of this problem.

As the neofascists came back into the political fold, and then entered government after 1994, in various phases, furious debates followed over the legacy of the resistance, its memory, and its meaning. Apart from straightforward attempts to simply rehabilitate fascism itself, the right in power chipped away piece by piece at the monuments of a state "born from the resistance." The fact that this process took place without provoking mass opposition (apart from in an early period, as with the huge demonstration of April 25, 1994, in Milan) was an indicator that the resistance myth itself had not penetrated very deep into Italian society.

It was also significant that many on the left—and particularly those from the communist left—also attempted to heal the divisions of the past. But just as the culture of community had been crucial to the fragile construction of a "civic religion" of the resistance, especially in central and parts of northern Italy, the break-down of those communities in the 1970s and 1980s dealt a fatal blow to these traditions. Rural society disappeared with great speed in the 1960s and 1970s, and the urban working-class followed in the 1980s. The former were intimately linked to the experience and memory of the resistance, with its "mountains and landscapes . . . peasant bands . . . weeping women dressed in black, the simple houses."[20] The urban working class provided the base for the left after the war, and with its decline resistance myths were suddenly working in a void. Italy's postindustrial, individualist society had little connection with the ideals of the resistance.

In 1996, Paggi argued that

> political public space has now become completely permeated with a spirit of spectacularization which induces an irreparable divorce between past and present. The result is memory without praxis, memory without politics. The past is dehistoricized and slotted into any consumer device to become part of the eternal return of the same. This politics of deliberate forgetting, physiologically linked to a postmodern society founded on the contraction of space and time, poses the urgent question of how to find an adequate symbolic reformulation in step with the present-day reality of democracy. On this score, the Italian right seems at present to have most of the cards in its hand.[21]

The decade or so since these words were written have proven that he was absolutely correct.

While many aspects of the resistance had been remembered and debated throughout the postwar period, there were also a number of areas that were forgotten, silenced or even hidden.

Forgetting the Resistance: Three Silences

Enemies

Civil war was something that happened in countries such as Greece or Spain. Italy had had instead a War of National Liberation, to free the country from the foreign invader. Those who had collaborated with the invaders were by definition traitors. They were not even worthy of being considered proper enemies. The enemies were the Germans, the Nazis, sometimes the *nazifascisti*. The RSI was labelled *Repubblica di Salò* (to stress its operetta-like nature); its supporters were called *repubblichini*.

—Guido Franzinetti, "The Rediscovery of the Istrian *Foibe*"

In 1999, Passerini identified three areas of "silence" within the history—and the memory—of the resistance.[22] The first was to do with the image of the enemy. As Colombara has written, "The stories of the winners do not include the stories of the losers, and often they cancel them out."[23] For a very long time, the Italian enemies of the Resistance, the fascists, were not given the (historical) status of a real combatants.[24] This was a by-product of the denial—above all by the communists—of the civil war aspects of the resistance. Other participants in the resistance—the Action Party, the socialists, those loyal to the king—were much less reticent about the fact that 1943 to 1945 had also been a civil war. For writers like Meneghello and Fenoglio, the civil war was the most important part of the resistance, not the war against the Germans. By denying that the enemies were—in part—also Italian, the resistance created problems in terms of the transmission of memory.

Perhaps the most marginalized group of all, in terms of public memory, were those who chose to return from internment in Germany on the "wrong side." Generally, these men are dismissed as a "small minority," which they were. But tens of thousands did say "yes," and their story has rarely been told, or been the object of historical study. According to Santo Peli some 186,000 soldiers made this choice after they were rounded up by the Germans, and many served in the German army. Those who decided to fight "on the wrong side" made this pledge: "I adhere to the republican fascist ideal and I declare that I will fight voluntarily in the new Italian army of the Duce, without reserve, as well as under the German Supreme Command against the common enemy." These men—along with those who signed up in Italy itself—were the celebrated "boys of Salò," about whom there has been so much debate in recent years.

A series of groups and individuals thus opted to fight on the side of the RSI and the Nazis (or were forced to do so) after September 8, 1943. Some were convinced fascists, many of whom joined the voluntary fascist militia. Many were from the Alto Adige region, and these were grouped together in the German army itself. Others made this choice for more practical reasons, to escape from internment camps, or after being taken in by the promises of the regime and the Germans. Some made a tactical decision, hoping to desert once back in Italy. Often, these stories were hidden for years, and often by the protagonists. Roberto Vivarelli, an eminent historian with impeccable antifascist credentials (for example, he edited the works of the antifascist historian Gaetano Salvemini) only published his memoirs detailing his role in the RSI as a young boy in 2000.[25]

A variety of reasons led a myriad of different kinds of men and women to support the RSI, with different levels of commitment. To cite Ganapini, "To understand the importance of the RSI in Italian history we must recognise its breadth and also—in a certain sense—the legitimacy of the very different choices that were made (neo-fascists, militant anti-fascists, those who didn't choose for reasons which ranged from noble motivations to other less dignified reasons)."[26] Morally, of course, these Italians were on the wrong side of the war. But subjectively, their reasons for staying with Mussolini could be traced back to a whole series of justifications and individual choices, not all of which were necessarily those of militant fascists. After all, the very concepts of the nation and the state were in flux in Italy after 1943. In Vivarelli's words, "Being on one or the other side of the barricades often depended on chance: the reasons of individual lives do not coincide with those of history."[27]

In terms of historical research, many of the reasons behind the long running hostility to serious study of the RSI are clear. Just as the neofascists themselves were taboo, untouchable for most of the postwar period, so was their history. On the one hand, the RSI was seen as the Republic of *Salò*, a minor phenomenon not to be taken seriously. On the other, the fear of a return of fascism led to a desire to use the experience of the RSI merely as a warning for the future, as the ultimate evil. Moreover, the experience of civil war had left a legacy of hatred, an idea of these enemies as inhuman. As Ganapini has written, the antifascists had "a deep repulsion for those who had been guilty of massacres and killings, alongside the Nazi army."[28]

Much of this has changed in recent years. A number of important studies of the RSI have been published by Italian historians and this research has often been supported by the network of institutes set up to study the Resistance. It is impossible—now—to claim that the RSI has not been studied or is not worthy of the attention of scholars. The seminal work of Ganapini is now the first reference point for all those who are working on this period.[29]

Neofascist historians, for their part, were unable to make a break with nostalgic and celebratory visions of the RSI—as a tragedy but also a heroic defeat—with its long list of martyrs. The memory of the RSI was above all, for neofascists, a memory of their dead.[30] Stories of RSI "martyrs" conflated those who died in the war with those killed during the *resa dei conti*, and these were presented above all as the dead from a civil war. In many ways, this cult linked up with that adopted by the fascists after World War I and with the "fascist martyrs" during the 1920s. But it no longer had the visibility of that period, nor was it promoted by the state. To cite Santomassimo, "The many veterans' associations, with their language which remained unchanged through time, operated in the open and not secretly, even if their material had a limited circulation."[31]

Nazis were more unambiguously an enemy, although even here there were silences and denials. The image of "German bullets" turns up again and again in the memories of dead partisans, and in resistance memory. But there were also processes that marginalized the role of the Germans. The "good German" stereotype is a constant in accounts of the war, as a (psychological) attempt to humanize a dehumanized army. Moreover, the massacres by the Nazi army in Italy frequently led to divided memory, where survivors "forgot" about the German role and blamed others—usually partisans—for provoking the Nazis. In this way, the Nazis were excluded from the story. These tendencies were contradictory. On the one hand, there was a desire to make the enemy into a foreigner, or to represent all enemies as foreigners. On the other hand, a scapegoat was usually found within, or close to, the local community.

A further level of this silence with relation to enemies was linked to justice and retribution. International political issues led to a long "pact of silence" at a government and judicial level. Apart from a few important names (and then only partially), leading Nazis were not prosecuted for war crimes in Italy and—in return—Italy did not extradite any of its potential war criminals to Greece, Yugoslavia, or Albania. This pact began to break down in the 1990s (with the exception of Trieste, where a trial was held in the 1970s), with the Priebke trial and numerous other trials where the ex-Nazis were usually absent, very old, or dead. The other side of the pact of silence—with regard to Italian war crimes—took even longer to break down.

Forgetting the Resistance: Violence and Conflicts within the Resistance

A second area of silence, or resistance inside the history and memory resistance, also identified by Passerini, has to do with conflicts within the resistance. This is a difficult subject, with gray zones, areas of silence, lies, taboos, tensions, and false stories. There were a number of well and lesser-known cases of violent clashes within the resistance and—as Dondi has shown in detail—this is not surprising given the deep divisions at a political, social, and military level among those who took part.[32] The very form of war fought by the partisans—with its spontaneous, fragile and improvised organization—lent itself to conflict. Partisans were not always as popular with the local populations as they have been painted, as the divided memories after the massacres in Tuscany and elsewhere revealed with great clarity. Moreover, political and ideological divisions often led to a desire to suppress or marginalize those who didn't follow the party line. Some partisan leaders were dictatorial and ambitious, and willing to do anything to keep control. A number of cases of murder and violence were covered up, or simply forgotten.

As research began to be carried out into killings within the resistance, some patterns began to emerge. Violence was largely over control of territories and often involved the taking out of rival, powerful, and charismatic partisan leaders. In order to carry out these crimes, farcical trials were set up and false accusations aimed at the partisans in question. After their deaths, the partisans' bodies were often hidden. These killings usually "worked," in the sense that the bands or partisan groups linked to these leaders collapsed after their death. Silence and cover-ups usually followed these events, which were accompanied by a combination of shame and intimidation of possible witnesses or testimonies. Sometimes there were also trials, but it often took fifty years or so for the truth to emerge, at least publicly.

Partisans operated with their own sets of laws, rules, and regulations. They created their own forms of justice, held their own trials and handed down their own sentences. They had no prisons, and were constantly on the move. Authority and legitimation were moveable feasts in this world and rules were open to interpretation and manipulation. Moreover, partisan life was extremely dangerous. Life was cheap, and death everywhere. Partisans were armed and often inexperienced. It was easy for arguments to end in violence, and this happened far more often than post-Resistance history and memory was ready to acknowledge. Only rarely, however, did these conflicts lead to mass killings within the resistance. The most common forms of violence were individual murders, and trumped up charges were used to eliminate rivals. Some partisan leaders became too big for their own boots, and their local power led to accusations of arrogance and abuse of authority.

This type of violence is linked to the wider issue of the *resa dei conti*—the postwar settling of accounts. Inter-resistance violence, in other words, did not always stop with the end of the war. As in Spain, the communists were not averse to the elimination of its political opponents. These acts of violence were covered up or lied about, creating shared silences and these silences were sometimes orchestrated from above. Partisans often became politicians in the postwar period, and many were mayors, councillors, or parliamentarians. Others were journalists. They were thus in a good position to control discussions about the past as well as commemorations and memorialization. These stories, finally, help us understand the reality of the 1943 to 1945 period. The resistance only becomes real when its whole story is told, warts and all. The history of the resistance—and its memory—is "troubled, complex and contradictory." [33]

I will tell three stories here.

Reggio Emilia, 1945–1946

Who killed Azor?

—Giorgio Morelli, *La nuova penna*, October 11, 1945

"Azor" was a partisan. He was shot in the back of the head on March 23, 1945, with his hands tied behind his back, it was said with wire. His body was found four and a half months after his death, some way from where he actually died.[34] Azor—Mario Simonazzi—was a Catholic antifascist and factory worker, fighting in a zone dominated by the communists. Although there had been a German round-up in March 1943, Azor's killers were not the official enemy, but "fellow" partisans. With the war over, a friend of Azor's and fellow Catholic began to rock the boat. Giorgio Morelli, who called himself "Il solitario" (the solitary one), had been the first partisan to enter liberated Reggio in April 1945, carrying the Italian flag.

Morelli wanted to become a journalist, and began to publish a series of striking articles in a small local paper called *La Nuova Penna*. These articles did not mince their words. "Who killed Azor?" was the title of the first piece. These open accusations did not make *Il solitario* a popular figure in Reggio. First, the newspaper itself was attacked. Then it was the turn of *Il solitario*. Two men on bikes fired six shots at him one night in January 1946. These shots—three of the six hit their target—were to eventually kill him in August 1947. He was twenty-one years old. Before that, *Il solitario* had been thrown out of the local partisans' association and refused the category of partisan. We still do not know for sure who killed Azor. The trial held in the 1950s was unconvincing—similar to many other trials where the wrong people were convicted over post-1945 murders[35]—and some partisans escaped to Czechoslovakia to escape investigation. In terms of memory, the postwar fate of Azor and *Il solitario* was one of almost complete silence, but a series of books have been published in recent years and the story is now fairly well-known, locally and nationally. The only official memory for Azor remains a small plaque that states that he was "murdered," but not by whom or in what context.

Piacenza, June 5, 1944

On June 5, 1944, four men were shot dead in two separate areas in the hills near Piacenza. In itself, this was not a particularly unusual event. A war was in course, after all. The four men all belonged to a partisan band known as "Piccoli," but their execution was not the work of the German army, or Italian fascists. The order to kill the four men was probably given by a partisan leader from a different group, Fausto Cossu. Materially, the executions were carried out by uniformed "Carabinieri," some of whom had earlier deserted or been captured by the partisans. Cossu himself had been a *carabinieri* lieutenant who had escaped from a German concentration camp in 1943.[36] As Dondi writes, "These deaths were not accidental. The clash was not by chance, but covered up and organised from above."[37] Dondi calls these murders the "second worst episode of conflict" within the resistance.[38]

One of those shot was Giovanni Molinari—a communist antifascist whose father had been socialist mayor of Fiorenzuola and whose brother had been killed by fascist *squadristi* in 1921. Molinari had been instrumental in organizing partisan resistance in the Piacenza area. After being shot, Molinari was pushed into a shallow grave, face-down. Another three men were killed—without any kind of trial—in a different zone. In order to justify these murders, Cossu (as with other interpartisan killings) accused the dead partisans of "theft and violence." This was the version put forward during various investigations held during and after the war. It is a version of events that is almost certainly a lie.

Cossu became the head of the police force in Piacenza after the liberation. But the embarrassing killing of the four partisans would not go away, and the local CLN was forced to open a further enquiry in 1945. In the meantime, Cossu had become an important partisan leader, who had also managed to "avoid reprisals," a fact that made him popular with the local population. Memories were divided about Cossu. He was a "gentleman," "a man of honour," but he carried the mark of the killing of Molinari for his whole life.

After the war, the four dead members of the Piccoli group had a plaque dedicated to them (at the place where three of them were shot). This place is the site of regular official commemorations. But, as with other interresistance murders, the way in which these men were killed is omitted from the plaque's inscription—where they are described (somewhat ambiguously) as "partisans who fell for the cause of freedom." This ambiguity can also be seen in other monuments to dead partisans, one where Molinari's name appears in Fiorenzuola and another in Castel San Giovanni (with one of the other dead).[39] For Dondi, a kind of reciprocal silence helped overcome the divisions created by these events. Everyone knew what had happened, and they even celebrated the lives of those killed, but the facts themselves were not publicly—or at least officially—acknowledged.[40] The *resa dei conti*—including that within the resistance itself—produced collective silence (Figure 7.3).

But is the Piacenza-Molinari plaque really a lie, or an omission? Anyone who had taken part in the resistance knew how easy it was for people to

Figure 7.3   Moiaccio (Piacenza): Plaque (with fascist graffitti) relating to the killing of four partisans. The inscription reads, "In your honour immortalised by the glorious anti-fascist struggle" and "Partisans who fell for the cause of freedom." The lower plaque was placed by the "Comrades of Pecorara" in 1983. The upper plaque is officially sanctioned by the partisan's association, *Associazione Nazionale Partigiani d'Italia* (ANPI).

die, even at the hands of their own side. There are almost certainly numerous other cases that we don't yet know about, which have remained within the realms of private or group memory. So the plaque in question, put up and used for commemorations by fellow partisans, was an expression of a specific way of understanding the resistance. It was also a form of counter-memory. It said this: those four men also died *as part of the resistance*. They took the risk that they would be killed, even by their "comrades in arms." Thus, they should be remembered as "partisans who fell for the cause of freedom." Second, this plaque is telling us that the official version of this killing is wrong. The men were not thieves or common criminals, but partisans, and they died as such. This is also the case with the various memorials dedicated to Molinari. So the messages being sent out by this small plaque are complicated, and change in relation to who is doing the remembering, and when. Where an element of omission and silence emerges is with relation to those who don't know the story of the four men—outsiders. For someone simply coming across this plaque in the hills, the (false) assumption would be that these men were killed by the fascists or by the Germans. Herein lies the ambiguity of this plaque. So, by not telling the whole story publicly—or by telling one version of the story—the plaque leaves open the possibility of misinterpretation. It is a kind of cover-up, but only for those outside of the story itself, or on the outskirts of a particular community.

Partisan Facio: A Hero, His Death, and His Afterlife

He was young and thin, and not very tall, with blond-brown hair. I remember the shape of his face with its signs and hard features, sweetened by his smile and his black eyes.

—Laura Seghettini, "Al vento del Nord.
Una donna nella lotta di Liberazione"

Dante Castellucci was a renowned partisan, a hero, a semimythical figure. His partisan name was *Facio*, and he first took up the antifascist struggle alongside the equally mythical Cervi brothers. Castellucci participated in the extraordinary "Battle of the Holy Lake," in the mountains above Parma, in March 1944. As leader of a group of nine partisans, Facio organized the defense of a mountain refuge against sustained German attack. The Germans lost sixteen men and suffered thirty-six injuries before retreating. The plaque placed on the refuge is "unusual . . . as it does not remember the dead, but intrepid and brave fighters for liberty" as Capogreco wrote in *L'argento e il piombo. La vera storia del partigiano Facio* (The Silver and the Lead. The True Story of Partisan Facio).[41]

> From this refuge nine partisans
> After twenty hours of fighting
> Fought off overwhelming enemy forces
> The victory cry echoed down the nearby valleys and a New Italy was born
> 18 March 1944

In May 1963, nearly nineteen years after his death, Dante Castellucci's aged mother, dressed in black, accepted a silver medal from the state in his memory, in Cosenza. The inscription of the medal, which was read out loud at the ceremony, was the following:

> Discovered by the enemy, he defended himself stoutly: outnumbered and having refused to surrender, he was killed there and then. A shining example of the purest heroism. The Zone of Pontremoli, 22.7.1944.

This might seem like a "normal" story from the resistance. As Pezzino has written, "Facio was a charismatic leader, loved by his men and by the local population"[42] and was "the most worthy . . . partisan leader in the area."[43] He was depicted as a brave soldier who had died "heroically" on the battlefield, like so many other partisans. But there was a key problem with this medal, and its inscription. It was a lie. Apart from the date itself, every other part of the medal was false, and knowingly so. Castellucci—the "legendary hero," the "teacher of democracy"[44]—had not been killed by Nazis, nor by Italian fascists. He was executed by a firing squad made up of fellow partisans, all of them Italian communists. At 5 AM on the morning of July 22, 1944, he was taken to a small hollow in the hills above Pontremoli (behind a cemetery), shot, and buried. His crime, according to the "tribunal" that had judged him, was to have stolen guns intended for the resistance. The story of Facio is a story of embarrassment, of petty jealousies, of internecine divisions within the resistance, but also of cover-ups, silences, fear, and half-truths.

Castelucci's story began in the south of Italy, a long way from Pontremoli. He was born in an isolated village in Calabria, Sant'Agata d'Esaro, in 1920. When he was just two years old, Dante's father, a blacksmith, struck a powerful local notable in public. The family was forced to emigrate to France as a result and they remained there until 1939. In 1940, after the family's return to Italy, Dante was called up to take part in the invasion of the country where he had lived for most of his life (and whose language he spoke perfectly)—France. After being given sixty days' leave in 1940, Dante befriended a man who had been exiled for his political views, Otello Sarzi. The two men discussed politics and antifascism. In 1941, Dante was called back to the army and sent to the Russian front. Injured, he returned to Italy at the end of 1942. Thanks to his friendship with Sarzi he even became an actor for a time, before coming into contact with the Cervi family, convinced antifascists from the Po Valley, between Parma and Reggio Emilia.

Dante went to live with the Cervi family on their farm (where there is now a museum) and took part in some early partisan activities there. The Cervi farm was a refuge for many soldiers on the run or ex-POWs after September 8, 1943. On November 25 of that fateful year, all seven Cervi brothers were arrested and taken to the Carcere Dei Servi in Reggio Emilia. Castellucci was with them, but he was held in Parma with other "foreign" prisoners, after pretending to be French. After a month, he managed to escape from there, on Christmas Day. The seven Cervi brothers were not so lucky and were executed in Reggio Emilia on December 28, 1943.

As a partisan, Dante operated in the area between Parma and La Spezia, where he developed into one of the most respected resistance leaders in Italy. He became Facio and took command of the Picelli group, one of the most important in that area. Dante was arrested in July 1944. This time, his captors were not the Germans, nor the fascists, but communist partisans. Tricked into a meeting that did not happen, and then beaten up and disarmed, Facio was accused of theft and of "sabotaging patriotic actions and in this way helping the enemy." After a brief trial, which Capogreco has compared to the activity of a "mafia cupola" and which many have defined as a farce, Facio was condemned to death.[45] He seemed to accept his fate, within the logic of the "higher cause" of the resistance. His death would serve the cause of the struggle, like Rubashov in Koestler's *Darkness at Noon*, or the fictional "hero" in Bertolucci's *La strategia del ragno*. There are, in fact, many similarities with the "trial" of Castellucci and a Stalinist show trial, apart from the fact that this trial was covered-up almost immediately.

After a last night in the company of his partner, Laura Seghettini, and some guards, during which he refused to escape, despite being given the opportunity to do so, Facio was shot. Before dying, he wrote a letter to his mother and told Laura that "one day someone will shed light on this story." Many local partisans and antifascists were shocked by this execution. Facio was popular with his men (and perhaps this was one of the reasons he had been eliminated) and had become a semimythical figure among the local population. In August 1945, Dante was reburied in Pontremoli, and a large crowd attended his funeral. Seghettini, his partner who had fought alongside him, wanted justice. She forced arrests and collected evidence, but nothing happened, either judicially or politically.

Facio's execution had an immediate effect on the collective memory of the area known as Zeri. On August 3, something like 200 people were killed in a round-up in the Zeri zone by Nazis and Italian fascist troops. Over time, the blame for the massacre among the survivors fell on "Tullio," one of those involved in the trial and execution of Facio. As Contini has written, "The community conserves the memory of Facio as that of an heroic victim: if he had still been alive, the massacre would not have happened."[46] Thus the divided memories that appeared so often in Italy after massacres in this case became a division between "good" and "bad" partisans. Facio was a mythical figure, who "could have saved" this area from disaster. "Tullio" became an antimyth—a traitor, a frequent visitor to brothels, the individual scapegoat.[47]

"Salvatore" (Antonio Cabrelli), Facio's main "accuser," was arrested after the war (Seghettini actually took him to the police station herself, with the help of others) but he was soon released, and the inquiry petered out. There was little enthusiasm for the opening up of a case of inter-Resistance violence in the 1940s and 1950s. This was a left-wing area, there was the cold war, the Resistance myth was being constructed. And this was true of almost every case of violence (and even of conflicts) within the resistance. Historians also largely ignored the case, or took part in cover-ups around the life and death of Facio. The combination of the need to keep the heroic memory of Facio alive (the Facio of the holy lake, and the Cervi brothers with whom his story was linked) while ignoring and forgetting the circumstances of his death, led directly to the shameful silver medal in 1963.

After that moment, the story of partisan Facio was silenced, despite (or perhaps because of) the "false" medal. This silence was from above, and from below. One of the side-effects of the "false" medal was to reduce even Seghettini to silence. She later wrote that, after the medal, "At that point I understood, nearly twenty years after the event, that nobody wanted to shed light on what had happened, and so my words became useless." As she pointed out, if Facio deserved a medal of this kind, how could he also have been guilty of "sabotaging patriotic activities and therefore helping the enemy"? The other reason Seghettini stopped her "Facio" campaign was for fear of damaging the Resistance. She added this comment: "It was also a story which was personal to me, and I decided not to speak out any more above all because I was encouraged to do so by those who wanted to exploit the affair for political ends."[48]

This silence continued throughout the 1960s and 1970s, at least officially. Some of those involved in the trial and execution of Facio became important local political figures. There were signs of a thaw in the Facio case, such as when local communist Luigi Porcari wrote in 1974 that Facio had been "betrayed and killed," or the research of Giulivo Ricci,[49] but generally the silence held. Facio failed to appear at all, for example, in the huge *Enciclopedia dell'antifascismo*, published in the late 1960s. Things began to open up slowly in the 1980s, as time and distance forced a breach in the wall of *omertà* around the "Facio case." An ex-comrade of Facio and a poet built a small monument with their own hands at the place where he was shot, and they added a photo of Dante to this simple site of memory.

Then, finally, in the 1990s, something started to move. Articles appeared in the local and national press. Two books dedicated to Facio appeared, by Capogreco and Seghettini. These books were an occasion for an open discussion about the case. A play was produced and performed. Left politicians took a stand on the case of Facio and the false medal.[50] A number of leading historians called for the old medal to be handed back, and replaced with a "true" (and gold) medal. The time seemed ripe for a discussion around the issue of violence within the resistance itself.

These debates led to concrete forms of public memory. The last survivor from the "trial" of Facio died in 2003 (he had a barracks named after him). In 2007 a new, official monument was dedicated to Facio at Adelano di Zeri, and inaugurated after a large-scale ceremony. The inscription was accurate, but still ignored the exact circumstances of Dante's death (you could easily assume from the words on the plaque that Facio was one of the many partisans who "fell" in battle):

DANTE CASTELLUCCI
"FACIO"
PARTISAN
COMMANDER
OF THE "PICELLI" BATTALION
RESISTANCE HERO
AN EXAMPLE OF COURAGE AND OF LOVE FOR SOCIAL JUSTICE,
LIBERTY AND DEMOCRACY
A SYMBOL OF GOOD
HE LIVES ON IN THE MEMORY OF THE PEOPLE OF THESE
MOUNTAINS
AS A SYMBOL OF ARDOR AND LOVE
THE PARTISANS OF THE "PICELLI" BATTALION AND OF THE
PROVINCES OF
MASSA CARRARA LA
SPEZIA AND PARMA
ON THE 63° ANNIVERSARY
22/7/1944 – ADELANO – 22/7/2007

The truth had gone so far, but no further. A commemoration was also held for Facio in Calabria. There are many conspiracy stories in circulation about the Facio story, which claim that Cabrelli was an agent provocateur, or a spy. Ever since his death, as the plaque states, Facio has continued to "live on in the memory of the people of these mountains," despite everything.

The story of the partisan Facio provides us with another example of divided memory, this time fused with silences, shame, and the political decision (within the Resistance and the post-Resistance) to cover up an uncomfortable event. But the Italian resistance needs to be analyzed warts and all, as in the works of Meneghello, Fenoglio or Calvino, "in all its glory and in its wretchedness, its truths and its errors."[51] It was a movement with light and shade, heroism and glory. Castellucci was one of the heroes of that resistance, but we should also remember the way in which he was killed. The study of those who—as the plaque at Porzus says—were "suffocated in blood by the a murdering fraternal hand," and their stories, allows us to see the Resistance as it really was. Valiant, yes, but also nasty, brutish, and short.

A further area of silence has to do with violence after the end of the "war" itself—the thousands of people killed, for a variety of reasons, after the military side of the conflict was over. These killings have been given a generic name—something that covers a wide variety of events—the *resa dei conti*.

The *Resa Dei Conti*

Partisan violence against Nazi-Fascists invariably raises normative questions about the ethics of violence committed in what its adherents believed to be a just cause. In short, what differentiates fascist acts of violence from partisan violence?

—Robert Ventresca, "Mussolini's Ghost.
Italy's Duce in History and Memory"

War did not end with the official day of liberation. Violence continued for days, weeks, and sometimes years, and left a trail of bitterness in its wake. This was above all true of the civil war and class war aspects of the resistance. The period immediately after liberation in particular was a time of the *resa dei conti*: the settling of accounts. As in other countries, Spain (in 1936–39), Greece, France (1945), thousands of people were killed, for a whole variety of reasons. The memories created by the *resa dei conti* were contradictory and problematic. More often than not, the settling of accounts led to a shared silence, above all in official and public circles. The *resa dei conti* is also an area where the public and political use of history has been especially acute.[52] For many Italians, April 25 was not a victory at all, but yet another defeat.

How many people were killed after the war had officially ended, a date that was different in different parts of Italy? The simple answer is—as with the *foibe*—we don't know. Numbers were played down by postwar governments and by those involved in the *resa dei conti*, for obvious reasons. Mario

Scelba, interior minister, claimed that only 1,762 had died in this war in a report to parliament in 1952. Meanwhile, huge—absurd—figures (of up to 300,000 people) were produced on the right, or by the church. The real answer probably lies close to the estimates of Bocca and Ginsborg, who settle on a figure of something between twelve and fifteen thousand.[53]

A realistic count of how many people were killed depends on how we define the term "*after the war*." Two of Pavone's three wars (class war and civil war) did not end on April 25 and were never "declared over," nor did they begin during World War II. Moreover, even the war of national liberation was not over on April 25. German troops took some time to leave Italian territory (there were massacres by Nazis well beyond April 25) and many of those fighting in the resistance defined fascists as "internal enemies" and traitors. These same definitions had been used by the fascists themselves for the socialists and *disfattisti* since 1918 (and even before fascism). Many Italians disagreed that "the war" had actually ended—their kind of war—and went on fighting it, on their terms for days, months, and sometimes years.

This was, therefore, a time of blood-letting, and there would be many bodies to bury and thousands of families who wanted answers about their relatives. How had they died? Who had killed them? Where were they? In most places, apart from a few isolated cases, the *resa dei conti* came to a pretty sudden halt with the arrival of democracy and the filling of the power vacuum left with the end of the war. However, some zones, above all Emilia-Romagna, saw a violent civil and class war continue, and its effects were still being felt at the end of the 1940s. These regions have been the focus of much attention from scholars and politicians, and of public debate, often mediated by the mass media.

How were these people killed? Most were taken out and shot, in the period immediately before or just after the liberation. Some were lined up and executed. Others were "executed" in planned attacks; "people were very rarely killed by chance."[54] Who was killed, and why? Revenge, political calculations, anger at the mild nature of the purges, a sense of power, social hatred going back decades, class war. All of these reasons could lead to assassination. Beyond the killings, there were beatings and humiliations, especially for women. Revenge killings were also a way to overcome the loss of loved ones, a brutal form of therapy.

The vast majority of those killed had some links with fascism. Locally, partisans often finished off a few fascist leaders in the immediate postwar period. Important fascist leaders were killed—sometimes after summary trials—after they were captured trying to escape, Farinacci in Vimercate outside Milan, a group of leaders in Dongo on Lake Como, Mussolini on the hills above the same lake. Others were saved from a similar fate by the

Allies. But violence sometimes exploded against those who were either not compromised with the regime, or who had actively opposed it. As Crainz has shown, postwar killings were usually linked to immediate memories of the war, but also to those of fascist violence after World War I, and often contained elements of class hatred, going back even further in time.[55] Pavone's three wars produced three forms of *resa dei conti*: three kinds of violence that were to continue after the war itself had—officially—ended. Memories were long, and it was not easy to forgive, or forget. As one witness remembers, "There were people whose fathers had been beaten in 1920, had had their houses burnt down, or worse . . . when we had the popular trials some prisoners went missing."[56]

Mirco Dondi, whose work is the only attempt to carry out a systematic, national survey of the *resa dei conti*, has divided postwar violence into three phases—insurrectional violence, April 20 to May 20, 1945, inertial violence (spring–summer 1945), and residual violence (autumn 1945 through to autumn 1946).[57] There were no clear boundaries between these phases of violence, just as there was no clear gap between the end of the war and the postwar period. Arms were not laid down, on either side, but kept well-oiled. July 1948 was another occasion for a settling of accounts, with many deaths across Italy. Many landowners and their families were killed for reasons that had little to do with fascism, and the same goes for the priests, Catholics, and non-communist politicians and trade unionists murdered in parts of central Italy after April 1945. And not all of those killed were to the right of the communists. Dissidents and antifascists were also murdered, such as Mario Acquaviva in Piedmont and others.

The Resa Dei Conti and Memory

You have to kill them, all of them, because not one of them deserves less. I say death is the mildest punishment even for the least bad of them . . . whoever isn't stained in blood up to his armpits on that great day can't come to me and tell me he's a great patriot.

—Beppe Fenoglio, *A Private Affair, Modern Voices*

And any little thing, a false step, a momentary impulse, is enough to send them over to the wrong side.

—Italo Calvino, *The Path to the Nest of Spiders*

The *resa dei conti* produced an enormous amount of silence among its perpetrators. It was spoken about, if at all, in hushed tones. It was something that, it was thought, had had to be done but that could not be celebrated for judicial, political, and personal reasons (apart from a few isolated cases, such as with Mussolini himself). A desire for revenge and justice had been satisfied, and those who had pulled the trigger were rarely brought to trial. The partisans—and others—had wanted to impose their own justice, and they had proceeded to do so, in a situation where the state (once again, as in 1919–22) was unable to either keep order or protect its citizens, where it was unclear who exactly was in charge, and who represented law and order.

People were often picked up at home and taken away for "interrogation," something from which they were not to return. This was a period when the dividing line between the state and the resistance was particularly blurred, especially in certain areas of Italy, and where the state itself had lost control of society (in 1946 over 6,000 murders were reported to the authorities, with over 4,000 in 1947) and there was "the rare sight of the breakdown of the state monopoly over the use of violence."[58] The law itself was contested terrain. As De Luna has written, "Violence ran amuck in the absence of legality."[59] Slowly, and it took some time, the new republican state gained control of society (and it did so, often, through repression).

But the victims, and those linked to the victims, did not remain silent. For those political groups who identified with fascism and neofascism after the war, the *resa dei conti* became a key element of propaganda. In part, this was a continuation of the cult of death that had been so strong under fascism. But the *resa dei conti* was central to the attempt to depict the resistance not as a national struggle, but as a civil war. Moreover, the violence of the *resa dei conti* was used to undermine the moral claims of the resistance and antifascism. Although official narratives about the *resa dei conti* minimized what had happened, it was clear that this period was important to many Italians. The phenomenal publishing success of Giampaolo Pansa's books about the *resa dei conti* in the twenty-first century was not merely an example of revisionism, but another indicator of the failures of the resistance myth to win over the majority of Italians.

Among neofascists, and the families of those killed, there were attempts to preserve and celebrate the memory of their dead. Special sections of cemeteries were set aside for those who died during and after the war (war and civil war were collapsed into one period, as they had been by fascism after 1918), and were used for commemorations. There were also occasional small monuments to those who died in the *resa dei conti*, a small, simple cross at the point where Mussolini and Claretta Petacci were shot, plaques, and some monuments, but nothing on the scale of the galaxy of memorials dedicated to the resistance. Extensive research was also carried out by neofascist historians like Pisanò (who travelled up and down Italy collecting material) and others, much of which is now available on the internet.[60] Detailed lists of "martyrs" were published for many Italian cities.

As Isenghi has written, "Those who were shot on that side had a separate death and continue to have a separate memory."[61] Other memories of the civil war sometimes mirrored those of the resistance itself, as with the use of martyrologies, the language used to describe the dead, and the publication of "last letters" from those condemned to death.[62]

During and after the war, a series of systems and forms of justice were in competition with each other. Partisans were used to carrying out executions, and the type of war they had fought meant that they had, as Secchia said, "no prisons." No prisons, no prisoners. German troops rarely took prisoners in the war with partisans, who were often simply lined up and shot after being captured. The same was often true of Italian troops involved in the civil war in the north.[63] Popular tribunals used violence to quench desires to *see* immediate justice being done.

After the war, these immediate forms of "justice" came into conflict with the slow workings and weak institutions of the official justice system. Trials of fascists often became, as Dondi has put it, "a public display of impunity."[64] In 1945 and 1946 these conflicts and frustrations led to suspects being marched out of court rooms and shot, or prisoners being killed inside or outside of the prison walls. Occasionally the "wrong person" was murdered.[65] With time, the state imposed its own form of justice, and the other methods dissipated, although there were still those, such as *La Volante Rossa* group in Milan, who believed that they had the right to dish out "proletarian justice." Some of the language (and the practices) used by ex-partisans immediately after the war would be recycled by red terrorists in the 1970s.

In this chapter, I will look at a number of stories from the *resa dei conti*.

An Undivided Memory: Grugliasco and Collegno (Turin), 1945

Memory also . . . works in different ways, in terms of displacement and forgetting.

—Bruno Maida, "Prigionieri della memoria"

By the end of April 1945, in Piedmont, it felt like the war was over, and for some, the celebrations had already begun. Turin was liberated and in the hands of the partisans, and sections of the German army were retreating through the area around the city. But on April 29–30, 1945, sixty-seven[66] people were killed in a Nazi massacre in Grugliasco, just to the west of Turin. This was one of the last killings carried out by retreating German troops. Twenty of the victims were residents of Grugliasco, thirty-two were from nearby Collegno, and fifteen were partisans from elsewhere. Amid the chaos of the end of the war, partisans had clashed with the Germans at various moments during their retreat. Some of the dead Italians were killed in direct skirmishes with the Germans, but the vast majority were civilians who were taken prisoner and then executed just outside the town, at three separate sites.

As news of the massacre spread, an angry crowd gathered. Led by some partisans, a group of people converged on Collegno, where a number of young ex-RSI soldiers were being held in a local factory. Most of these prisoners were in their twenties, and none were armed. On May 1, at least twenty-nine of these prisoners were taken out, marched through the streets and shot in front of the *casa del popolo* (formerly a fascist building) before a crowd of locals at about 6:30 PM. The bodies were buried (according to some versions in a mass grave, according to others in unmarked plots), after being displayed in the open for a time. This was a rare case of a direct partisan reprisal (or counterreprisal) after a Nazi massacre, although many of the deaths during the *resa dei conti* were connected to specific acts of fascist violence, often going right back to the period after World War I.

The first of these massacres has always produced considerable levels of public memory, monuments, street names, schools (such as the Scuola Media "66 Martiri" in Grugliasco), ceremonies, and annual commemorations. The other collective killing, the "reprisal" against RSI soldiers, has not. Memory of the first massacre began immediately, as the central piazza of Grugliasco had its name changed from Piazza Umberto I to *Piazza 66 martiri* two days after the killings. In some ways, that event defined the postwar history and identity of the town. Meanwhile, "the killings of the 1 May were forgotten, despite that fact that everyone, or nearly everyone, knew about them."[67] Or, as an official document put it, "this story has always been well known, at least amongst the older people from Collegno and Grugliasco, but its memory has been kept underground for decades and many have repressed it; nobody talks about it willingly."[68] The RSI victims were denied proper funerals. Their bodies were displayed, and then hidden, and the relatives of the victims were prevented from collecting them. This "double death," as Dondi has called it, "with the intention of cancelling out memory itself," was fairly common during the *resa dei conti*.[69] The hiding of fascist bodies, the denial of burial and memory, was also the result of twenty years of exaltation of the fascist dead and their "martyrs" by the regime. Methods were aped, in a parody of what had come before. From the overexposure of those who had "died for the fascist nation," the *resa dei conti* responded with the opposite strategy—complete oblivion, even of the body.

These bodies emerged metaphorically from the below the ground in the 1980s and 1990s, at first in the local press and then through histori-cal research, although there had been attempts to discover the truth by relatives of the victims right from the start (and some continued these efforts for years). Historian Bruno Maida was asked in 1999 to look into the massacres by both local councils, and produced an account (in 2002) that used documents and also analyzed the memories produced by the two massacres. His book was not acceptable to the families of the Grugliasco victims, who boycotted its presentation in a unique joint sitting of the two councils. In this case, then, a historian was asked to look into the memory of *two* massacres. Yet, unlike with Guardistallo, the community was not ready to deal with one part of their past. This was "a silent memory, uniform, self-defensive."[70]

At times, over the years, active steps were taken to cancel the memory of the RSI soldiers. Their graves were attacked. Even after death, the civil war continued. On one grave this inscription—"on the way home insane hatred on the 1 May cancelled out this young life"—was defaced and "some time later the family was forced to cancel the phrase 'insane hatred' in the face of threats to knock down the plaque and other threats."[71] But with time, these cancellations themselves have faded. The enemy was killed twice. They had no right to a grave, or even to private memory after death. Often, civil wars have seen this type of silence. Only in recent years have a number of mass graves been opened up from the Spanish civil war.

One memory seemed to exclude the other. As Maida argues, "The myth of the 66 martyrs—that is the mythical construction of a communitarian memory of that event—has remained intact, and in this way there is no risk that the other part of the memory will emerge"[72] This is not a case of forgetting. Publicly, the reprisal was never mentioned, but privately it appears that the memory of the reprisal was ever-present, if unspoken, an open wound. To cite Maida again, "When Collegno had to come to terms with the less noble part of its liberation history, a sort of short-circuit of memory was created thanks to the difficulty of explaining and narrating an experience which had been repressed for so long."[73]

There was no divided memory, it seems, in Grugliasco or Collegno like that which emerged in Guardistallo or Civitella, despite the fact that it appears that the partisans had attacked the retreating German troops, leading to a reprisal. And one reason for this "lack" may well have been that the "desire for justice" had been satisfied, immediately, by the second killing. Twenty-nine soldiers had paid the price for the sixty-six "martyrs," and this allowed the community to develop a compact memory based around sacrifice, struggle, and a shared past that was not allowed to become public.

Rovetta, April 28, 1945

"No, absolutely not, they had surrendered, according to military rules."
"Rules, *regulation*, what do you mean by 'rules'? There are no rules in a war of Italians against Italians, no rules."

—Discussion between a partisan leader and a British agent about the possible shooting of a group of fascist prisoners, 1945, in Bendotti, "Come un lavoro da fare"

In Rovetta, a small town in the Val Seriana, not far from Lago d'Iseo, forty-three Italian soldiers from the *Tagliamento Assault Legione* (Italians fighting for the RSI) were shot by partisans, against the wall of the local cemetery, on April 28, 1945. The shooting took an hour or so to complete. Three younger men were spared. These soldiers had previously come down from the mountains to surrender, waving a white flag, and had been disarmed and arrested. Giuseppe Mancini, son of Mussolini's sister, was the last to die. These deaths were an example, during the *resa dei conti*, of "the use of an extreme form of the armed struggle, in which sentiments such as those inspired by revenge and rage found ample space."[74]

As with so many other cases of this kind, this shooting led to recriminations, endless debates over the facts, mysteries, silences, and divided memories. It was "a difficult story . . . a story which does not fit, does not find place in the memory of the conflict as it has been constructed and affirmed."[75] A long judicial inquiry in the 1940s and 1950s came to the conclusion that the shooting had been an "act of war" (and that no trial was needed).

In 1947, the bodies of the dead were dug up from mass graves (although none could be identified) and were later transferred to Rome's Verano cemetery. Among the partisans who had carried out the shootings, silence reigned. It appears that this event was simply not discussed. The shooting never became a story (for the partisans) and the multiple memories that resulted were revealed when the protagonists were interrogated by investigating magistrates and others in the late 1940s and early 1950. No adequate narratives were developed by the partisans that could be expressed collectively, or in public. Meanwhile, other memories, those linked to the victims of this shooting, were much clearer about who they were remembering, and why. In 1995, after the case had been reopened by journalists and politicians and following a number of books dedicated to the killings, a cross was unveiled in the cemetery of Rovetta, with a photo of Mussolini and a list of names, as well as some explicit fascist symbols (which were later partially covered with flowers).

Rovetta's shootings thus produced a series of divided memories, and silences, ranging from those of the families, those of the neofascists (with explicit reference to Mussolini's nephew), to those of the partisans (who had their own dead to mourn) and that of the local priest. As with other massacres and similar stories, a complicated mystery was created, this time around an enigmatic figure known as "the mohican," an Istrian antifascist who was working for the British Secret Services. The role of "the mohican" has produced pages and pages of text, much of it in contradiction with other versions.[76] Silences and omissions led here to a story without end, without closure, where the facts themselves were continually questioned and highly flexible.

Schio Prison: The Veneto Region, July 6–7, 1945

Narratives diverge . . . in two ways—because, quite simply, facts are suppressed, and because moral discourses are set up that refuse certain explanations.

—Sarah Morgan, "The Schio Killings: A Case
Study of Partisan Violence in Post-War Italy"

They found the prison warden in a bar, and he had his keys with him. It wasn't difficult to force him to go back to the unguarded prison, perhaps with a few drinks inside him, and open up for the ten or so armed and masked partisans (another ten or so turned up soon afterwards). The "prison" was not a real prison at all, and is now the local library. Ninety-nine prisoners were crushed in here, and the overcrowding had led the Allies to decide, it seems, to release most of them in the near future. Ninety-one were there for political reasons, while eight were accused of "normal" crimes.

What exactly happened in the prison that night has been shrouded in mystery and myth ever since. Dozens of versions exist. There was certainly an argument among the partisans, probably about who to kill. Discussions with the prisoners themselves also took place. But someone probably decided that enough was enough, and opened fire. About seventy prisoners were lined up in different parts of the building. A long rattle of gun fire was heard in the night, and then the partisans made their escape.[77]

After the shooting had finally ended, forty-seven prisoners lay dead. Fifty-four of those who were shot eventually died, including fourteen women.[78] Many were fascists of some sort, but not all by any means (Dondi describes the fifty-four dead as "fascist prisoners").[79] Many had not even been formally accused of any specific crime. For Morgan, some "were obviously war criminals [but] . . . the majority were small-time supporters of the Republic."[80]

There were many explanations for the massacre, which was not sanctioned nationally (where it was criticized by Togliatti and others): frustration at the slow pace of the purging process and the imminent release of the prisoners, revenge, personal hatreds, and a sense of class war. The return of a man who had been deported to Mauthausen, weighing a mere thirty-eight kilograms, the only survivor of those who had been taken to that camp, saw emotions rise in the city. Angry crowds gathered outside the prison, and at one demonstration a placard was displayed that read "*vogliamo vendicare i martiri di Mauthausen*" (we want to avenge the martyrs of Mauthausen).[81] The funerals of the prison victims took place in a climate of civil war. It is said that not even the funfair rides stopped as the coffins went by. This was "a settling of accounts within the community itself with the tacit approval of a large part of the town once the event had finished."[82]

After an investigation by the Allies, a number of arrests were made.[83] A trial was held in September 1945, and two life and three death sentences were handed down, although the death penalties were never carried out. Some of those who were accused of being responsible had already escaped to Czechoslovakia or Yugoslavia. The Italian state held a further trial in 1952 in Milan, at which Ruggero Maltauro, who had been extradited from Yugoslavia in 1949, was given a life sentence, along with seven others (not present at the trial). Maltauro's sentence was later reduced to "29 years." This trial gained national press coverage, and formed part of what has been called the "war against the resistance" in the 1950s. The PCI leadership had changed tack a number of times over Schio, and pressure from below forced them to carry supportive articles in the communist press, although the reaction to the massacre was a clear case of *doppiezza* (duplicity). In the wake of the massacre, *L'Unità* blamed "false partisans" and "Trotskyists" of the killings. Local support for the partisans accused of the killing remained strong.

Unlike in Grugliasco, the national impact of the "facts of Schio" meant that they could not be publicly forgotten, or dealt with through collective silence within the local community. As such, the "facts of Schio" have inspired endless debate, *dietrologia* and arguments over if they should be remembered, and if so how, and where those events were to become part of public memory. As Croci has written, "The ambiguities of facts, roles and judgements were inevitably reproduced—and often magnified—in terms of memory." But, as with Rovetta, "for a long time the memory of these events represented a kind of 'black hole' in which cover-ups and forgettings were contained, as well as accusations of all kinds, silences, memories and scandals."[84]

Public Memory and Schio, 1945

As with so many other events in Italian history, the killings from the *resa dei conti* produced debates over the facts themselves, as well as how to remember and interpret them. In Schio, the prison killings were not reflected at all, officially and locally, in any forms of public memory until the 1990s. After a long battle (largely waged by the families of the victims, who had formed an *Associazioni familiari delle vittime dell'eccidio di Schio*), a plaque was put up in 1994 on the wall of what had been the prison. But the story did not end there. A long debate followed (and preceded) this inauguration around the text of the plaque. These debates were linked to different ideas about the meaning of the resistance, but also to "Schio itself and its relationship with the past."[85] They were patterned by and part of contemporary political struggles. Only a small ceremony was held when the plaque was unveiled, reflecting the lack of agreement over the text itself.

This is the current plaque's inscription:

In this building, which was once a prison and is now dedicated to study, on the night of the 6–7 July 1945, 54 people were killed, men and women who had not stood trial, in attempting to obtain justice, more barbarity took place, the city places this not in memory of hatred but as a sign of pity

7.6.1994

Two parts of this plaque were particularly controversial, especially for the families of the victims. First, the word "ingiudicati" (had not stood trial). Most of those in the prison were about to be released, and would not have stood trial. This word seems to imply some sort of guilt on the part of the victims. Then, there was the line "*in attempting to obtain justice,*" which seems to absolve or at least explain the actions of the partisans. There is also an explicit call for pacification in the plaque.

The families of the victims preferred a more neutral and descriptive inscription, and waged a political battle to remove the phrase "*in attempting*" and to have the names of the victims added to the plaque.[86]

In this building which was a prison on the night of the 6–7 July 1945 unarmed people were murdered, the city places this to remember those killings and as a sign of pity

The 1994 plaque was, as one local commentator argued, a compromise between two extreme positions. There were, in fact, a number of texts or "virtual plaques" doing the rounds that were also part of an ongoing debate over the past, and how to remember that past. ANPI's "plaque" was in part an antiwar message, which laid the blame for the massacre at the door of the conflict (and therefore on those who started the war). Its message was one of "never again." Meanwhile, at the other extreme (if we are to ignore neofascist requests) there was another proposal from the Lega, who had recently won elections across the northeast of Italy. The Lega "plaque" contained a plea against a repetition of the horrors of war, but the language was much stronger and accusatory. Above all, the plaque underlined the fact that the war had been "over" and the fifty-four had been "barbarically murdered."

Of all the events of the *resa dei conti*, the Schio killings are among the best known. But this is within the context of very little public debate, at least until recently, about the whole period. The far right has made Schio the site for marches in favor of the victims of the 1945 killings, a tradition that continues to this day. For neofascists, Schio remains one of the symbols of the injustices of the *resa dei conti*. The difference between the Schio killings and most of the other events during the *resa dei conti* was one of scale. Moreover, unlike most of the killings after the liberation, the Schio massacre led to two trials, long debates, and various forms of public memory.

Other prisons saw similar massacres, albeit on a smaller scale, a fact that has led some to claim that there was a national plan to carry out such attacks. There were also frequent episodes of civil war-type violence within the overcrowded prisons of Italy in this period, and a number of serious prison riots, leading up to Togliatti's amnesty in 1946. Prison massacres took place at Cesena (seventeen dead, May 5), Carpi (sixteen dead, June 17), Ferrara (end of June, eighteen dead). In Imola at the end of May, sixteen fascists were taken from a carabinieri truck (they were under arrest) by an angry crowd. Twelve were killed. Fascist prisoners were also shot dead in Liguria and in other parts of Emilia Romagna and the Veneto.

Explaining the *Resa Dei Conti*: The Power of Memory

No ferocity can justify any successive ferocity.

—Istvan Bibo, in Crainz, *L'ombra della Guerra*

Memory was central to the patterns of violence during the *resa dei conti*. Many people were killed precisely because of specific memories of their actions in the past. Time and again, deaths were directly linked to the rise of fascism, and struck out at local exponents of the regime. But memories of the recent war, of spies, of deportations and massacres also mattered.

The partisans and others involved in the *resa dei conti* were frequently very precise about who they killed, where, and when. Their reprisals were not usually organized according to the "rules" adopted by the Nazis or the Italian fascists. Here, the numbers were often the same, as with the sixteen fascists attacked in Imola, in revenge for sixteen antifascists murdered during the war, or the fifteen fascists shot at Dongo and brought back to Piazzale Loreto, just like the fifteen partisans whose bodies had been left in the sun, close by, in 1944. One for one. Not ten to one. Partisans operated with the ancient rule of an eye for an eye, a tooth for a tooth. But this was not always the case. At Rovetta in the Val Seriana in 1945, forty-three unarmed fascist soldiers were shot by partisans (in part, it seems) as a reprisal for the earlier deaths of a smaller number of partisans.

This was not wild or uncontrolled violence, but organized popular justice, although the rituals of the killings often contained elements of premodern rituals—humiliations, hair-shavings, public exhibition of bodies (and then their disappearance). In this way, the *resa dei conti* aped the fascists and the Nazis, copying some of their methods. Places of memory were important in the *resa dei conti*, time and time again. The leading fascist in Turin, Giuseppe Solaro, was hung from a tree in the city in the same square were four partisans had previously been hung.[87] Sometimes, memory also played a part in *how* people were killed, with the same method of death as before being employed.

Most famously of all, Piazzale Loreto was used to display the bodies—usually killed elsewhere—of Mussolini and other fascist leaders.[88] This was no casual choice, but made direct reference to the partisan bodies left in the same square by the Nazis in 1944, which in itself had been a reprisal for a partisan attack in the city. Memories of Nazi killings had thus inspired the "spectacle" of the strung-up bodies in Piazzale Loreto. And that spectacle became a memory in itself. For some, Piazzale Loreto (1945) was linked to emotions of pride and happiness, even joy, and the image of the dead fascists was reproduced on photographs and posters. A woman widowed by the Civitella massacre kept the image by her bedside for the rest of her life. As Leonardo Paggi wrote (about his own mother), "Revenge came therefore, 10 months later, for her, as well as for that crowd who rushed to Milan to see those bodies for themselves. The destruction of one's own family only makes sense as part of a national tragedy."[89] For others, what had happened in Piazzale Loreto was a source of shame. After the war, only the partisan dead were remembered, with a large monument at the side of the piazza, at which annual ceremonies were held.

The more celebrated display of fascist bodies was not remembered publicly, apart from by neofascists. For the movement of the 1960s and 1970s, Piazzale Loreto was sometimes used as a warning, and as an event to be remembered for political ends. The students of the movement informed their political enemies that "there is still room" in Piazzale Loreto. In the piazza itself, all trace of what had happened was removed, and it is now difficult to tell where the bodies themselves had been suspended from. Sometimes, after 1945, revenge was generic, but still linked to memory, as in the calls to "avenge Matteotti" that were frequently heard during the *resa dei conti*. Local and national memories often merged, and hatred took time to dissipate. Fascists returning home throughout 1946 were subject to attacks and even murders, sometimes by large groups of people.

So, in many cases, the *resa dei conti* felt the need to display the bodies of the dead to show that they had been killed, publicly. In many other cases, killings took place at night, and secretly, and bodies were either dumped or hidden. Often, these two strategies were combined. Many leading fascists were denied a proper burial, in an attempt to inflict a kind of "double death" upon them. Mussolini's body was the best-known object of this strategy, and the subsequent "theft" of the dead Mussolini by neofascists confirmed fears that the power of the Duce continued even after his death. It was not until 1957 that the Italian state felt safe enough to allow Mussolini finally to be buried in Predappio.[90] As Luzzatto has argued, some of this was spectacle. How many of those in Piazzale Loreto also attended the huge fascist rallies in the 1920s and 1930s? A public display of hatred toward fascists was a good way of deflecting attention from one's own murky past.

But if memory of the past was crucial to understanding the *resa dei conti*, its methods, its places of death, and its rhythms, the memory of the *resa dei conti* took different forms. Usually, the postrevenge attitude was one of public silence. Private memories, moreover, were rarely expressed. Justice had been done, and had been seen to be done, it was felt by many, but this was not a reason to rejoice. Many felt ashamed or guilty, and these emotions rarely found expression in collective or public narratives. Little public memory was allowed for these victims or for the *resa dei conti* in general. These memories were only carried forward by families or by political groups closest to many of the victims, usually neofascists. The failure to acknowledge the extent of the *resa dei conti*—publicly—created the space for huge interest in the question both in the 1960s (as was seen with the success of Giorgio Pisanò's journalism) and in the early twenty-first century with the extraordinary sales of Pansa's books beginning with *Il sangue dei vinti* in 2003. The hostility to Pansa's work allowed him to claim that the left had tried to (and was still trying to) suppress knowledge about the *resa dei conti*, and this allegation in itself formed the basis for a long series of other books.[91]

Before Pansa, Pisanò's books had also sold extremely well. *Sangue chiama Sangue* went through eight editions in the early 1960s after first seeing the light of day in the popular magazine *Gente*, in a series of eighteen articles in 1960 and as a book sold with that magazine in 1961.[92] Interest in and demand for this type of material was already very high just fifteen years after the resistance had ended.[93] For a long time, after all, historians had ignored the *resa dei conti*, which was only discussed in works of fiction. And, as Isnenghi argued, "where historians are silent or deny things, something else takes their place: stories . . . scandalistic journalism or—in the best of cases—literature."[94]

Pansa's *Il sangue dei vinti* did not entirely ignore the fascist and Nazi crimes that gave birth to the *resa dei conti*, nor did it fail to cite some of the many books that have dealt with this subject. Pansa was also aware already with this first book that he would create controversy[95] and claimed right from the beginning that he was breaking a wall of silence by discussing "the facts that anti-fascist historiography have always purposely ignored."[96]

In the 1990s, Nicola Gallerano had warned other historians of the danger of ignoring or playing down the power of public history and the public use of history. As he wrote, "The public use of history is not something which should be demonised or rejected tout court: it can be a place of debate and conflict which involves the participation of citizens, and not just specialists, around important themes: it can also tell us about deep divisions in terms of memory."[97] Many of the reactions to Pansa's work played into his hands. Pansa is an acknowledged expert on the Resistance, whose study of the partisan war in the Alessandria region was introduced and praised by none other than Guido Quazza, who wrote that Pansa was "attracted, in a enthusiastic way, by the generous and courageous values of the partisan struggle."[98]

Moreover, Pansa had been interested in these issues for years, although they had only found an outlet in his novels. His book *Ma l'amore no* was an extended account of the murder of the antifascist militant Mario Acquaviva in Piedmont in 1945.[99] The criticism of Pansa's later books, beginning with *Il sangue dei vinti*, was above all linked to the supposed lack of context to the violence he described, as well as the absence in the books of reference to historical research in these areas. Pansa was accused by many of "overturning" the history of Italy.[100] But this fact alone is not enough to explain the incredible success of these volumes. His books are not only read or purchased by neofascists, or revisionists. Clearly, forty years of public silence (because the work of historians such as Storchi, Crainz, and Dondi have remained largely confined to an academic audience) have created a mass need for information and accounts of the *resa dei conti*, but these sales also showed just how fragile the resistance myth had become.

The Strategy of Tension and Terrorism

Piazza Fontana and the "Moro Case"

On December 12, 1969, a bomb exploded in a bank in Piazza Fontana in the center of Milan. Sixteen people eventually died and more than ninety were injured. This was the first act in what later became known as the "strategy of tension." Although much is still unknown about the series of bombs that exploded throughout the 1970s, most commentators now agree that they were placed by neofascist activists as part of a plot inspired by sections of the secret services.[1] These events took place in the middle of the most radical moment of late 1960s, with student and worker movements active across the whole of Italy.

Immediately after the bomb, a nationwide roundup of left-activists took place, with more than 4,000 arrests. One of those arrested was Giuseppe "Pino" Pinelli, a forty-one-year old railway worker in Milan. Pinelli was an anarchist. Three days after the bomb, Pinelli fell to his death from the fourth floor window of Milan's central police station. The first official police version of the death was suicide. Another anarchist, Pietro Valpreda, had been arrested on December 15 and charged with the bomb attack. He was to remain in prison, without trial, until 1972, and was only finally cleared in 1981. Eight trials have been held with relation to Piazza Fontana, with no guilty verdicts being confirmed by the courts.

Ever since Pinelli's death in December 1969, controversy has raged on about how he died, and why. The facts themselves have never been the subject of agreement. Numerous versions exist of this event and new ones continue to appear, nearly forty years after the original massacre. These divisions have continued to separate the ways in which Pinelli is *remembered*, culminating in the existence of two very similar plaques dedicated to the anarchist, in the same place, but with different messages about the circumstances of his death.

A first dividing line can be drawn between two contrasting versions of Pinelli's dramatic "fall" from the police station window in 1969. The police said immediately that Pinelli had committed suicide; they added (falsely) that he was "deeply compromised" with the Piazza Fontana bombing. Meanwhile, suspicions soon emerged that something different had happened. Another version took shape, which claimed that Pinelli had been murdered. The evidence for this version lay above all in the tangle of lies and jumbled versions issued by the police, and in the refusal to believe that Pinelli was the type of person who would have committed suicide. Moreover, many blamed the police for Pinelli's death, irrespective of the fact that he had been murdered or not. After all, he was being held illegally, for a crime he had nothing to do with, and had been under interrogation for three days and nights. More extreme versions talk of torture of various kinds. The police denied any wrongdoing.

The last judicial word on the Pinelli case came in 1975, and it was a compromise between the two broad versions offered by the police and the "movement." According to Italian justice, Pinelli had neither committed suicide *nor* had he been murdered. He had suffered from an "active illness," in part due to the treatment of the police, and had "fallen" from the window to his death. This is an extract from the 1975 sentence: "The air in the room was heavy, oppressive. The window was opened [Pinelli] went over to the balcony for a breath of fresh air, he felt dizzy, he put out his hands in the wrong direction, his body fell over the railings . . . all the evidence points in this direction." This version satisfied almost nobody, and has been the object of ridicule ever since. We still have no clear idea of the events in that small police room that night. Many people know what happened, not least the policemen who were there with Pinelli, but an acceptable version of the truth has not materialized.[2] This uncertainty has only exacerbated the conflict over the *memory* of the Pinelli case, symbolized by the "war of the plaques" in Milan after 2006.

Pinelli's death became a central event during the 1970s in Italy for a number of historical and cultural reasons. First, the dramatic, almost cinematic nature of the event aroused interest and debate, as did the botched cover-up and police lies, which were easy to rebut. Second, Pinelli's death was intimately connected with other shocking events of that period: not only the Piazza Fontana bomb for which he was arrested but also the 1972 murder of police inspector Luigi Calabresi, blamed by many for Pinelli's "murder." Third, the form of the Pinelli case tapped into left-wing mythology and history. Many drew parallels with the unexplained death of other anarchists in similar circumstances in Italy and America. Pinelli's "fall" was part of a longer story: arousing memories and passions beyond the event itself. Finally, the Pinelli case was a fascinating detective story, with twists and turns, mysteries and misrepresentations, and a cast of shady personalities.

The iconography of "Pinelli" was powerful, inspiring paintings, books, films, plays, poems and songs. Pinelli's campaign developed quickly into a crucial component of the movement for justice (and revenge) linked to Piazza Fontana and the "strategy of tension." Moreover, the campaign kept the case open, leading to the creation of unforgettable images and the raking over of macabre details. A number of myths became part of left folklore. The Pinelli case also contained other characters who helped the drama of the story: above all Pinelli's wife, Licia, and their two young daughters.[3] Within months of his death, the Pinelli case had became part of the very identity of the left. To position yourself politically meant taking sides on Pinelli. There could be no gray zone here. Language itself became an object for discussion, a dividing line between left and right. For many, Pinelli had not just fallen; rather, he had "fallen," he had "been suicided," he had "precipitated."

Bodies dominate the Pinelli case. Photos of Pinelli's corpse were used in propaganda posters produced by the left. The injuries, or supposed injuries, to Pinelli were gone over in minute detail, as were his various fractures. One strong left myth, that Pinelli had been killed by a karate chop, was linked to the examination of a swelling on the anarchist's shoulder. The x-rays of his back were published in the press. Everyone knew Pinelli's exact height: 1m 67cm. Pinelli's body was buried, then reexhumed for new autopsies, then reburied, then reexhumed and finally reburied in Carrara. The first reexhumation was described in minute and gory detail in all the major newspapers. A dummy representing Pinelli was thrown out of a window four times in front of photographers and film cameras. Pinelli's last journey to the hospital was rerun by the investigating judge. Images of Pinelli's face dominated demonstrations, posters, and obituaries for years.[4] Many remained convinced, despite the various investigations and the 1975 sentence, that Pinelli had been murdered. Since 1969, the Pinelli and Piazza Fontana cases have inspired books, articles, campaigns, songs, demonstrations, public inquiries, novels, plays, paintings, and monuments, some of which will be discussed here.

The 1970s saw deep divisions emerge in the city around the interpretation of Piazza Fontana and the death of Pinelli. Many have compared post-1969 Milan to the Paris of the Dreyfus case. The post-Piazza Fontana period was marked by conflicts over all forms of memory, including plaques, memorials, and monuments. As Van Hass has written in her study of the Vietnam War Memorial in Washington DC, the reactions to "the wall" constitute a kind of "restless memory . . . a conversation about post-Vietnam America" and a "continuing public negotiation about patriotism and nationalism."⁵ *But some memorials are more contested than others.* Many plaques barely merit a mention even when they are unveiled. Conflict and attention has arisen when a plaque or other kind of memorial is closely connected to recent political and social controversies, which have divided the city, society, or the nation. Obviously, these reflections also apply to the Pinelli case, and it is no surprise that a plaque dedicated to Pinelli, a small and simple marble slab containing just twenty or so words, has been the most discussed plaque in the history of the city.

One further violent event underlined the atmosphere created by Piazza Fontana and the Pinelli case. On May 17, 1972, Luigi Calabresi, the policeman who had arrested Giuseppe Pinelli in 1969, was shot dead outside his house in Milan. Calabresi had been on his way to work. A huge crowd attended Calabresi's funeral. Despite long investigations by the police, nobody was charged with the murder, although many in the city had no doubts that the revolutionary left were responsible. The press campaign (particularly that of the newspaper *Lotta Continua*) against Calabresi was blamed by many for his murder, and journalists such as Camilla Cederna were accused of being the "moral mandates" of his execution. Calabresi's murder became the subject of a second extraordinary series of trials and campaigns in the late 1980s, when three ex-militants of the left-wing organization, *Lotta Continua* were arrested, charged and eventually convicted of the murder of the policeman.⁶ The story of the memories linked to the Calabresi case shadow those linked to Pinelli. It is more or less impossible to tell one story without reference to the other. The debates over their memory were separate, in theory, but in reality the two cases were intertwined. Demands for recognition of "truths" from one side of the divide often coincided, as we shall see, with requests for the removal of or alteration to the memories of the other. Memories and commemorations were divided, but they lived in a kind of symbiosis, in continual reference to each other.

In 1977, after a discussion between what remained of the 1968 student movement, some ex-partisans and anarchists, an unofficial plaque to Pinelli was placed in the piazza during a demonstration, close to the official plaque dedicated to the bomb attack (it appears that the organizers wanted to put the plaque outside the police station, and then on the bank itself, but both locations were refused). As Mario Martucci, student activist and one of the organizers of the ceremony, put it, "We were obliged to put the plaque there because of what had happened: there were plaques for the victims of the bomb and we considered Pinelli a victim of those who had organised the attack."⁷ Those who had created and erected the plaque informed the police and local authorities, whose lack of action on the day amounted to tacit acceptance of it.

However, the Pinelli plaque was "unauthorized," without official permission to be where it was. The event caused little comment in the papers, even the revolutionary press, at the time. But protests began to mount almost immediately. The Christian Democratic Party issued a statement that called for the plaque's immediate removal and complained about "the arbitrary placing of a plaque in Piazza Fontana . . . where once again the memory of an innocent citizen—Pinelli—has been exploited."[8] One magistrate made two official written protests; another magistrate complained four times. This was the text of the 1977 plaque (Figure 8.1). To

GIUSEPPE PINELLI
ANARCHIST RAILWAY-WORKER
AN INNOCENT MAN MURDERED IN THE ROOMS OF THE CENTRAL
POLICE STATION
ON THE 16.12.1969

MILAN'S STUDENTS AND DEMOCRATS

Why all these protests? The problem was that the plaque gave one side of the Pinelli story. Pinelli had been "killed" in the "rooms of the police station." This was a version that had not been proven by any inquest or

Figure 8.1   Piazza Fontana, Milan: Plaque dedicated to Giuseppe Pinelli.

judicial inquiry, but it was also the version that most of those involved in the Pinelli case believed. *The plaque presented one side of a extremely contested fact that had divided the city, and it presented it as a uncontested fact.* This was why the plaque has caused so much controversy. Over the years, numerous attempts were made by judges, police organizations, and political groups to have the plaque removed, leading to demonstrations in favor of the plaque, guards around the site, and debates. Anniversaries commemorating Pinelli began to focus around the plaque, as numbers dwindled. The plaque became the only means of keeping the Pinelli case, or at least some memory of it, alive. Memory was divided over what had happened to Pinelli, but only one side of that divided memory had been given form as a commemorative object.

In 1981, traffic police discovered the plaque in pieces one morning (this was presumably the work of fascists). The original organizers paid for a new plaque and relaid it after a new ceremony. In 1986, the city mayor admitted the plaque had not been officially authorized. In November 1987, a different mayor started a huge controversy by announcing that the plaque would be removed and placed in Milan's Museo di Storia Contemporanea. Paolo Pillitteri argued that by 1987, the plaque was part of history. Huge protests followed. Dario Fo organized a new run of his *Accidental Death of an Anarchist*, which opened in record time in early December. For Martucci, one of those who had prepared the plaque, "removing the plaque from Piazza Fontana is a way of murdering Pinelli, because a man dies when his memory is cancelled out . . . we used to say that history is written in the streets, and today they would like us to believe that it is learnt in museums."[9] Pillitteri retreated. The plaque remained.[10] It mattered.

In 1994, the plaque was at the center of attention once again. Work in the Piazza had meant the plaque had been temporarily removed. A left-wing councillor placed a motion in the city council guaranteeing its replacement in the same place. Thanks to the abstention of one right-wing party, the motion was passed and an unofficial plaque was given institutional status.[11] The latest threat to the plaque came in the same year, with a campaign by one of the police trade unions for a plaque for Luigi Calabresi. After threatening to remove the Pinelli plaque themselves, or place a Calabresi plaque nearby, the unions retreated and placed their own plaque to Calabresi (again without official permission) on the barracks in Piazza Sant'Ambrogio.[12] Their requests called for the wording to be changed (e.g., to "died innocently in the Questura") or the incriminating phrase simply to be crossed out. Some took the law into their own hands, altering the words on the plaque. Liberal Party councillor Luca Hasda claimed that "the removal or correction of the plaque dedicated to Pinelli should be the duty of all people who respect history and reality."

The debates over Pinelli's plaque reflected the divisions opened up in the city after 1968 and 1969, but the claims made for the plaque by its supporters revealed how far the plaque had become overloaded with political and symbolic value. Camilla Cederna wrote that to remove the plaque would "wipe out history itself," Salvatore Veca described the plaque as "a part of collective memory." The anarchists, who had their own Pinelli plaque, called the removal proposal a provocation and an attempt to rewrite history. The plaque was unofficial and "anarchist": "We had put it there, as a challenge, as a way of affirming our own truth."[13] Alternative proposals emerged. One was for a combined monument to the victims of Piazza Fontana (an idea that was circulating on the left back in the 1970s), another mentioned a vague category of "victims of the 1960s." Pinelli's plaque (and the demand for a monument for Calabresi) became part of the identity of different generations. It was "our past" and "our truth." To admit to doubts, to allow more than one truth to emerge, was to wipe out part of that identity. The veterans from the 1968 student movements were anxious about defending that past, even if many of them had become someone else in the meantime. They were no longer political militants in the vast majority of cases, but the Pinelli plaque was something they still wished to be militant about.

Official and unofficial memorials of all kinds reflected the dividing lines set up in the city by the massacre and the Pinelli case. Often, the unofficial attempts to keep certain memories alive, or to press certain version of events, caused more controversy and led to more debate. As the movement faded and the Pinelli case lost its power over the city, monuments became the center of attention, and no longer reflections of wider campaigns. The importance attached to the Pinelli plaque is understandable, but reflects a kind of desperate last stand in a supposed battle against the loss of memory. It is as if the whole case, the trials, the debates, and the hundreds of books produced about the case have been reduced to a bitter discussion about a few (important) words: "killed" or "died"? "In the rooms" or not? In some ways the whole saga of the plaque is a sign of the way the Pinelli case *no longer* occupies the minds of the citizens of Milan, or divides the city itself as it used to. It is not an immediate, burning political issue, but a question of *divided memory*. One "side" felt defrauded by a version presented in the plaque. Its very presence was a threat to their own memories and narratives. In spring 2006, this "other" side had a (brief) victory.

Just when it seemed that the whole affair had come to a close, there came another coup de theatre. At four o'clock in the morning on March 18, 2006, local government workers removed the old Pinelli plaque, in secret, and put up another one in its place. The new plaque sported a different wording. It read as follows (Figure 8.2).

Figure 8.2   Piazza Fontana, Milan: New plaque dedicated to Giuseppe Pinelli, 2006.

Milano: Milan City Council
To

GIUSEPPE PINELLI
ANARCHIST RAILWAY WORKER
AN INNOCENT MAN WHO DIED TRAGICALLY
IN THE ROOMS OF MILAN'S CENTRAL POLICE STATION
ON THE 15.12.1969

News spread fast of the substitution, and a debate ensued. Three days later, anarchists and other protesters gathered in Piazza Fontana to demonstrate. The demonstration ended with an old plaque being erected right next to the new one. This was not *the* old plaque that had been removed by the council, but an older example that had been replaced some years earlier. The Piazza now had two—nearly identical—plaques to Pinelli, and the "old" plaque had become technically illegal, again. Much rhetoric surrounded the protests. *L'Unità* called the old plaque "the true plaque." The new plaque was described as "a fake" created by "the stupid stubbornness of a form of revisionism which some people are trying to substitute for reality."

Gabriele Albertini, center-right mayor of Milan from 1997 to 2006, who had tended to ignore the Piazza Fontana anniversaries, claimed that he had made a promise to Luigi Calabresi's widow, Gemma, that he would have the plaque removed, as it constituted "an insult" to the memory of her dead husband. For Albertini, "That plaque, which accused Calabresi of being a murderer, threw mud at his memory. In this way the Council has re-established historical truth."

Protests and messages of support split down political lines, although some on the right doubted the wisdom of the change in the middle of an election campaign. Many argued that the substitution of the plaque was a form of forgetting, or revisionism, although it could be argued that the new plaque was a more accurate reflection of the judicial position with regard to Pinelli's death (while repeating the factual error that he had died in the rooms of the Questura, when Pinelli actually died in hospital) and that the official recognition of a plaque to Pinelli in some ways represented a form of victory after years of campaigning.

Once again, the great difficulty Italy has in producing consensus, and therefore a shared memory, over past events had been revealed by the ways in which those events—the very *facts* of the past—were still the subject of controversy and politicization. Albertini's position was undermined when he unearthed the old story of Pinelli's suicide. Was the "tragic" phrase in the new plaque an underhand reference to the discredited suicide theory? Pinelli's widow expressed "shock" at the whole affair and added that "not even in this way will they succeed in eliminating Pino's memory from the heart of Milan." The center-right majority on the city council refused to suspend the work of the council to allow some members to participate in the session. The center-left councillors left anyway, and the sitting was cancelled, as it was not quorate. On his way out of the chamber, Green Party councillor Basilio Rizzo repeated the phrase "Milan will not forget." But what exactly was being remembered, and forgotten, and by whom?

Since 2006, more than one commentator has argued that the two plaques should be retained, as they reflect continuing divisions over the way those events are remembered. As I write (in 2009) this is, in fact, what has happened, providing Milan's residents with a daily and evocative reminder of the divided memories (and other factors) around the experience of the 1960s and 1970s (Figure 8.3). Divided memory was being reflected in public memory, in the perfect image of two plaques, side-by-side, with different (but not necessarily *incompatible*—apart from the date) versions of the same event. Each period had produced multiple narratives, which demanded recognition. A fragile form of consensus could be achieved, through the acknowledgement of division. No organization—the state, the justice system, the media—had been able to impose a single, acceptable version of what had

Figure 8.3   Piazza Fontana, Milan: Both plaques dedicated to Giuseppe Pinelli, 2008.

happened. Neo-fascists continued to stick to a version that blamed the left for many of the massacres, despite overwhelming evidence to the contrary.[14]

Collective memory is not just the sum of individual memories, and memories themselves are mediated through time by political beliefs, personal experiences, myths, traumas, pleasure, and pain. These memories are often difficult, and many were simply not allowed to forget, such as the wives of the two victims—Licia Pinelli and Gemma Calabresi. Licia Pinelli began to leave the city on the anniversary of Piazza Fontana to avoid the "usual questions."

There is no such thing as a collective memory to be maintained through time, independent of personal experience. In divided Milan, with its contested facts and political and social fissures, there were *many* collective memories, many of which competed with others, or even excluded other versions of what had happened and who was responsible. Facts were often adapted to fit certain versions. Myths were commonplace. Sometimes, this competition has been within the same apparent set of forces. After the 1974 Brescia massacre, for example, many victims' families refused the generic label of "victim" and pressed home the political views of their relatives, who had died *because they were antifascist*, not because they happened to be in the wrong place at the wrong time.[15] Memories are also collected and shaped in other ways, through monuments, language, slogans, film, traumatic moments such as funerals, plays, artworks, books, speeches, photographs, and records. Certain places have become crucial as "places of memory"—contested and fought over, sometimes literally, for the right to commemorate or to impose one version of events over another.[16]

The mass of trials, articles, analyses, and demonstrations linked to the events of the 1970s in Italy have led to a profound sense of alienation and cynicism in the state and its institutions. It is almost as if the mass of paper produced, and the length of the trials themselves, is inversely related to any sense of justice or satisfaction in the whole process or its protagonists. *The more "information" that has been produced, the less it has seemed to matter.* Judge Salvini's long investigation, and even the apparent discovery of the actual bomber, continued amid almost total indifference.

By 1999, the legal documentation in the Piazza Fontana trial alone amounted to some 107 boxes each containing 1,000 pages—at least 107,000 pages in total. Lawyers were facing bills of £5.000 merely to photocopy the documents available. Some have even argued that the official set of anniversaries has had the effect of brushing under the carpet the collective movements that accompanied the period of the massacres.[17] The old cliché that the lack of official or judicial truth has been an incentive to remember has not been born out by the post-1969 experience. Certain groups in Brescia simply stopped going to the official ceremonies altogether.

In the meantime, there were developments in the public memory relating to Luigi Calabresi. In 2007, two official plaques dedicated to Calabresi were inauguarated. One was in the central offices of Milan's Provincial government (where the left were in the majority) and the other close to the spot where the policeman was killed in 1972. This simple monument reads as follows:

Here, in front of his house, while he was on his way to work, on the 17 May 1972, Police Commissioner Luigi Calabresi fell victim to terrorism. Milan. 17 May 2007

Meanwhile, in the offices of the Province of Milan, this was the wording of the plaque:

To Luigi Calabresi, faithful servant of the State, who fell victim to the spiral of political violence which covered the streets of Milan with innocent blood 35 years on from his vile murder, the Province of Milan remembers and honours him

In one way, this proliferation of monuments seems to herald a plurality of opinions and memories, a kind of pacification. But they also symbolize the continuation of a conflict over the past and over how to interpret that past. In the same year, a best-selling book by his son Mario Calabresi, *Spingendo la notte più in la*, opened up the debate around the ways in which Luigi Calabresi (and Pinelli) had been remembered (2007). In 2008 was the first day of memory for the victims of terrorism in Italy (a day fixed for May 9, the day Aldo Moro's body was displayed in the center of Rome). No official list of these victims exists, and the category of "victims of terrorism" was linked to a nonofficial organization.

Norberto Bobbio has drawn a distinction between dead and live memories. The first consists of memorials, history books, testimonies, plaques, and so on. This memory "only has meaning if it helps to keep internal memory alive. It can stimulate this memory, but not substitute it. One is dead memory, the other is live memory." A tomb only takes on meaning when it is visited by a relative, or created, or moved, or some flowers are left nearby. In the Piazza Fontana case, conflict has kept memory alive—there has been a considerable amount of activity around the various plaques in the square and elsewhere. But in other areas there has been silence, and forgetting, especially with regard to the victims of the bomb itself. Some writers have wondered why the whole period has not produced a major work of fiction, and why the massacres have no longer been told as stories. Even one of the bank workers who had seen the bomb had not told his own children. The massacres had a devastating effect on the whole of Italy, leading directly to terrorism that dominated all else and pervades the accounts of the students who knew nothing about Piazza Fontana. As intended, the massacres created confusion, violence, silence, and fear.

For the Italian state, Piazza Fontana was a turning point. For Bobbio, "The degeneration of our democratic system began after Piazza Fontana."[18] For Marco Revelli, in 1969 "a significant part of the state apparatus passed knowingly into the camp of illegality."[19] Politicians, secret servicemen, army officials, policemen, journalists, and others all combined to cover up and organize the strategy of tension. The state had plotted against its own citizens, imprisoned innocents, set false trails, and manipulated evidence. This series of events, from Piazza Fontana onward, undermined fatally the faith in the institutions that had been an important part of postwar Italy after the defeat of fascism. This was not just a legitimation crisis, but the end of legitimation altogether. By the 1990s, the truth concerning the dark side of the state was available for all to see, laid bare by documents, documentaries, inquests, confessions, and trials. Yet nobody was listening any more. The link between "justice," "truth," and memory had been broken.

Do we need to forget Piazza Fontana to be able to finally understand it? Is there a right to forget? The best-known victims of the bomb, the Pizzamiglio children, refused to answer journalists' questions in 1994, on the twenty-fifth anniversary of the massacre, and they stated that "for years now we have decided to stay silent. Another relative of a victim claimed that "at Catanzaro (where the Piazza Fontana trials had been moved in the 1970s in order to distance them from the press and the attention of the public), my father has been killed for a second time." The very phrase "do not forget" has now become obsolete. As we have seen with the Milanese students, many simply have never known what happened. You cannot forget something you have never learned. A deeper process of historical understanding can only arise through the rekindling of Bobbio's "live memory." Certainly, the post-Piazza Fontana victims—Pinelli and Calabresi—dominated discussions, while those who were killed by the bomb itself were forgotten, their uncontroversial and wordy plaque rarely noticed by passers-by. As with San Miniato, the two plaques in Piazza Fontana are a dramatic example of how divided memory has become part of public memory.[20] They are testimony to the power of those events to divide and of the weakness of the justice system in reaching a shared judgment on these cases. Yet the conspiracy theories and debates over Piazza Fontana were nothing compared to the mass of material and debates that surrounded the dramatic events of March 1978, in the capital city, Rome.

Aldo Moro and the Memory of the "55 Days"

Whatever the whole truth of the Moro kidnapping and the reasons behind it, it is fair to say that Aldo Moro has not gone away: he continues to haunt the cultural psyche of the Italian nation.

—Alan O'Leary, "Tragedia all'italiana:
Cinema e terrorismo tra Moro e Memoria"

It is a paradox of the Moro case . . . that investigations lasting more than twenty-five years [now more than 30] have produced greater knowledge of the events but less consensus about their interpretation. The lack of consensus is regularly conveyed by public skirmishes between the members of two camps: the supporters of the "official version" and the "conspiracy theorists."

—David Moss, "Il caso Moro 1978–2004: Witchcraft, Oracles, and Magic"

Fifty-five days. "The 55 days."[21] Most Italians, if they have reached "a certain age," know what this length of time means. In 1978, from March 16 to May 9, one of the most powerful and well-known Italian politicians from the postwar period was held hostage by a terrorist group in the center of Rome. He was then shot, covered with a blanket, and left in a car boot in the center of the capital. Ever since that moment (as well as during the kidnap itself) the "Moro Case" has been the subject of claims and counterclaims, political and historical debate, conspiracy theories and counterconspiracy theories, and, some argue, a series of other murders and court cases. The Moro case was crucial to the continuing success of these forms of reportage and political analysis in Italy (although this type of reasoning had been around for some time in Italy)—*dietrologia, behind-thescenes-ology.*[22]

In prison, Moro wrote numerous letters and a long "memoriale," documents that were censored and manipulated to serve the needs of different people and different groups at various times. All of these letters were copied by hand, and many also photocopied. Some were delivered to their intended destination, others were never sent (although Moro often thought they had arrived). A number turned up in a flat in Milan in October 1978 in Via Montenevoso, and another series in the same flat in October 1990. On the latter occasion, some 421 pages of copies of writings by Moro (without the originals) were discovered by a Neapolitan building worker (in a fake wall) on the first morning of the first day of work on the apartment, which had been sequestrated by the state for twelve years.[23]

A number of films have been dedicated to the Moro story, as well as a long TV "fiction" and documentaries. Intellectuals took a stance on and dedicated books to the Moro Case such as Sciascia, Arbasino, Eco, Marco Belpoliti, and Bruno Pischedda.[24] Eco's best-selling novel, *The Name of the Rose*, was also strongly linked to a rereading of *Il caso Moro*. Members of Moro's family have also contributed to the literature around the case, including his daughter and his grandson. A lengthy parliamentary inquiry carried out investigations and produced various reports, in addition to the seemingly interminable legal proceedings that dragged on for years. There were five trials and two parliamentary commissions, as well as numerous books, testimonies, and investigations. As with Piazza Fontana, innumerable documents, testimonies, versions, films photographs and analyses have done little to clear up ambiguities and doubts. More "information" and less clarity has been the pattern here as well.

Moro's kidnapping—and his death—were Italy's "Kennedy moment." Everyone remembers where they were, and what they were doing, when they heard the news. Everyone has seen the images, and the celebrated self-referential photo of Moro holding up a copy of a newspaper with the headline *Moro Assassinato*? *Il caso Moro* led to various forms of public memory. Plaques stand where he was kidnapped and where his body was dumped, and these are the focus of official ceremonies on certain key dates. All over Italy, there are squares and roads dedicated to Moro. By 1998, an estimated 2,438 places had been named after Moro.[25]

The two key plaques in Rome are located in the two sites of memory linked to the 55 days, and the Moro case—Via Fani and Via Caetani. These two sites are also linked to two annual ceremonies on March 16 and May 9. The first plaque in Via Fani was put up (rather strangely) on the anniversary of *Moro's* death, and not of that of the five bodyguards and driver. May 9, 1978, saw this plaque unveiled in Via Fani (with photos of the dead, but not Moro, and their names). The plaque is in a difficult position in terms of access and visibility, at ground level.

ORESTE LEONARDI
FRANCESCO ZIZZI
DOMENICO RICCI
RAFFAELE IOZZINO
GIULIO RIVERA
IN THIS PLACE
AT 9.05 ON THE 16 MARCH 1978
FIVE MEN
WHO WERE FAITHFUL SERVANTS OF THE STATE AND DEMOCRACY
WERE KILLED WITH COLD FEROCITY
WHILE THEY WERE DOING THEIR DUTY
THE ROME TOWN COUNCIL PLACES THIS PLAQUE
9 MAY 1979
[Photos of the victims]

One strange feature of this plaque is the use of a specific time (something extremely rare in public memorials), the lack of reference to Aldo Moro, and the failure to specify who the perpetrators of the murders were. In 1979, terrorism was still seen as in the ascendancy, and the lack of reference to terrorists or the Red Brigades (BR) was probably a mixture of a desire not to provide publicity, as well as an acknowledgement of their continued power.[26] A very different kind of plaque is to be found in Via Caetani:

54 DAYS AFTER HIS BARBARIC KIDNAPPING
THE BULLET-RIDDEN BODY OF ALDO MORO
WAS FOUND IN THIS PLACE
ON THE MORNING OF THE 9 MAY 1978
BORN IN MAGLIE ON THE 23 SEPTEMBER 1916
PROFESSOR OF THE UNIVERSITY OF ROME
POLITICAL SECRETARY AND LATER PRESIDENT OF THE CHRISTIAN
DEMOCRATIC PARTY
MANY TIMES PRESIDENT OF THE COUNCIL OF MINISTERS OF THE
ITALIAN REPUBLIC
FOR MORE THAN THIRTY YEARS HE CONTRIBUTED TO THE POLITICAL
LIFE, IN A COUNTRY REBORN AS FREE AND DEMOCRATIC, WITH
HIS LUCID INTELLIGENCE, HIS MORAL FIBRE AND HIS EXQUISITE
SENSIBILITY HE WAS ABLE TO REMAIN FAITHFUL TO HIS PROFESSED

BELIEFS HIS SACRIFICE WAS CARRIED OUT WITH COLD AND INHU-
MAN FEROCITY BY THOSE WHO TRIED IN VAIN TO PREVENT THE
REALISATION OF A COURAGEOUS PROGRAMME OF CHANGE FOR
THE BENEFIT OF THE ENTIRE ITALIAN PEOPLE
HE WILL REMAIN AS A WARNING AND AN EXAMPLE FOR ALL CITIZENS
IN TERMS OF A RENEWED COMMITMENT TO NATIONAL UNITY,
JUSTICE, PEACE AND SOCIAL PROGRESS
THE ROME TOWN COUNCIL ON THE 1ST ANNIVERSARY OF HIS DEATH

Nearby there is an image of Moro to add to this long description of his life. But, once again, the Red Brigades are not mentioned, and appear only as generic "murderers." These two plaques are the focus for public commemorations every year. For Cavallaro, "Every 16 March and 9 May the same rituals are repeated, various laurel wreaths are laid under the two plaques, the highest representatives of the State visit these places and pronounce a few words which remind people of what had happened there, while other politicians visit as private citizens. Beyond this, we know very little about the way the city understands these symbols which represent part of its history."[27]

A further memory of the Moro case is linked to the car in whose trunk his body was found: a red R4.[28] That specific R4 was given back to its owner in 1982, and is still preserved in a garage in Rome. It is, for Luzzatto, a "metallic place of memory."[29] But not all the sites of memory linked to the Moro case are remembered or marked. In Via Camillo Montalcini, the place where Moro was killed in an underground garage, there is no trace of what happened thirty years ago.

Conspiracies and Anti-Conspiracies

The Moro Case's most controversial legacy was in terms of its link to ideas of conspiracy. Over time, those looking to interpret what happened and why during the "55 days" have divided into conspiracy theorists and anti-conspiracy theorists. These two broad positions are now quite clear. One side claims that we still "don't know everything" about the Moro case, and argue that Moro's death was useful for many different groups and individuals. Here the emphasis is placed on the role of the state—in infiltrating the Red Brigades, in "not finding" Moro, in hiding or manipulating his letters. But it is also claimed that there was—and is—an unwritten pact of silence (or of confusion) between the terrorists and the state to cover-up certain elements of the case (and to murder Moro at the time). Dietrologists concentrate on key elements of the case, the discovery of a Red Brigade hideout during the 55 days, the "false comunique," and other mysterious moments including a so-called séance where indications were supposedly given about where Moro was. These details are obssessively repeated and mulled over, and anybody who downplays them is dismissed as naïve, or in some way part of the conspiracy.

On the other side of the fence stand the antidietrologists (an increasingly powerful and influential group). This group argues that we "know everything" about Moro; there is nothing left to be discovered. Moreover, for these analysts, the idea that "we don't know everything" is part of an ongoing myth, *in itself.* One key problem in the Moro case is thus the huge gap between what is said to have happened, and *rumors* about *what actually happened.* The official line is that no negotiations with the kidnappers took place, while evidence points toward a series of attempts to deal with the terrorists. These gaps are most obvious in terms of the letters themselves, which were manipulated by the terrorists and by the state, as well as by the press and numerous politicians. But the gap is also about details—the exact number of days of the kidnap, the position of the car where Moro's body was found, myths about facts that have entered into the official, public narratives about the case. These debates have also had an effect on how Moro and the Moro case have been remembered.

Public Memory, Private Memory, Guilt

One got used to the unavoidable impression that the Moro *affaire* had already been written, that it was already a completed work of literature.

—Leonardo Sciascia, "La Sicilia come metafora"

Memories of the Moro case and are mixed with silences and guilt, given that a number of people on the Left were (at the time) indifferent to, or even satisfied with the kidnapping. These attitudes were publicly unacceptable, and were thus hidden or suppressed. This private (but collective) shame remained in some cases, and has rarely been investigated by historians.

Given its dates, Moro and the Moro case had a significant influence on the commemorations and memories linked to 1968, especially in 1978 and in 2008, when a far greater quantity of material was dedicated to Moro than to the uprisings associated with that year a decade earlier. These memories are often selective. For example, memories connected to the murders of Moro's four bodyguards and driver have been weak in relation to the death of Moro himself. Moro was often attacked for his supposed failure to take these deaths seriously, especially his letters, although this "omission" is in itself a myth.[30] There are very few Italians who can name any members of "la scorta." (The bodyguards and driver killed in Via Fani.) Their memory is collective, but also anonymous. Moro's death dominates everything else in this case, especially as it was a death that "lasted 55 days," had been announced many times and was intensely visual in terms of the display of the politician's body.

Collective memory relating to the funerals of "la scorta" is more or less nonexistent, while memories of Moro's "fake funeral" (his body was not there) are strong, thanks in part to the images from Bellocchio's film *Buongiorno, Notte* (2003). Competing memories of the Moro case have also appeared through a number of publications by the terrorists themselves, many of whom have brought out semiautobiographies.[31] O'Leary argues that the very nature and length of the Moro kidnapping, and its obsessive reporting in the media, "partly accounts for the traumatic persistence of the memory of the Moro events in the Italian consciousness."[32]

There are those who argue the Moro case was more "memorable" than right-wing terrorist events such as the Bologna bomb. But how can we measure what was or is "memorable" and what is not? Certainly, the choice of a day of memory for the victims of terrorism was a significant moment, in May 2007. Parliamentary debate centered on two alternatives: December 12 and May 9. In the end, the "Moro" date was chosen, marking a political shift toward a concentration on left-wing terrorism at the expense of the massacres, as well as a focus on the spectacular and not on the more mundane but far more numerous deaths of ordinary policemen or bodyguards. Nonetheless, the choice of the Moro date probably reflected public opinion, which had not been created spontaneously, and the way Italians saw the past and "terrorism" in general. The continuing interest in, if not domination of, the Moro case was also explicit in the flood of books, films, and discussions that coincided with the thirtieth anniversary of the kidnapping in 2008.

Over time, memory of the massacres became increasingly local and de-politicized and ritualized. The number of films dedicated specifically to the Moro case is relatively low—one in 1986 and two in 2003—plus the two-part drama aired on TV in 2008. Analysis of *Il caso Moro* has above all been carried out in the form of *texts*, with interventions from weighty intellectuals and writers: Sciascia, Eco, Arbasino, Belpoliti, Pischedda, and Sofri. In the Moro case, the scapegoat for the crime was often seen as the state itself, and not the Red Brigades. As with many wartime massacres, blame shifted.

Was Moro's memory somehow "Catholic-Communist," a reflection of the historic compromise of which he was the political architect? This was the image portrayed by the controversial statue erected in 1998 in Maglie (his hometown in Apulia), where Moro is depicted carrying a copy of *L'Unità*. In a strange form of protest, a center-right Catholic politician replaced the ex-communist paper with a copy of the ex-DC paper *Il Popolo*.[33] Debates have continued about Moro's legacy, and about why he had died. Divisions have also been inevitable, as the monolithic DC and the equally monolithic PCI broke up in the 1990s into a mosaic of different parties and groups.

The other great division over Moro's memory was between parts of the DC leadership (in particular) and the relatives of the dead politician. This split was created during the 55 days of the kidnap, where the family became increasingly frustrated by the hard-line adopted by the DC and the PCI and tried to push for negotiations to save Moro's life. Here there was not even a dialogue, as the family refused to share a stage or a platform with certain DC politicians, such as Andreotti. Relations between Moro's family and the state broke down. This fracture has never been healed.

These divisions were not just at the level of language, or the media, but took concrete form in separate ceremonies and commemorations. Most famously, Moro was the subject of a "double funeral." Moro himself had asked for a private, family funeral. The state and the Vatican were thus excluded from the real funeral, but nonetheless went ahead with a similar form of ceremony. On May 9, 1978, Moro's family had issued this statement (in line with the wishes of Moro himself, as expressed in his letters): "No public demonstration or ceremony, or speech, no national mourning, no state funerals or medals dedicated to his memory. The family will remain in silence. History will be the judge of Aldo Moro's life and death."

The next day, May 10, 1978, a small private funeral was held for Moro at Torrita Tiberina, fifty kilometers north of Rome. The ceremony lasted some forty-five minutes and leading DC politician Amintore Fanfani attended after half an hour. The other "funeral" was a much more pompous affair, and is most famous for its depiction (with music) in Bellocchio's *Buongiorno, Notte*. This was also the last public appearance of Pope Paul VI (a key player during the 55 days) who entered the church carried on a chair.

The two "funerals" were a dramatic illustration of the deep fissures that had opened up between representatives of the state and Moro's family. By holding a huge, filmed ceremony in the center of Rome, the state was ignoring Moro's last wishes. Once again, this was a sign that Moro had become a "non-Moro" during his captivity—according to the leaders of the DC—and thus everything he had written in his many letters was to be ignored. As Cavallaro has written, many of the private memories around this event are deeply confused.[34] There is very little memory—given the privacy of the event—of the real funeral for Moro. It is the *fake* funeral— thanks largely to the mass media—that has become part of collective memory. This ambiguity is repeated in the final scene of *Buongiorno, Notte. Il caso Moro* had become a spectacle, a theatrical production in which various actors played out their roles. As Debord wrote, "The whole life of those societies in which modern conditions of production prevail presents itself as an immense accumulation of spectacles. All that once was directly lived has become mere representation."[35]

The whole Moro case is crisscrossed by truths and half-truths, and also by theatrical creations of false events. Thus, the Red Brigade hideout was flooded to attract the attention of the police, but the "flood" was a setup. And then there was the infamous false BR communiqué. These fakes sent out messages, especially to the BR itself, and have been analyzed time and time again, especially by the "dietrologists." A fake communiqué. A fake water leak. A fake séance. A fake funeral-ceremony (without a body) that looked more like a funeral than the real one. And then there were a series of twin events, negations of each other. The two seventh communiqués, the photo of Moro holding up a newspaper that asked if he was dead, the two funerals, the DC and PCI offices as fulcrum of the staging of the discovery of the body, the two Gradolis (a street name, and a town).

The dietrologists—of course—claim that the *whole Moro kidnapping and murder* was fake, a setup, a *mise-en-scene* (in collaboration with the state, which *directed*—quite literally—the whole operation). Many commentators have interpreted the false BR comuniqué as a mise-en-scene, as a way of preparing, or testing, public opinion about the real death of Moro. The state's often grotesque and botched attempts to "find" Moro, are also often interpreted in the same way. Meanwhile, the nondietrologists or "realists" argue that this whole event was "as it seemed" (with some mysterious elements—how could there not be, in Italy?). Then there are the two public sites linked most strongly to the tragedy: Via Fani and Via Caetani. At one site, five people were killed, while at the other a body was found, in a car.

In their subsequent activity, the Red Brigades themselves also made specific reference to the Moro case, sometimes as a warning to others. Roberto Peci, brother of BR supergrass Patrizio Peci, was kidnapped and held for fifty-four days in 1981, and murdered with eleven shots. Both these macabre statistics were reminders of the Moro case.

In general, the "55 days" was a creator of contradictory memories; as Gotor has written, they were "a paradoxical place of Italian memory because, on one hand, everyone is ready to affirm the symbolic and actual importance of those 55 days for the history of the republic, while on the other there is probably no other subject which provokes such differing interpretations or bitterly divisive arguments."[36] The history of Moro's kidnapping and death has become something else—*Il caso Moro*—"a literary-historical-cinematographic phenomenon."[37] In this way, as O'Leary argues, films such as *Buongiorno, Notte* are not about Moro at all, but studies of *Il caso Moro*. Or, to put it another way, "that which remains in terms of collective memory is not Aldo Moro but the Moro Case."[38]

Conclusions: The "Curse" of Via Fani and the Photos of Moro

I will still be here.

—Aldo Moro, in *Aldo Moro. Lettere della prigionia*

Many Romans believe that Via Fani, where the four members of Moro's "scorta" and his driver were killed, is a cursed place. It is said that plants fail to grow there, businesses close down, a tree died soon after the kidnapping. For Giuseppe D'Avanzo, "It is said that from that day onwards, in via Mario Fani on the corner of via Stresa, there is the long shadow of a curse. They say that nothing is as it should be . . . it seems that who lives there moves out, as soon as they can. The bar which used to be called 'Olivetti' became a restaurant 'La Camilluccia.' It has since closed down."[39]

Two photos of Moro were released by the Red Brigades during the 55 days. As Belpoliti has shown, these images have developed into a key part of the memory of that kidnapping. The Red Brigades managed the kidnapping of Moro as a kind of advertising campaign, within which the photos played a key role. As Belpoliti writes, "The Red Brigades sent out an advertising photograph."[40] This symbolic level had been understood, at the time, by the cartoonist Vincino who had produced a satirical version of the photo with this by-line (a joke that was never published): "Sorry, usually I dress Marzotto." But this is not the only way of reading this photo, which is "an historical document, for us, today."[41] In those photos, as Belpoliti argues, Moro seems to be looking at us, asking us questions with his eyes, haunting us with his fixed gaze. Moro still casts his shadow over contemporary Italy, just as the Moro Case is still discussed, written about, and commemorated to this day.

Conclusion

End of the Voyage

Facts, Memory, History

A common history and memory are a key part of recognising ourselves as
a nation.

—Gian Enrico Rusconi, "Se cessiamo di essere una nazione"

The problem for my generation and the next . . . is to integrate Proust with
the work of the historian. We are used to saying that on the one hand there is
memory and on the other there is history: but it isn't like that.

—Pierre Vidal-Naquet, "Assassins of Memory"

July 22 1944, July 22 2008

At dawn, on July 22, 1944, Dante Castellucci was shot dead by a firing squad made up of other partisans. In 2007, he had a plaque dedicated to his memory near his place of execution. The sixty-three years
in between these two events had been marked by a combination of lies,
silences, and attempts at rehabilitation. In 1963, the state awarded him a
medal accompanied by a false set of motivations. Most local historians had
ignored or glossed over the truth about Facio's death, until two books in
the 1990s opened up the case. Memory and history have come together in
this instance, although the case is still marked by omissions and mysteries.

Later that same morning in San Miniato, Tuscany, in 1944, an explosion
in the cathedral, packed with people, claimed fifty-five victims. Ever since
that moment, the town has been divided over the facts of the killings, and
consequently over how to remember them. These divisions were over both
history and memory. A plaque in 1954 laid out one version of the "facts,"
but failed to satisfy those who did not recognize those "facts" as true.
Numerous books, further plaques, and various commissions of inquiry all

looked into the case, and failed to agree. Documents were produced and reproduced. Insults flew. In 2008, a second plaque "corrected" the first one, overturning the facts but leaving memories not only divided but institutionally divided (see Figure 1.1). The debate continues over San Miniato, despite these attempts to close the gaps over the understanding of the past.

In one day, there were two tragic events. As on so many other occasions in contemporary Italian history, the past would not go away. The ghost of *Facio* and the ghosts of the victims of the Cathedral in San Miniato haunted many of those who survived for years. Some tried to forget, others falsified the past, many looked to create forms of memory or contest those forms that had already been created. The debates over the past and how to understand it were restless, ceaseless, and without closure. They were also deeply politicized and informed by short-term considerations and opportunism. For the historian, Italy provides a rich and complicated kaleidoscope of debates over the past. Our task is not to look for overarching theories or outcomes that suppress these competing visions and narratives, but to understand, explain, and study how the past has been experienced and narrated over time. This is the real stuff of history, and without these experiences, however contradictory or uncomfortable they may be, history makes no sense.

On July 22, 2008, the sixty-fourth anniversary of the deaths in the cathedral, the new plaque was finally unveiled in San Miniato. It was of identical size to the original and was placed at the same height, just to the right (Figure 9.1). A small group of politicians, residents, journalists, and some survivors attended the ceremony, which was followed by two speeches and a Mass in the cathedral, where a wreath was laid. The cathedral square itself resembled a concentration camp, complete with barbed wire and guard towers, scenery for a play by Jean-Paul Sartre being performed in that public space.

Nobody in San Miniato was under any illusions that the new plaque would end the controversy over the events of 1944. Mayor Angelo Frosini, in his speech, defended his decision to retain the original plaque. In doing so, he made explicit reference to the idea of "divided memory." The plaque was a part of history. "The two plaques are testimony," Frosini said, "to a divided memory which was generated by the painful experience of the massacre in the Cathedral and which will continue to exist . . . but above all they show us how difficult and complicated it is to create what is called public memory."

As everyone expected, including the mayor, the codification of divided memory in marble did not mark an end to the controversy over the Duomo killings. The run-up to the unveiling saw a series of debates in the press, with criticism from the left and some historians (who maintained that there were doubts about the facts of July 1944) and from the right (who wanted the old plaque removed, as well as criticized the text of the

Figure 9.1   San Miniato: The two plaques dedicated to the deaths of 1944. Council Building, 2008.

new plaque).[1] On the day of the unveiling ceremony, a pamphlet was distributed that consisted almost entirely of an attack on another pamphlet about the case. The authors claimed that "everyone has always known in San Miniato that the killings in the cathedral were caused by an American cannon and not by a German mine or artillery."[2] Paolo Pezzino, the leading expert on Nazi massacres of civilians in Italy, argued that there were ambiguities in the evidence concerning the U.S.-bomb version of events. He also accused the city's administration of hypocrisy. If they believed that the U.S. bomb had been responsible, then why not remove the original plaque?[3] As Frosini was well aware, the plaque was a contribution both to the end of divided memory *and* to its codification. Debates were far from over, but now both versions of the past had their own forms of public memory, after one "side" had been excluded in this way for over sixty years.

Those who called for the removal of the old plaque were also—explicitly or implicitly—criticizing the form of the new plaque. Scalfaro's new text only works in comparison with the old plaque. Alone, it would make no sense, and would not work as a commemorative plaque for the massacre by itself. Thus, if the original plaque were to be removed, this would create a need for a new "second" plaque. The plaques referred to each other, and were not entirely contradictory (e.g., both were antifascist). As so many still voiced their doubts about what had happened and who was responsible, surely the two plaques—with all their ambiguities—were perhaps the only way to capture this uncertainty about the past itself, and about the memories of that past.

Divided Memories and Shared Memories

The real conflict is not between memory and forgetting, but between different memories.

—Nicola Gallerano, *La verità della storia*

Does Italy need a shared history, and a shared memory, in order to survive as a country? For Pietro Scoppola, "Every time that the attention of the public looks back towards the past, arguments open up which often lead to the sad collapse of any sense of national identity."[4] According to Rusconi, "The most serious problem with contemporary Italian culture is the inability to narrate our national history in a convincing way, so as to create an identification with that history."[5] Others disagree, arguing, as Tommaso Detti and Marcello Flores have, that such consensus is impossible: "As historians and teachers of history we think that the search for truth, which is part of every historical reconstruction, can only come about through a plurality of interpretations which also take on board different and counter-posed memories."

During this journey into the past and how it has been understood in Italy, we have looked at the memory wars after 1918, with violent struggles over how to understand and remember World War I. In the 1920s, fascism succeeded in imposing its own version of history, but after July 1943, other memories were to reappear and seek their revenge. Since 1945, the battle over memory has been a constant feature of Italian politics and its historiography, from the women of Civitella, to the contested bomb of San Miniato, from the plaques for Pinelli and Calabresi. All of this has been the subject of debates and sometimes violence but also silences and forgetting. Material for the study of memory is all around us, in every nook and cranny of Italy's cities, villages, cemeteries, and ex-battlefields. Memory wars will continue, and it is only through studying and interpreting divisions over the past that we can fully understand the present. And we should always remember the words of George Orwell: "Who controls the past . . . controls the future, who controls the present, controls the past."[6]

Notes

Chapter 1

1. Rousso 1991, 3.
2. Stern 2006, 3–4.
3. But see the fundamental work of Tota, 2001, 2003, 2007.
4. Pezzino 1997, 223.
5. Clemente and Dei 2005.
6. Dogliani 2006, 269.
7. Brooke-Rose 1992.
8. Dogliani 2006, 274.
9. Ibid., 269.
10. Huyssen 2003, 9.
11. Passerini 1999, 289, 295.
12. Winter 2006, 5–6.
13. Detti and Flores 1999, 51.
14. Portelli 1997, viii.
15. Connerton 2008.
16. Pes 1998, 50–51.
17. Portelli 1985, 1991, 1997; Montaldi 1994; Ginzburg 1974, 1980; Levi 1993.
18. Portelli 1991, viii.
19. Portelli 2007.
20. Benjamin 1999, 247.
21. Cappelletto 2005, 113.
22. Tonkin 1992, 67.
23. Portelli 2006, 38.
24. Rusconi 1995; Pezzino 2002.
25. Paggi 1996.
26. Klinkhammer 2006, 195–202.
27. Clemente 2005, 49–61, 312–24.
28. Contini 2006.
29. Portelli 2003, 2005; Foot 2000.
30. Orlandi 2005, 134–62; Petrizzo 2005, 163–90.
31. Rousso 1991, 58
32. An estimated 3,500 people died in political and social violence in the 1919 to 1922 period that preceded the rise of the fascists to power in 1922. Gramsci, however, claimed that around 10,000 were killed. The majority of these victims

were thanks to fascist violence, although a not inconsiderable number of people were shot by the police and army and a smaller number (probably around 100) of fascists were killed by socialists or the forces of law and order. See Franzinelli 2004, Tasca 2002; Tobagi 1963; Gentile 1989, Albanese 2006.

33. Bermani 1997.
34. Presto 1995, 148–81; Ranzato 1994.
35. Crainz 1994, 1995.
36. Pavone 1991.
37. Gribaudi 2005.
38. Gundle 1996.
39. Habermas 1988, 46.
40. The original plan of this book included a chapter dedicated to memory wars in the northeast of Italy, which has had to be cut for reasons of space. The same fate befell a further chapter concerning memories of colonialism and the extra-European aspects of Italian historical memory and forgetting, which helps to explain the somewhat Eurocentric nature of this book.
41. Kertzer 2001, 408.
42. Samuel and Thompson 1990, 4.
43. Mason 1995, 274.
44. Ibid., 294.
45. Luzzatto 2004, 21–25.
46. Cited in Contini 1997, 257.
47. Galli della Loggia 2002, 14.
48. Tremlett 2006; Aguilar 2002; Deaglio and Cremagnani 2008.
49. Rousso 1991, 2002; Clifford 2008.
50. Judt 2002, 157–83.
51. McBride 2001.
52. Mazower 2000, 212–32; Van Boeschoten 2007, 39–48.
53. Herf 1999.
54. Rev 2004.
55. Bet-El, Ilana R. 2002.
56. Judt 2007, 803–31.
57. Levi 2000, cited in Jones 2003, 13.
58. Petrizzo 2005, 167.
59. Battini and Pezzino 1997, xix, 105–40; Portelli 2007, 185 n. 66; Klinkhammer 2006, 175 n. 39, 178–79.
60. Paoletti 2000; Biscarini and Lastraioli, 1991, 2001.
61. Orlandi and Petrizzo 2005.
62. Paggi 2004.
63. Ibid.
64. Morelli 2002.
65. Paggi 2004.
66. Contini 2004, 39–87.
67. Paoletti 1998, 14.

Chapter 2

1. Isola 1990, 171.
2. Winter 2006; Isnenghi 1997, 273–309; Leoni and Zadra 1986; Leed 1979; Fussell 1975.
3. Winter 1995, 51.
4. Mondini 2006, 273.
5. Winter 2006, 2.
6. Ibid., 288.
7. Sabbatucci 2002, 107–25.
8. Forcella and Monticone 1998; Procacci 1981; Isnenghi 1999.
9. Isnenghi 1967, 1970, Procacci 1999.
10. Galli della Loggia 1999; Satta 1980.
11. Malaparte 1995, 119.
12. Procacci 2002.
13. Mussolini 1920, cited in Luzzatto 1998, 3.
14. Mussolini 1932, cited in De Paolis 1975, 337.
15. Procacci 2005, 139.
16. Maione 1975, 62; Mantovani 1979, 138–42.
17. Fabi 2005.
18. De Micheli 1978, 124; Scalarini 1920.
19. Isola 1990.
20. Sabbatucci 1974, 78–86; Vivarelli 1991, 303–4; Tasca 1965, 19–20, 541–42; Gibelli 1998, 317–36.
21. Minniti 2000.
22. Isola 1990, 168.
23. Audoin-Rouzeau and Becker 2002, 175.
24. Mignemi 2006, 13–61, 95.
25. Ibid., 31.
26. Ibid., 35.
27. Colombara 1989, 168.
28. Moranino 1991.
29. Abse 1991, 133, 144.
30. Bocci 1991, 46.
31. Mignemi 2006, 18.
32. Mosse 1991; Mosse 1979; Vidotto 1998; Marchesoni 1998; Isola 1997.
33. Canal 1981.
34. Baldassari 2006.
35. Ibid., 14
36. Gibelli 1998, 332
37. Ibid., 335
38. Isola 1990, 180.
39. Meneghello 1998, 78.
40. Fabi 1998.

41. Gentile 1993, 1996; Mosse 1979, 1991.
42. Todero 2002, 8.
43. Audoin-Rouzeau and Becker 2002, 211.
44. Winter 1995.
45. Todero 2002, 10.
46. Bregantin 2006, 391.
47. Todero 2002, 27.
48. Fabi 2005, 24.
49. Isnenghi 1989, 382.
50. Todero 2002, 68.
51. Fabi 2005, 28.
52. Brice 1998; Tobia 1998; Dickie 1994; Cosgrove 1996.
53. Tobia 2002: 111.
54. Gentile 2005.
55. Cattaruzza 2007, 111.
56. Dogliani 1996, 384.
57. Fabi 2005, 25.
58. Ballinger 2002, 53–55.
59. Pupo 2006, 109–18; Borsatti 2003.

Chapter 3

1. Amendola, killed by fascists at Montecatini in 1926, had to "wait" for twenty-
   two years before his murderers were brought to trial and his body could be
   brought back in Italy. He is now buried in Naples.
2. Gentile 2005.
3. Isnenghi 1997, 311–30.
4. Berezin 2003; Suzzi Valli 2008.
5. Suzzi Valli 2008, 102–3. The official figure was a highly inflated 425 with this
   year-by-year breakdown: 1919, 4; 1920, 36; 1921, 232; 1922, 153. Franzinelli
   2004, 169.
6. Isnenghi 1997, 463.
7. *Enciclopedia Treccani 1934*, 457.
8. Baldassari 2006.
9. Gentile 1993, 1996, 41–42.
10. Suzzi Valli 2000, 139.
11. Suzzi Valli 2008, 112.
12. Miriam Serni Casalini, http://www.coopfirenze.it/informazioni/informatori/
    articoli/3742.
13. *Enciclopedia Treccani 1934*, 457.
14. Parsons 2007, 482.
15. Isnenghi 1996, 5.
16. Gentile 1989, 489–90.
17. Gribaudi 1987, 37, 150.
18. Passerini 2001, 114.

19. Cited in Tobagi 1973, 57.
20. Caretti 1997, 13.
21. Zaghi 1990, 432–46.
22. Sciascia 1989, 3.
23. Luzzatto 1998, 7.
24. Caretti 1994, 43.
25. Cited in Caretti 1994, 44.
26. Caretti 1994, 2004; Luzzatto 1998, 6–9.
27. Luzzatto 1998, 48.
28. Colombara 2009, 21.
29. Ibid., 18.
30. Franzinelli 1997, 225.
31. Colombara 2009, 17–48.
32. Franzinelli 2004, 169.
33. Cited in Tobia 2002, 215.
34. Tobia 2002, 217.
35. Isnenghi 1997, 463.
36. Crainz 2007, 74–110.
37. Dondi 2008, 148.
38. Crainz 2007, 110–12; Dondi 2008, 156–57.
39. Dondi 2008, 149.
40. Gentile 2007, 257.
41. Dickie 1997, 7–14.

Chapter 4

1. Di Sante 2001, 205.
2. Ibid., 206.
3. Collotti 2005, 9.
4. Galimi 2005, 225.
5. Ibid., 227.
6. Capogreco 2004; Galluccio 2002.
7. Finzi 2004.
8. Capogreco 1996, 2004; Grande 1997.
9. Grande 1998, 3.
10. Folino 1985; Capogreco 1989, 1996, 1998, 2001; Volpe 1997.
11. Capogreco 2001, 92.
12. Capogreco 1991.
13. Capogreco 2001.
14. Galluccio 2002, 120.
15. Capogreco 2003, 81.
16. Finzi 2004, 9.
17. Capogreco 2001, 78.
18. Kersevan 2003; Oliva 2007; Burgwyn 2006; Ferenc 2000; Gombač and Mattiussi 2004; Gobetti 2007; Rodogno 2003.

19. Judt 2007, 808.
20. Bernabei 1997.
21. Gilman 1980; Balestracci 2006, 63–79.
22. Bernabei 1997, 237.
23. Di Stasi, cited in Ugolini 2004, 154.
24. Ugolini 2004, 151–66.
25. Meletti 2008.
26. Bernabei 1985.
27. Bernabei 2001, 53–59; 1997, 230–32.
28. Balestracci 2006; Sponza 2000, 2005; Hickey and Smith, 1989; Bernabei 1997, 2001, 2002. Bernabei's two-part documentary was transmitted on Channel 4 in 1987. The second part was dedicated to the *Arandora Star, People to People: Dangerous Characters, Part 2, The Sinking of the Arandora Star.*
29. See the documentary *Arandora Star. La tragedia dimenticata* (NoiTV/ Fondazione Paolo Cresci, 2004). A play called *L'Arandora* was staged in 2006 in Prato (R. Caccavo, I. Danti, M. Magistrali, V. Receputi, F. Rotelli), and a musical play premiered in 2008, *Una storia da raccontare* (F. Festa con testi di M. Fois).
30. Venegoni 2005, 7.
31. Ibid.; Pfeifer 2004; Tibaldi 1994; Happacher 1979.
32. Villani 2006, 138–48.
33. Galluccio 2002, 90.
34. Franzinelli 2002, 239
35. Pantozzi 2002.
36. Some were also used for an RAI program and Web site, http://www.testimonianzedailager.rai.it. More testimonies were collected in conjunction with the legal processes and trials held in Verona.
37. Venegoni 2005.
38. Pfeifer 2005, 408–9.
39. Mezzalira and Romeo 2002; Franzinelli 2002, 234–69, 302–7; Galluccio 2002.
40. Franzinelli, 2002; Focardi and Klinkhammer 2008, Battini 2008; Borgomaneri 2006; Giustolisi 2004.
41. Giacomozzi 2007.
42. Ratti 2006.
43. The Alto Adige is the only region in Italy where antifascist monuments are routinely translated into German.
44. Giacomozzi 1995; Happacher 1979.
45. *Il segno della memoria* 1995.
46. Venegoni 2005, 19; Gibertoni and Melodi 1996, 96–119.
47. Mayda 2008, 421.
48. Horwitz 1994; Bensoussan, 2002.
49. A different version of these events attributes the "salvation" of the Gusen site to ex-deportees and their families from Bologna. See G. Serrani, "Le villette non soffocano la memoria," *La Repubblica*, January 27, 2007.
50. Mayda 2008, 421–22.
51. Aldebert 2002, 11

52. Restelli 2006.
53. http://www.gusen.org, http://www.mauthausen-memorial.at/
54. http://audiowalk.gusen.org
55. http://centrostudistreben.blogspot.com/search/label/Memorial
56. De Luna 2008a
57. De Luna was much more conciliatory toward the monument in a later article (2008b).
58. E. Ruffini, "Auschwitz. L'eredità di un memoriale da difendere," http://www .deportati.it/mem_auschw.html.
59. Clifford 2008a, 2008b; Gordon 2006.
60. Gordon 2006, 109–11.
61. Ibid., 109.

Chapter 5

1. Isnenghi 1989, 41–45.
2. Revelli 1966, 1993, 1997; Rigoni Stern 1993.
3. Rochat 1997.
4. Ibid., 374.
5. Ibid., 379; Giusti 2000.
6. Bedeschi 1963; Mondini, 2008.
7. Cited in Facchinetti 2006, 21.
8. Snowden 2002, 2008.
9. Gribaudi 2005, 26.
10. Gribaudi 2005, 532.
11. Bravo 2000, 268–82.
12. Ibid., 269.
13. Ibid., 269.
14. But for France, see the study by Virgili 2002.
15. The Imi were those Italian soldiers who refused to fight for the German or Italian fascist armies after August 9, 1943. Over 600,000 were held in camps in Germany and elsewhere for the duration of the war as a result of this refusal.
16. Contini 2007, 197.
17. Mangiafico and Gurrieri 1991.
18. Gribaudi 2005, 625.
19. Portelli 2006, 34; Forgacs 2005, 19–20.
20. Gribaudi 2005, 385.
21. Rosati 1990.
22. Portelli 2007, 170.
23. Gribaudi *Memorie private*, 20.
24. Ibid.
25. Gribaudi 2005; Burdi 2000–2001.
26. Gribaudi 2005, 33.
27. Forgacs 2005, 18–24.
28. Marucci 2004; Negri 2004.

29. Boneschi 2004, 143.
30. Portelli 2006, 32.
31. Ibid., 38.
32. Portelli 2007, 171; 2003; Forgacs 2003, 2005; De Simone 1993, 2007.
33. Forgacs 2005, 16–17.
34. But see the account of the visit and the photo in De Simone 1993, 253–55.
35. Cited in Vergani 2004, 113.
36. Marucci 2004, 51–52.
37. Gioannini and Massobrio 2007; Patricelli 2007; Bonacina 2005; Rastelli 1994, 2000; Ferrara and Stampacchia 2004; Versolato 2001; Passarin and Sandrini 1995; Gentiloni, Silveri, and Carli 2007. For the bombing of Foggia in 1943 that left over 20,000 civilians dead, see Cicolella 1983; Odorico Tempesta 1995; Guerrieri 1996; De Santis 2007.
38. Grayling 2006; Friedrich 2006.
39. Forgacs 2005, 20.
40. Santarelli 2004, 295.
41. Finaldi 2002.
42. Cited in Pavone 2008, 93.
43. Satta 2003, 19.
44. Camera dei Deputati 1998, 29.
45. Pavone 1991, 2008.
46. Aga Rossi 1993, 157.
47. Galli della Loggia 1996; Schreiber 1992.
48. Altman 1970, 9.
49. Bloch 1970, 167.
50. Quazza 1979, 15.
51. Franzinelli 1997, 244
52. Ibid., 257.
53. Pavone 1991.
54. Ibid., 36.
55. De Felice 1995; Bersellini 1998.
56. Rusconi 2004; Rochat 2006.
57. Rusconi 2004; Salotti 2001; Romano 2001; Rochat 2006, 7.
58. Rochat 2006, 6.
59. Ibid., 10–11.
60. Heer 2008.
61. Rusconi 2004, xii–xiii.
62. Galli della Loggia 1996; Pavone 1991; De Felice 1995.
63. Ciampi 2001, 7.
64. Caruso 2000.
65. Pirani 1999; Ghilardini 1960, 5; Camera dei Deputati 1998.
66. Gallotta 2005, 101–2.
67. Moscardelli 1945; Ghilardini 1960; Giraudi 1982; Colombari 1990; Sfiligoi 1993; Rochat and Venturi 1993; Monni 2000; Endrizzi 2000.
68. Santomassimo 2001.

69. Ponzani 2003, 2, 11.
70. Battaglia 1964, 109.
71. Rodogno 2003.
72. Cited in Giraudi 1982, 187.
73. Ghirlardini 1960.
74. Speech in Verona on October 23, 1966, inauguration of the *Monumento ai novemila Caduti della Divisione Acqui.*
75. Taviani 1982, 5–7.
76. *Ai soldati della Divisione Acqui. Marinai e Finanzieri di presidio nell'Isola/ Offertisi volontariamente in fraterna comunanza con I patrioti Elleni nella lotta contro gli agressori tedeschi/Caduti dal 15 al 26 settembre 1943/In combattimento Uf. 68, sottouff e soldati 1250/Fucilati Uff. 342 Sottouff e soldati – 6000/ Dispersi in mare, 3000/L'Italia riconoscente.*
77. Francini 2006, 7–12.
78. Rochat 2006, 8–9.
79. Klinkhammer 2008, 185.
80. Ibid., 188
81. Ghilardini 1960, 5.
82. Cited in Klinkhammer 2008, 187.
83. Cited in ibid., 186.
84. Triarius 1945, 36.
85. Filippini 2004.
86. Paoletti 2003.
87. Venturi's book was in turn based to some extent on Ghilardini 1952.

Chapter 6

* The literature about massacres in Italy is vast, with a large number of texts being produced over the last twenty years. Here is a selection of texts that I have used in this work (with a particular focus on memory): Klinkhammer 2006; Contini 2007: Pezzino 2007; Baldissara and Pezzino 2005; Schreiber 2000, 2004; Gribaudi, ed., 2003; Fulvetti and Pelini, eds., 2006; Paggi, ed., 1996; Pezzino 1997 (new edition 2007); Portelli 1999; Paggi, ed., 1997; Paggi, ed., 1999; Forti 1998; Cappelletto 2005; De Simonis 2004; Matta, ed., 1996; Battini and Pezzino 1997; Clemente and Dei 2005; Todorov 2003; Rovatti 2004.
1. Contini 2001.
2. Clemente and Dei 2005, 9–49, 49–60; Paggi 1996, 71–72.
3. Contini 2001.
4. However, the first public airing of these narratives—which also contributed to divisions—was carried out with the clear intent to undermine resistance myths from the right, above all with the journalistic work of Pisanò in the 1960s.
5. Clemente 2005.
6. Todorov 1995.

7. Portelli 1996, 101.
8. Paggi 1996, 74; Contini 1987, 251; Balò Valli 1994.
9. Paggi 1996, 60, 72; Contini 1987, 251.
10. Paggi 1996, 64–74; Portelli 1997, 123–24.
11. Bentivegna 1996, 2006.
12. The board was placed by the motorway in February 1995.
13. Pezzino 2003, 34–85; 2009; Rovatti 2004, 19–47; Cappelletto 2005, 101.
14. Cappelletto 2005, 16.
15. Paoletti 1998, 265–85.
16. Cipollini 2006.
17. De Simonis 2004, 142; Cipollini and Guidi 1996, 69–81.
18. Residori 2007.
19. Contini 2007b, 42.
20. Cappelletto 2005, 16.
21. Ibid., 104–6.
22. Battini and Pezzino 1997; Klinkhammer 2006.
23. Contini 2007b, 42.
24. Contini 2004b, 6.
25. Rovatti 2004, 117–21.
26. Law 39 (August 12,1991) set up the *Comitato per le Onoranze ai Martiri di Sant'Anna di Stazzema* (Committee for the Honoring of the Martyrs of Sant'Anna di Stazzema) and made possible the opening of a *Museo Storico della Resistenza* (Resistance Historical Museum) in the old elementary school building.
27. Cappelletto 2003, 7; 2005, 112. Sant'Anna had also been the subject (or the object) of specifically anti-resistance narratives in the 1960s. Giorgio Pisanò, the neofascist journalist and historian, visited Sant'Anna, carrying out interviews that he later used to write a series of well-publicized articles in *Gente* (1960, numbers 34–51) magazine as well as a chapter of his book *Sangue chiama sangue* (1964, 123–37). Pisanò argued that partisans had provoked the massacre with the manifesto pinned up in place of the Nazi evacuation order. After these articles appeared, according to Cappelletto, the villagers stopped giving interviews. Cappelletto 2005, 113.
28. Contini 2004b, 8; Rovatti 2004, 111–14.
29. Rovatti 2004, 138.
30. Leopolda Bertolucci, cited in Rovatti 2004, 175.
31. Cipollini 2003.
32. Palla 2003; *La Domenica degli italiani*, December 9, 1945.
33. Calamandrei, cited in Cipollini 1996, 74.
34. Mancini 2003, 193–99.
35. Pezzino 1997, 2007; Battini and Pezzino 1997, 87–104.
36. Cited in Pezzino 2007, 9.
37. Ibid., 130.
38. Ibid., 15.
39. Ibid., 79

40. Bondani and Bondani 1992; Pezzino 2007, 50–56, 101–5.
41. Pezzino 2007, 164.
42. http://ius.regione.toscana.it/memorie_del_900/eccidi_nazifascisti/geografia/
715.htm (accessed January 8, 2009).
43. Gribaudi 1999, 139; Rossi-Doria 2000; Pezzino 2007, 131–32; Paggi 1996,
69–71; Gribaudi 2005.
44. Paggi 1996, 70.
45. A number of the other names do not tally with other lists, such as that in Pezzino 2007, 283–85. The list in Bondani and Bondani 1992, 78–79, makes no
distinctions between partisans and others. The total of sixty-six names on the
plaques is also anomalous.
46. Contini 1997, 14.
47. De Grazia and Paggi 1991, 153–69; Bilenchi 1984; Paggi 1996, 60–61; De Grazia 1992, 286–88.
48. Passerini 1996, 2003.
49. Paggi 1996, 12.
50. Ibid.
51. Ibid., 5, 47, 52–53.
52. Contini 1987, 81.
53. Cappelletto 2003, 9
54. Von Boeschoten 2007, 47–48.
55. Pezzino 2007, 277.
56. Contini 1987, 18.
57. Von Boeschoten 2007, 48.
58. Portelli 2003, 15.
59. Portelli 1999, 18.
60. Portelli 2008.
61. Orlandi 2005; Petrizzo 2005.
62. Von Boeschoten 2007, 47.
63. Cappelletto 2005, 9.
64. Contini 2007b, 48–52; 2006, 315–44.
65. Von Boeschoten 2007, 40.
66. Pezzino 2007, 229
67. Tonkin 1992, cited in Capelletto 2005, 108.

Chapter 7

1. Dogliani 1995, 21–36, 97; Gundle 2000, 120.
2. Cooke 2005, 126.
3. Ibid., 127.
4. Germinario 1999, 2005.
5. Dogliani 1995, 28.
6. Gundle 2000, 120.
7. Dogliani 2005; Gundle 2000, 119–20.
8. Dogliani 2006, 97.

9. Nizza 1995, 12.
10. Colombara 2009, 162.
11. Ibid., 190.
12. Cooke 2007.
13. Gundle 2000, 125, 127.
14. Cooke 1998, 2005, 120–31; Scoppola 1995; Rusconi 1995; Focardi 2005; Luzzatto 2004; Chiari 2005; Cavaglio 2005; Ponzani 2004; Santomassimo 2001; Peli 2004; Pezzino 2005; Peli 2006.
15. Cited in Focardi 2005, 30.
16. Gundle 2000, 114.
17. Cooke 2000, 161–73.
18. Focardi 2005, 49.
19. Cooke 2006 175–80.
20. Gundle 2000, 127.
21. Paggi 1996b, 109–10.
22. Passerini 1999, 288–96.
23. Colombara 1999, 17.
24. There was a long-running debate about the legal and political status of those who had fought for the RSI, and attempts to pass laws awarding such status failed in 2005 and 2006. In 2008, a similar law was presented to parliament again, but then withdrawn under political pressure.
25. Vivarelli 2000.
26. Ganapini 2000, 12.
27. Vivarelli 2000, 104.
28. Ganapini 2000, 2.
29. Ganapini 2002; Annali della Fondazione L. Micheletti 1986; Bugiardini 2006.
30. Fondazione della RSI 2003; Germinario 2008.
31. Santomassimo 2001; Minucci 2000.
32. Dondi 2004, 2007; Franzinelli 1995.
33. Passerini 1999, 295.
34. Storchi 2005; Pansa 2003; Simonazzi 2004; Pansa 2005, 430–43.
35. Sessi 2000.
36. Dondi 2004, 199–227.
37. Ibid., 199.
38. Dondi 2007, 233; for Porzus, see Dondi 2004, 122–31; Gervasutti 2002; Padoan 1965.
39. Dondi 2004, 377.
40. Ibid., 377–78.
41. Capogreco 2007, 6.
42. Pezzino 2007.
43. Contini 2001, 42.
44. Capogreco 2008, 185.
45. Ibid., 181.
46. Contini 2006, 327–29.
47. Contini 2007, 49–50.

48. Seghettini 2006, 73.
49. Ricci 1978, but see Capogreco 2007, 145–46, and Vietti 1980.
50. Ranieri 2007.
51. Capogreco 2007, 155; see also Guccini and Machiavelli 2007.
52. Pavone 1991, 413–514; 1999; Dondi 1999; Crainz 1992, 1994, 1995, 1997, 2001, 2007; Storchi 1992–93, 1995, 1998; Bertucelli 1999; Alessandrini 1999; Fantozzi 1990; Gorrieri 2005; Onofri 2007; Peli 2006.
53. Ginsborg 1990, 68; Bocca 1977, 339.
54. Bertucelli 1999, 293.
55. Crainz 1992, 1995.
56. "Bruno," cited in Storchi 2001.
57. Dondi 2008, 91–183.
58. Pavone 1991a, 31.
59. De Luna 2006, 174–75.
60. http://www.italia-rsi.org/arpabirmana/databasecadutirsi.htm (accessed January 28, 2009).
61. Isnenghi 1990, 234.
62. Associazione Nazionale Famiglie Caduti e Dispersi delle Repubblica Sociale Italiana, 1990 (first published in 1960). This, of course, was a direct response to the highly successful edition of last letters by partisans published by Einaudi in the 1950s, Malvezzi and Pirelli in 1952, and Franzinelli in 2005.
63. Residori 2007.
64. Dondi 2008, 32.
65. Ranzato 1997.
66. As with many of the other massacres, there are different versions of the number of the victims for Grugliasco.
67. Maida 2002, 198.
68. "Istanza alla Presidenza della Repubblica di concessione di Medaglia al merito civile alle citta' di Grugliasco e Collegno Provincia di Torino. per l'eccidio dei 67 martiri tra il 29 e il 30 aprile 1945 da parte di una divisione Tedesca in ritirata."
69. Dondi 2008, 99.
70. Baldissara 2003.
71. Maida 2002, 199.
72. Ibid., 185.
73. Ibid., 201.
74. Ibid.
75. Ruffini 2008, 149
76. Bendotti 2008, 93–133.
77. Morgan 2000, 2002; Villani 1994; Dondi 2008, 143–44; Crainz 2007, 94–95; Croci 1999.
78. Once again, these figures differ depending on which source you use.
79. Dondi 2008, 143
80. Morgan 2000, 147.
81. Dondi 2008, 144.
82. Ibid.

83. Croci 1999, 10–11.
84. Morgan 2002, 49.
85. Ibid., 8.
86. A further official plaque was put up in the local cemetery in 2000: *Comune di Schio. Questo cimitero accolse e diede sepoltura alle 54 vittime dell'eccidio di Schio avvenuto nella notte del 6–7 luglio 1945.*
87. Pansa 2003, 95–99.
88. Dondi 1990, 1996; Isnenghi 1994, 1994, 366–70; De Luna 2006b; Ventresca 2006.
89. Paggi, writing about his mother, 1996, 53.
90. Luzzatto 1998.
91. Pansa 2004, 2005, 2006, 2007.
92. Isnenghi 1990, 233.
93. Ibid., 231–44.
94. Ibid., 244.
95. Pansa 2003, 22.
96. Ibid., ix.
97. Gallerano 1999, 39.
98. Quazza 1967, vii.
99. Pansa 2007.
100. Storchi 2007, 246; D'Orsi 2006; De Luna 2006; Luzzatto 2008, 105–7.

Chapter 8

1. Giannuli 2008; Boatti 1999; *La strage di stato.*
2. Sofri 2008.
3. Scaramucci 1982.
4. *L'Unità*, December 15, 1979.
5. Van Hass 1998, 1, 3.
6. Sofri 1993; Ginzburg 1991; Cazzullo 2004; Marino 1992; Capra 1990; Sofri 2009.
7. *Corriere della Sera*, November 19, 1987.
8. *Corriere della Sera*, December 21, 1977.
9. *Corriere della Sera*, November 19, 1987.
10. There was talk of removing it again in 1988 and in 1989, when a threat from the police union led to an all-daylong "guarding" of the plaque.
11. *Il Giornale*, October 26, 1994; Giannattasio 1994.
12. *Il Giornale*, October 26, 1994; *Corriere della Sera*, November 1, 1989.
13. Oliva 1987, 10.
14. Bull 2007.
15. Milani 1994, 17–22.
16. Nora 1984; Isnenghi 1997; Palumbo 1997.
17. Cerami 1994, 85.
18. Bobbio 1980, 202.
19. Revelli 1996, 22.

20. There are signs that some of these tensions are also coming to an end. In May 2009 the wives of Luigi Calabresi and Giuseppe Pinelli met (for the first time) at a ceremony for the victims of terrorism hosted by the Italian president, Giorgio Napolitano. This symbolic moment was widely interpreted as a sign that the conflicts of the 1970s were "closed."

21. Controversy also reigns about exactly how many days Moro was held prisoner for, with many fixing the total at fifty-four days, including the Brigatisti themselves who killed Roberto Peci after fifty-four days in a macabre "homage" to the Moro case.

22. "The Moro affair offers one of the most extensive and diverse samples of conspiracy literature, and the basic facts of the events remain hugely controversial to this day. Indeed it is no coincidence that it was only shortly after the haunting 55-day kidnapping and assassination that the term *dietrologia* was coined." Johnson 2008a; see also Johnson 2008b.

23. Gotor 2008, 2009.

24. Belpoliti 2001, 3–51; 2007.

25. Cavallaro 2007.

26. Ibid., 152–58.

27. Ibid., 157.

28. Luzzatto 2007, 402–3.

29. Ibid., 402.

30. Gotor 2008, 315–16.

31. Braghetti and Tavella 2003; Mosca and Rossanda 1994; Morucci 1994; Gallinari 2008.

32. O'Leary 2008, 37.

33. Cavallaro 2007, 161–66.

34. Cavallaro 2007, 79–84, 137–39.

35. Debord 1995, 12.

36. Gotor 2008, xii.

37. Ibid., xiv.

38. Santomassimo 2004, 236.

39. D'Avanzo 2008.

40. Belpoliti 2008, 6.

41. Ibid., 30.

Conclusion

1. Baroni 2008; *Il Tirreno*, July 19, 2008; July 20, 2008; July 22,2008; *Nazione Pontedera*, July 19, 2008.

2. Lastraioli and Biscarini 2007.

3. *Corriere Fiorentino*, July 23, 2008.

4. Cited in Di Nucci and Galli della Loggia 2002, 13–14.

5. Rusconi 1993, 14.

6. Orwell 1989, 37.

References

Abse, T. 1991. *Sovversivi e fascisti a Livorno. Lotta politica e sociale (1918–1922)*. Milan: FrancoAngeli.

———. 2007. The Moro Affair: Interpretations and Consequences. In *Assassinations and murder in modern Italy: Transformations in society and culture*, ed. S. Gundle and L. Rinaldi, 89–100. New York: Palgrave.

Aga Rossi, E. 1993. *Una nazione allo sbando. L'armistizio italiano del settembre 1943*. Bologna: Il Mulino.

Aguilar, P. 2002. *Memory and amnesia: The Role of the Spanish Civil War in the Transition to Democracy*. Oxford: Berghahn.

Albanese, G. 2006. *La marcia su Roma*. Bari: Laterza.

Aldebert, B. 2002. *Il campo di sterminio di Gusen II. Dall'orrore della morte al dolore del ricordo*. Milan: Selene edizioni.

Alessandrini, L. 1999. The option of violence—partisan activity in the Bologna area 1945–1948. In *After the war. Violence, justice, continuity and renewal in Italian society*, ed. J. Dunnage, 59–74. Hull: Troubadour.

Altman, G. 1970. Preface. In *La strana disfatta. Testimonianza scritta nel 1940*, by M. Bloch. Naples: Guida.

Arendt, H. 1999. *Le origini del totalitarianism*. Turin: Edizioni di Comunità.

Associazione Nazionale Famiglie Caduti e Dispersi delle Repubblica Sociale Italiana. 1990. *Lettere di caduti della Repubblica sociale italiana*. Castelbolognese: Editrice L'Ultima Crociata.

Audoin-Rouzeau, S., and A. Becker. 2002. *La violenza, la crociata, il lutto. La Grande Guerra e la storia del Novecento*. Turin: Einaudi.

Baldassari, M. 2006. Percorsi di memoria: la guerra in piazza. Storie in corso. Workshop nazionale dottorandi in Storia contemporanea. Unpublished paper. http://www.sissco.it/fileadmin/user_upload/Attivita/Convegni/StorieInCorsoI/paper_Baldassari.pdf (accessed June 4, 2007).

Baldissara, L. 2003. Sissco, Annale, IV, review of Bruno Maida. http://www.sissco.it.

Baldissara, L., and P. Pezzino, 2004. *Crimini e memorie di guerra. Violenze contro le popolazioni e politiche del ricordo*. Naples: L'ancora del mediterraneo.

———, eds. 2005. *Giudicare e punire. I processi per crimini di guerra tra diritto e politica, l'ancora del mediterraneo*. Naples: L'ancora del mediterraneo.

Balestracci, M. S. 2006. *Arandora Star—una tragedia dimenticata*. Parma: Millenium editrice.

———. 2008. *Arandora Star. Dall'oblio alla memoria*. Parma: Monte Università Parma.

Ballinger, P. 2002. *History in exile: Memory and identity at the borders of the Balkans.* Princeton: Princeton University Press.

Ballini, P. L. 2004. Una riflessione retrospettiva sul caso di San Miniato. In *L'eccidio del Duomo di San Miniato. La memoria e la ricerca storica 1944–2004.*, ed. L. Paggi, 130–40. San Miniato: Comune di San Miniato.

Balò Valli, I., ed. 1994. *Giugno 1944. Civitella racconta.* Cortona: Editrice grafica L'Etruria.

Barbiano di Belgiojoso, L. 1996. *Notte, nebbia. Racconto di Gusen. Con venti disegni dell'autore.* Parma: Ugo Guanda Editore in Parma.

Baroni, C. 2008. Finalmente la lapide ristabilisce la verità. *La Nazione,* July 16.

Battaglia, R. 1964. *Storia della resistenza Italiana.* Turin: Einaudi.

Battini, M. 2008. *Peccati di memoria. La mancata Norimberga italiana.* Bari: Laterza.

Battini, M., and Pezzino, P. 1997. *Guerra ai civili. Occupazione tedesca e politica del massacro. Toscana 1944.* Venice: Marsilio.

Bedeschi, G. 1963. *Centomila gavette di ghiaccio.* Milan: Mursia.

Belardelli, G. 2005. L'8 settembre tragedia o festa. *Corriere della Sera,* September 13.

Belardelli, G., L. Cafagna, E. Galli della Loggia, and G. Sabbatucci. 1999. *Miti e storia dell'Italia unita.* Bologna: Il Mulino.

Bellocchio, M. 2003. *Buongiorno, Notte.* Feature film.

Belpoliti, M. 2001. *Settanta.* Turin: Einaudi.

———. 2007. Caso Moro. In *Annisettanta,* ed. M. Belpoliti, G. Canova, and S. Chiodi, 93–107. Milan: Skira.

———. 2008. *La foto di Moro.* Rome: Nottetempo.

Benassi, R. 2003. *Testimonianze dai lager.* Bolzano and Nova Milanese: Citta di Bolzano, Archivio Storico, Comune di Nova Milanese, Assessorato Cultura.

Bendotti, A. 2008. Come un lavoro da fare. Il Mojcano nella guerra civile in alta val Seriana. In *Gli ultimi fuochi. 28 aprile 1945, a Rovetta,* by A. Bendotti and E. Ruffini, 11–133. Bergamo: Il filo di arianna.

Benjamin, W. 1999. *Illuminations.* London: Pimlico.

Bensoussan, G. 2002. *L'eredità di Auschwitz. Come ricordare?* Turin: Einaudi.

Bentivegna, R. 1996. *Operazione via Rasella. Verità e menzogna: i protagonisti raccontano.* Rome: Riuniti.

———. 2006. *Via Rasella. La storia mistificata. Carteggio con Bruno Vespa.* Rome: Manifestolibri.

Berezin, M. 2003. Martiri del fascismo. In *Dizionario del fascismo,* ed. S. Luzzatto and V. De Grazia, 101–2. Turin: Einaudi.

Bermani, C. 1997. *Il nemico interno. Guerra civile e lotte di classe in Italia (1943–1976).* Rome: Odradek.

Bernabei, A. 1985. Tanti nemici, poco onore. *Panorama,* July 14.

———. 1997. *Esuli ed emigrati italiani nel Regno Unito. 1920–1940.* Milan: Mursia.

———. 2001. *"A gold watch is missing": Italian Scottish identities and connections.* Vol. 9. Edinburgh: Italian Cultural Institute.

———. 2002. L'isola, la tomba e l'italiano. *Diario,* April 11.

Bersellini, G. 1998. *Il riscatto: 8 settembre–25 aprile: le tesi di Renzo De Felice, Salò, la Resistenza, l'identità della nazione.* Milan: FrancoAngeli.

Bertucelli, L., et al. 1999. *L'invenzione dell'Emilia Rossa. La memoria della guerra e la costruzione di un'identità regionale (1943–1960)*. In *Le memorie della Repubblica*, ed. L. Paggi, 269–324. Florence: La Nuova Italia.

Bet-El., Ilana R. 2002. Unimagined communities: The power of memory and the conflict in the former Yugoslavia. In *Memory and Power in Post-War Europe. Studies in the Presence of the Past*, ed. J. Müller, 206–22. Cambridge: Cambridge University Press.

Bilenchi, R. 1946. La strage di Civitella. *Società* 2 (7–8): 787–819.

———. 1984. *Cronache degli anni nere*. Rome: Editori Riuniti.

Biscarini, C., and G. Lastraioli. 1991. *Arno-Stellung. La quarantena degli Alleati davanti a Empoli 22 luglio- 2 settembre 1944*. Empoli: BSE.

Boatti, G. 1998. Tra il prima e il dopo. Continuità e rottura degli anni della strategia della tensione con alcuni degli aspetti permanenti della storia unitaria italiana. Unpublished paper.

———. 1999. *Piazza Fontana. 12 dicembre 1969. Il giorno della innocenza perduta*. Turin: Einaudi.

Bobbio, N. 1980. La democrazia e il potere invisibile. *Rivista italiana di scienza politica* 2: 181–203.

Bocca, G. 1977. *La Repubblica di Mussolini*. Bari: Laterza

Bocchetta, V. 2003. *Testimonianze dai lager*. Bolzano: Citta di Bolzano, Archivio Storico.

Bocci, M. 1991. *La Casa del Popolo alla Fontana*. Milan: NED.

Bodei, R. 1996. *Il Noi diviso. Ethos e idee dell'Italia repubblicana*. Turin: Einaudi.

Bonacina, G. 2005. *Obiettivo: Italia. I bombardamenti aerei delle città italiane dal 1940 al 1945*. Milan: Mursia.

Bondani, V., and Vito Bondani, eds. 1992. *Mazzetto Rafanelli*. Livorno: Casa editrice San Benedetto.

Boneschi, M. 2004. Quando suonava la sirena. Le bombe nella memoria dei milanesi. In *Bombe sulla città, Milano in guerra 1942–1944*, ed. R. A. Marrucci, 143–51. Milan: Skira.

Borgomaneri, L., ed. 2006. *Crimini di guerra: il mito del bravo italiano tra repressione del ribellismo e guerra ai civili nei territori occupati*. Milan: Guerini e associati.

Borsatti, U. 2003. *Trieste 1953. I fatti di Novembre*. Trieste: Lint.

Braghetti, A. L., and P. Tavella. 2003. *Il Prigioniero*. Milan: Feltrinelli.

Bravo, A. 2000. Resistenza civile. In *Dizionario della Resistenza, vol 1.*, ed. E. Collotti et al., 268–82. Turin: Einaudi.

Bregantin, L. 2006. Culto dei caduti e luoghi di riposo nell'arco alpino. In *Der Erste Weltkrieg im Alpenraum. Erfahrung Deutung, Erinnerung. La Grande Guerra nell'arco alpino. Esperienze e memoria*, ed. H. Kuprian and O. Überegger, 383–96. Innsbruck: Universitätsverlag Wagner.

Brice, C. 1998. *Monumentalité publique et politique à Rome: le Vittoriano*. Rome: École Française de Rome.

Brooke-Rose, C. 1992. Palimpsest history. In *Umberto Eco. Interpretation and Over-Interpretation*, ed. Stefano Collini, 125–38. Cambridge: Cambridge University Press.

Bugiardini, S., ed. 2006. *Violenza, tragedia e memoria della Repubblica sociale italiana*. Rome: Carocci.

Bull, Anna Cento. 2007. *Italian neo-fascism: The strategy of tension and the politics of non-reconciliation*. Oxford: Berghahn Books.

Burdi, F. 2000–2001. *Storia e memoria della guerra. Il fronte di Cassino 1943–1944*. Unpublished undergraduate thesis, Facoltà di Sociologia, Università di Napoli "Federico II."

Burgwyn, J. 2006. *L'impero sull'adriatico. Mussolini e la conquista della Jugoslavia 1941–1943*. Gorizia: L. E. Goriziana.

Calabresi, M. 2007. *Spingendo la notte più in la*. Milan: Mondadori.

Calvino, I. 1956. *The path to the nest of spiders*. London: Collins.

———. 2002. *Il sentiero dei nidi di ragno*. Turin: Einaudi.

Camera dei Deputati. 1998. *55 anniversario della resistenza della Divisione Acqui a Cefalonia 1943–1988)*. Rome: Camera dei Deputati.

Canal, C. 1982. La retorica della morte. I monumenti ai caduti della Grande Guerra. *Rivista di Storia Contemporanea* 4: 659–69.

Canestrari, A. 2003. *Testimonianze dai lager*. Bolzano: Citta di Bolzano, Archivio Storico.

Capogreco, C. S. 1991. I campi di internamento fascisti per gli ebrei 1940–1943. *Storia Contemporanea* 22: 663–82.

———. 1993. L'internamento degli ebrei stranieri ed apolidi dal 1940 al 1943: il caso Ferramonti-Tarsia. In *Italia Judaica. Gli ebrei nell'Italia unita 1870–1945*. Rome: Ministero dei beni culturali e ambientali.

———. 1996a. Il campo di concentramento di Ferramonti. In *Un percorso della memoria. Guida ai luoghi della violenza nazista e fascista in Italia*, ed. T. Matta, 37–55. Milan: Electa.

———. 1996b. Per una storia civile dell'internamento fascista (1940–1943). In *Italia 1939–1945. Storia e memoria*, ed. A. L. Carlotti, 527–80. Milan: Vita e pensiero.

———. 1998. *Renicci. Un campo di concentramento in riva al Tevere 1942–43*. Cosenza: Fondazione Ferramonti.

———. 2001a. Una storia rimossa dell'Italia fascista: l'internamento civile nell'Italia fascista (1940–1943). *Studi Storici* 42: 203–30.

———. 2001b. L'entrata in guerra dell'Italia e l'internamento degli ebrei stranieri: il campo di Ferramonti. In *I campi di concentramento in Italia. Dall'internamento alla deportazione 1940–1945*, ed. C. Di Sante, 83–94. Milan: FrancoAngeli.

———. 2003. *Renicci. Un campo di concentramento in riva al Tevere*. Milan: Mursia.

———. 2004. *I campi del duce: l'internamento civile nell'Italia fascista, 1940–1943*. Turin: Einaudi.

———. 2007. *Il piombo e l'argento. La vera storia del partigiano Facio*. Rome: Donzelli.

———. 2008. Il caso Facio e il rovescio della medaglia. In *Vero e falso. L'uso politico della storia*, ed. M. Caffiero and M. Procaccia, 179–95. Rome: Donzelli.

Cappelletto, F. 2005. Public memories and personal stories: Recalling the Nazifascist massacres. In *Memory and World War II: An ethnographic approach*, ed. F. Cappelletto, 101–30. Oxford: Berg.

Capra, G. 1990. *Mio marito il commisario Calabresi. Il diario segreto della moglia dopo 17 anni di silenzio.* Ed. L. Garibaldi. Turin: Ediz. Paolini.

Caretti, S. 1997. Matteotti. In *I luoghi della memoria. Personaggi e date dell'Italia unita,* ed. M. Isnenghi, 187–206. Bari: Laterza.

———. 1994. *Matteotti. Il mito.* Casciana Terme, Pisa: Nistri-Lischi.

———. 2004. *Il delitto Matteotti. Storia e memoria.* Manduria-Bari-Rome: Piero Lacaita Editore.

Caruso, A. 2000. *Italiani dovete morire: Cefalonia, settembre 1943: il massacro della divisione Acqui da parte dei tedeschi. Un'epopea di eroi dimenticati.* Milan: Longanesi.

Cattaruzza, M. 2007. *L'Italia e il confine orientale: 1866–2006.* Bologna: Il Mulino.

Cavaglion, A. 2005. *La resistenza spiegata a mia figlia.* Naples: L'ancora del mediterraneo.

Cavallaro, F. 2007. *Hanno rapito Moro. Memorie a confronto.* Bologna: Bononia University Press.

Cazzullo, A. 2004. *Il caso Sofri. Dalla condanna alla "tregua civile."* Milan: Mondadori.

Celestini, A. 2005. *Radio Clandestina. Memoria della Fosse Ardeatine.* Rome: Donzelli.

Cerami, V. 1994. In *Le ragioni della memoria. Interventi e riflessioni a vent'anni dalla strage di piazza della Loggia.* Brescia: Grafo.

Chiarini, R. 2005. *25 aprile. La competizione politica sulla memoria.* Venice: Marsilio.

Ciampi, Carlo Azeglio. 2001. Discorso a Cefalonia, 1.3.2001. *Diario della Settimana,* May 4.

Cicolella, L. 1983. *E la morte venne dal cielo. Foggia 1943. Cronistoria di cento giorni di guerra.* Foggia: Bastogi.

Cipollini, G. 1996. Sant'Anna di Stazzema. In *Un percorso della memoria,* ed. T. Matta, 69–74. Milan: Electa.

———. 2003. Storia di un manifesto partigiano: l'assurda polemica sulle responsabilità della strage. In *Tra storia e memoria,* ed. M. Palla, 179–92. Rome: Carocci.

———. 2006. Sant'Anna di Stazzema: fantasie, menzogne e realtà sulla strage del 12 agosto 1944. In *La strage di Sant'Anna di Stazzema. 1944–2005,* by C. Buratti and G. Cipollini. Rome: Nuova Iniziativa Editoriale spa.

City of Bolzano. 2005. *The concentration camp in Bolzano: Pictures and documents of the Nazi concentration camp in Bolzano.* Bolzano: City of Bolzano.

Clemente, P. 2005. Ritorno dall'apocalisse. In *Poetiche e politiche del ricordo,* ed. P. Clemente and F. Dei, 49–60. Rome: Carocci.

Clemente, P., and F. Dei, eds. 2005. *Poetiche e politiche del ricordo. Memoria pubblica delle stragi nazifasciste in Toscana.* Rome: Carocci.

Clifford, R. 2008a. Creating official Holocaust commemorations in France and Italy, 1990–2005. Unpublished PhD thesis, University of Oxford.

———. 2008b. The limits of national memory: Anti-fascism, the Holocaust and the Fosse Ardeatine Memorial in 1990s Italy. *Forum for Modern Language Studies* 44: 128–39.

Collotti, E. 2001. Introduzione. In *I campi di concentramento in Italia,* ed. C. Di Sante, 9–13. Milan: FrancoAngeli.

Colombara, F. 1989. *La terra delle tre lune. Classi popolari nella prima metà del Novecento in un paese dell'alto Piemonte: Prato Sesia. Storia orale e comunità.* Milan: Vangelista.

———. 1999. L'identità del nemico nella memoria resistenziale del Piemonte nord-orientale. *L'impegno* 19: 11–17.

———. 2005. Il carnevale di Mussolini. 25 luglio 1943. Simboli e riti di una comunità nazionale. *L'Impegno* 25: 31–57.

———. 2006. Il fascino del leggendario Moscatelli e Beltrami: miti resistenti. *L'Impegno* 26: 33–62.

———. 2009. *Vesti la giubba di battaglia. Miti, riti e simboli della guerra partigiana.* Rome: DeriveApprodi.

Connerton, P. 1989. *How societies remember.* Cambridge: Cambridge University Press.

———. 2008. Seven types of forgetting. *Memory Studies* 1: 59–71.

Contini, G. 1997. *La memoria divisa.* Milan: Rizzoli.

———. 2001. Memorie in conflitto. *L'Impegno* 21: 38–42.

———. 2004a. L'esperienza della strage nella tradizione orale di San Miniato. In *L'eccidio del Duomo di San Miniato. La memoria e la ricerca storica 1944–2004*, ed. L. Paggi, 39–87. San Miniato: Comune di San Miniato.

———. 2004b. Prefazione. In *Sant'Anna di Stazzema. Storia e memoria della strage dell'agosto 1944*, T. Rovatti, 5–9. Rome: Deriveapprodi.

———. 2006. Toscana 1944: Una storia della memoria delle stragi naziste. In *La politica del massacro. Per un atlante delle stragi naziste in Toscana*, ed. G. Fulvetti and F. Pelini. 315–44. Naples: L'ancora del mediterraneo.

———. 2007a. Guerra totale. Contini legge Gribaudi. *Storica* 13: 191–200.

———. 2007b. I massacri di civili toscani nell'estate del 1944 e la loro memoria. *Politiche della memoria*, ed. A. Rossi-Doria and G. Fiocco, 37–66. Annali del Dipartimento di Storia, 3. Rome: Viella.

Cooke, P., ed. 1998. *The Italian Resistance: An anthology.* Manchester: Manchester University Press.

———. 2000a. Recent work on Nazi massacres in Italy during the Second World War. *Modern Italy* 5 (2): 211–18.

———. 2000b. The resistance continues: A social movement in the 1970s. *Modern Italy* 5 (2): 161–73.

———. 2005. The Italian State and the resistance legacy in the 1950s and 1960s. In *Culture, censorship and the state in twentieth-century Italy*, ed. Guido Bonsaver and Robert Gordon, 120–31. Oxford: Legenda.

———. 2006. "A riconquistare la rossa primavera": The Neo-Resistance of the 1970s. In *Speaking out and silencing: Culture, society and politics in Italy in the 1970s, Italian perspectives*, ed. A. Bull and A. Giorgio, 172–84. Leeds: Legenda.

———. 2007. What does it matter if you die? The seven Cervi brothers. In *Assassinations and murder in modern Italy: Transformations in society and culture*, ed. S. Gundle and L. Rinaldi, 84–95. New York: Palgrave.

Corriere della Sera. 1977. Protesta della DC contro una lapide in piazza Fontana. December 21.

———. 1987. Quella lapide dedicata a Pinelli. November 19.

———. 1989. Almeno mettiamo una lapide che ricordi Calabresi. November 1.

Corriere Fiorentino. 2008. Due lapidi, due verità. È la pace di San Miniato. July 23.

Cosgrove, D., and D. Atkinson. 1996. Embodied identities: City, nation and empire at the Vittorio-Emmanuele II monument in Rome. Imperial Cities Project Working Paper 4, Royal Holloway, University of London.

Crainz, G. 1992. Il conflitto e la memoria. "Guerra civile" e "triangolo della morte." *Meridiana,* 13: 17–55.

———. 1994a. La violenza postbellica in Emilia fra "guerra civile" e conflitti antichi. In *Laboratorio di storia. Studi in onore di Claudio Pavone,* ed. P. Pezzino and G. Ranzato. Milan: Franco Angeli.

———. 1994b. *Padania.* Rome: Donzelli.

———. 1995. Il dolore e la collera: quella lontana Italia del 1945. *Meridiana* 22–23: 9–47.

———. 1997. La violenza armata dopo la liberazione: problemi storici e storiografici. In *La guerra partigiana in Italia e in Europa,* ed. B. Micheletti, 453–65. Brescia: Fondazione Micheletti.

———. 2001. La giustizia sommaria in Italia dopo la seconda guerra mondiale. In *Storia, verità, giustizia, I crimini del XX secolo,* ed. M. Flores, 162–71. Milan: Bruno Mondadori.

———. 2006. L'Italia era piena di sangue. *La Repubblica,* November 8.

———. 2007. *L'ombra della Guerra. Il 1945, l'Italia.* Rome: Donzelli.

Croci, O. 1999. Alla ricerca del Turco: un modesto contributo al dibattito sulla Resistenza. *Italian Politics and Society* 52: 10–18.

———. 2004. Lo storico e l'investigatore. Sulle orme del "Turco." In *L'investigazione come scienza,* ed. F. Sidoti, 95–108. L'Aquila: Edizioni Libreria Colacchi.

D'Avanzo, G. 2008. Trent'anni dopo il rapimento Moro. *La Repubblica,* March 8.

D'Orsi, A. 2006. Rovescismo, fase suprema del revisionismo. *La Stampa,* October 18.

de Bernières, L. 1994. *Captain Corelli's Mandolin* (translated into Italian with the title *Una vita in debito.* Milan: Longanesi, 1996. Republished as *Il mandolino del capitano corelli.* Milan: Guanda: 2001).

De Felice, R. 1995. *Il rosso e il nero.* Milan: Baldini & Castoldi.

De Grazia, V., and L. Paggi. 1991. Story of an ordinary massacre: Civitella della Chiana, 29 June, 1944. *Cardozo Studies in Law and Literature* 3 (2): 153–69.

———. 1992. *How fascism ruled women. Italy, 1922–1945.* Los Angeles: University of California Press.

De Luna, G. 2006a. Resistenza. Hanno vinto i revisionisti. *La Stampa,* November 9.

———. 2006b. *Il corpo del nemico ucciso. Violenza e morte nella guerra contemporanea.* Turin: Einaudi.

———. 2008a. Se questo è un memorial. *La Stampa,* January 21.

———. 2008b. Il fascismo derubricato. *La Stampa,* March 28.

De Micheli, M. 1978. *Scalarini. Vita e disegni del grande caricaturista politico.* Milan: Feltrinelli.

De Paolis, E., et al., eds. 1975. *Tesi antitesi: argomenti e testi di letterature e storia per le scuole medie superiori, anni venti-anni settanta.* Messina/Florence: G. D'Anna.

De Santis, A. 2007. *L'immane tragedia dell'estate del 1943 a Foggia*. Foggia: Tipografia Valerio De Santis.

De Simone, C. 1993. *Venti angeli sopra Roma. I bombardamenti aerei sulla Città eterna 19 luglio e 13 agosto 1943*. Milan: Mursia.

De Simonis, P. 2004. *Passi nella memoria. Guida i luoghi delle stragi nazifasciste in Toscana*. Rome: Carocci.

Deaglio, E., and B. Cremagnani. 2008. *L'ultima crociata*. Documentary film.

Debord, G. 1995. *The Society of the Spectacle*. New York: Zone Books.

Dei, F. 2005. Poetiche e politiche del ricordo. In *Poetiche e politiche del ricordo. Memoria pubblica delle stragi nazifasciste in Toscana*, ed. P. Clemente and F. Dei, 9–49. Rome: Carocci.

Detti, T., and Flores, M. 1999, I crimini della storia. Lo storico, la verità e la memoria del passato. *I viaggi di erodoto* 38/39: 44–56.

Di Sante, C. 2001. I campi di concentramento in Abruzzo. In *I campi di concentramento in Italia. Dall'internamento alla deportazione 1940–1945*, ed. C. Di Sante. Milan: FrancoAngeli.

Dickie, J. 1994. La macchina da scrivere: The Victor Emmanuel Monument and Italian nationalism. *The Italianist* 14: 261–85.

———. 1997. "Largo Bottai": An attempt to construct a common Italian history. *Patterns of Prejudice* 31 (2): 7–14.

———. 2005. *Messina: A city without memory?* Documentary film.

———. 2006. Messina: A city without memory? Unpublished conference paper.

Dickie, J., J. Foot, and F. Snowden, eds. 2002. *Disastro! Disasters in Italy since 1860: Culture, politics and society*. New York: Palgrave.

Dogliani, P. 1995a. Monumenti alla Resistenza. Bologna e il suo territorio. In *La premiata resistenza*, 21–36. Bologna: Grafis.

———. 1995b. Il monumento come documento. Un percorso di ricerca per una mostra storico-didattica. In *La premiata resistenza*, 97–112. Bologna: Grafis.

———. 1996. Redipuglia. In *I luoghi della memoria. Simboli e miti dell'Italia unita*, ed. M. Isnenghi, 375–90. Bari: Laterza.

———. 2006. I monumenti e le lapidi come fonti. In *Storia d'Italia nel Secolo Ventesimo. Strumenti e Fonti, II, Istituti, Musei e Monumenti, Bibliografia e Periodici*, ed. C. Pavone ed., 261–78. Rome: Associazioni, Direzione Generale per gli Archivi.

La Domenica degli italiani. 1945. December 9.

Dondi, M. 1990. Piazzale Loreto 29 aprile: Aspetti di una pubblica esposizione. *Rivista di Storia Contemporanea* 2: 219–48.

———. 1996. Piazzale Loreto. In *I luoghi della memoria: Simboli e miti dell'Italia unita*, ed M. Isnenghi, 487–99. Rome-Bari: Laterza.

———. 2004. *La Resistenza tra unità e conflitto. Vicende parallele tra dimensione nazionale e realtà piacentina*. Milan: Bruno Mondadori.

———. 2007. Division and conflict in the partisan resistance. *Modern Italy* 12 (2): 225–36.

———. 2008. *La lunga liberazione. Giustizia e violenza nel dopoguerra Italiano*. Rome: Riuniti.

Enciclopedia dell'antifascismo e della Resistenza. 1968. Milan: La Pietra.

Enciclopedia Treccani. 1934. Martire, vol. 22, 456–60. Rome.

Fabi, L. 1998. *Gente di trincea. La grande guerra sul Carso e sull'Isonzo.* Milan: Mursia.

———. 2005. *Enrico Toti. Una storia tra mito e realtà.* Cremona: Persico.

———. 2005. *Redipuglia. Storia, memoria, arte e mito di un monumento che parla di pace.* Trieste: LINT.

Facchinetti, P. 2006. *Quando spararono al Giro d'Italia. Storie dal Giro.* Arezzo: Limina.

Fantozzi, G. 1990. *Vittime dell'odio. L'ordine pubblica a Modena dopo la liberazione 1945–1946.* Bologna: Europrom.

Fenoglio, B. 1992. *Una questione privata, Romanzi e racconti.* Turin: Einaudi.

———. 2006. *A private affair, modern voices.* London: Hesperus.

Ferenc, T. 2000. *Rab, Arbe, Arbissma, Confinamenti-Rastrellamenti-Internamenti nella provincia di Lubiana, 1941–1943.* Lubiana: Istituto di Storia Moderna.

Ferrara, E., and M. Stampacchia. 2004. *Il bombardamento di Pisa del 31 agosto 1943. Dalle testimonianze alla memoria storica.* Pontedera: Tagete.

Filippini, M. 2004. *La tragedia di Cefalonia: una verità scomoda.* Rome: IBN.

Finaldi, G. 2002. Italy's scramble for Africa from Dogali to Adua. In *Disastro!,* ed. J. Dickie et al., 80–97. New York: Palgrave.

Finzi, D. 2004. *La vita quotidiana di un campo di concentramento fascista. Ribelli sloveni nel querceto di Renicci-Anghiari (Arezzo).* Rome: Carocci.

Focardi, F. 2005a. *La guerra della memoria. La Resistenza nel dibattito politico italiano dal 1945 a oggi.* Rome-Bari: Laterza.

———. 2005b. La questione dei processi ai criminali di guerra tedeschi in Italia: fra punizione frenata, insabbiamento di Stato, giustizia tardiva (1943–2005). Università degli Studi di Bologna e Gedit Edizioni. http://www.storicamente.org/ focardi_shoa.htm.

Focardi, F., and L. Klinkhammer. 2008. *Criminali di guerra in libertà. Un accordo segreto tra Italia e Germania federale, 1949–1955.* Rome; Carocci.

Folino, F. 1985. *Ferramonti un lager di Mussolini.* Cosenza: Editore Brenner.

Fondazione della RSI, Istituto Storico Onlus. 2003. *Albo caduti e dispersi della Repubblica Sociale Italiana.* Bologna: Arturo Conti editore.

Foot, J. 2000. Via Rasella, 1944: Memory, truth and history. *Historical Journal* 43 (4): 1173–81.

———. 2001. La strage e la città. Milano e Piazza Fontana, 1969–1999. In *La memoria contesa. Studi sulla rappresentazione sociale del passato,* ed. A. Tota, 199–215. Milan: FrancoAngeli.

———. 2002a. The massacre and the city, Milan and Piazza Fontana since 1969. In *Disastro!,* ed. J. Dickie et al., 256–80. New York: Palgrave.

———. 2002b. Memoria e Funerali. Da Piazza Fontana a Enrico Baj, 1969–2000. *Il Mulino* 4: 640–48.

———. 2005. L'Italia degli ultimi trent'anni. In *1974 28 Maggio 2004. 30 Anniversario della strage di Piazza della Loggia. "Brescia: La Memoria, La Storia." Testimonianze, riflessioni, iniziative,* 224–30. Brescia: Casa della Memoria.

————. 2007. The death of Giuseppe Pinelli: Truth, representation, memory (1969–2006). In *Assassinations and murder in modern Italy: Transformations in society and culture*, ed. S Gundle and L. Rinaldi, 59–72. New York: Palgrave.

————. 2009a. Contested memories: Milan and Piazza Fontana, 1969–2006. In *Imagining terrorism in Italy: The rhetoric and representation of political violence in Italy, 1969–2009*, ed. P. P. Antonello and A. O'Leary, 152–66. Oxford: Legenda.

————. 2009b. *Fratture d'Italia. Un secolo breve di memoria divisa.* Milan: Rizzoli.

Forcella, E., and Monticone, A. 1998. *Plotone di esecuzione. I processi della prima guerra mondiale.* Bari: Laterza.

Forgacs, D. 2003. *San Lorenzo: Memory and place.* Documentary film.

————. 2005. Memory and place in San Lorenzo, Rome. Unpublished chapter.

Forti, C. 1998. *Il caso Padre Roques. Un eccidio del 1944 tra memoria e oblio.* Turin: Einaudi.

Francini, M. 2006. Per non metterci una pietra sopra. La memoria monumentalizzata della Resistenza: il caso di Cefalonia. *Quaderni di Farestoria* 8 (2): 7–12.

Franzinelli, M. 1995. *Un dramma partigiano. Il "caso Menici." Fiamme verdi, garibaldini e tedeschi in Alta Valcamonica: la zona france e il "Caso Menici."* Brescia: Fondazione Micheletti.

————. 1997a. Il 25 luglio. In *I luoghi della memoria*, ed. M. Isnenghi, 219–40. Bari: Laterza.

————. 1997b. L'8 settembre. In *I luoghi della memoria*, ed. M. Isnenghi, 241–70. Bari: Laterza.

————. 2002. *Le stragi nascoste. L'armadio della vergogna. Impunità e rimozione dei crimini di guerra nazifascisti 1943–2001.* Milan: Mondaori.

————. 2004. *Squadristi. Protagonisti e tecniche della violenza fascista. 1919–1922.* Milan: Mondadori.

————. 2005. *Ultime lettere dei condannati a morte a di deportati della Resistenza. 1943–1945.* Milan: Mondadori.

Franzinetti, G. 2006. The rediscovery of the Istrian *Foibe. JGKS, History and Culture of South Eastern Europe* 8: 85–98.

Friedrich, J. 2006. *The fire: The bombing of Germany, 1940–1945.* New York: Columbia University Press.

Fulvetti, G., and F. Pelini, eds. 2006. *La politica del terrore. Per un atlante delle stragi naziste in Toscana.* Naples: l'ancora del mediterraneo.

Fussell, P. 1975. *The great war and modern memory.* Oxford: Oxford University Press.

Galimi, V. 2001. I campi di concentramento in Toscana fra storia e memoria. In *I campi di concentramento in Italia. Dall'internamento alla deportazione 1940–1945*, ed. C. Di Sante, 207–27. Milan: FrancoAngeli.

Gallerano, N. 1999. *La verità della storia. Scritti sull'uso pubblico del passato.* Rome: Manifestolibri.

Galli della Loggia, E. 1996. *La morte della patria. La crisi dell'idea di nazione tra Resistenza antifascismo e Repubblica.* Bari: Laterza.

Gallinari, P. 2008. *Un contadino nella metropoli. Ricordi di un militante delle Brigate Rosse.* Milan: Bompiani.

Gallotta, V. 2005. Cefalonia: la strage, il processo, l'oblio. In *Ottosettembre 1943. Le storie e le storiografie*, ed. A. Melloni. Reggio Emilia: Diabasis.

Galluccio, F. 2002. *I lager in Italia. La memoria sepolta nei duecento luoghi di deportazione fascisti*. Rome: Libere edizioni.

Ganapini, L. 2000. La Rsi e l'ultimo fascismo. Una rilettura critica della storiografia. *L'Impegno* 20 (3): 1–12.

———. 2002. *La repubblica delle camicie nere. I combattenti, i politici, gli amministratori, i socializzatori*. Milan: Garzanti.

Ganapini, L., and M. Legnani. 1969. *L'Italia dei quarantacinque giorni*. Milan: Istituto Nazionale per la storia del movimento di liberazione.

Gentile, E. 1989. *Storia del partito fascista 1919–1922. Movimento e milizia*. Bari: Laterza.

———. 1993. *Il culto del littorio. La sacralizzazione della politica nell'Italia fascista*. Rome-Bari: Laterza.

———. 1996. *The sacralization of politics in fascist Italy*. Cambridge, MA and London: Harvard University Press.

———. 2007. *Fascismo di pietra*. Bari: Laterza.

Gentiloni Silveri, U., and M. Carli. 2007. *Bombardare Roma. Gli Alleati e la "Città aperta" 1940–1944*. Bologna: Il Mulino.

Germinario, F. 1999. *L'altra memoria. L'estrema destra, Salò e la Resistenza*. Turin: Bollati Boringhieri.

———. 2005. *Da Salò al governo. Immaginario e cultura politica della destra italiana*. Turin: Bollati Boringhieri.

———. 2008. Eros e Tanathos. La morte nella memorialistica della Repubblica sociale. In *La morte per la patria. La celebrazione dei caduti dal Risorgimento alla Repubblica*, ed O. Janz and L. Klinkhammer, 189–212. Rome: Donzelli.

Gervasutti, S. 2002. *Il giorno nero di Porzus*. Venice: Marsilio.

Ghilardini, Don L. 1960. *I martiri di Cefalonia. Esumazione dei Caduti in GRECIA*. Genova: Scuola tipografica opera.

Giacomozzi, C., ed. 1995. *L'ombra del buio: Lager a Bolzano 1945–1995/Schatten, die das Dunkel Wirft: Lager in Bozen 1945–1995*. Bolzano: Comune di Bolzano.

———. (n.d.) *I luoghi della memoria. Bolzano. Percorso 1943–1945*. Bolzano: City of Bolzano.

Giacomozzi, C., and G. Paleari. 2004a. Bolzano. In *Dizionario dell'Olocausto*, 96–99. Turin: Einaudi.

———. 2004b. *Conoscere e communicare i lager. Un'esperienza educativa, Assessorato alla Cultura e allo Spettacolo*. Bolzano: Ufficio beni culturali.

Giannattasio, G. 1994. Pinelli vince la guerra dei vent'anni. *Il Giornale*, October 26.

Giannuli, A. 2008. *Bombe a inchiostro*. Milan: BUR.

Gibelli, A. 1998. *La grande guerra degli italiani, 1915–1918*. Milan: Sansoni.

Gibertoni, R., and A. Melodi. 1996. Il campo di Fossoli e il Museo Monumento al Deportato di Carpi. In *Un percorso della memoria*, ed. T. Matta, 99–119. Milan: Electa.

Gilman, P., and L. Gilman. 1980. *"Collar the Lot": How Britain interned and expelled its wartime refugees*. London: Quartet Books.

Ginsborg, P. 1990. *A history of contemporary Italy: Society and Politics, 1943–1988.* London: Penguin.

Ginzburg, C. 1974. *Miti emblemi spie.* Turin: Einaudi.

———. 1980. *The cheese and the worms: The cosmos of a sixteenth-century Miller.* London: Routledge.

———. 1991. *Lo storico e lo giudice.* Turin: Einaudi.

Gioannini, M., and G. Massobrio. 2007. *Bombardate l'Italia. Storia della guerra di distruzione aerea 1940–1945.* Milan: Rizzoli.

Il Giornale. 1994a. Piazza Fontana cambia, ma la lapide di Pinelli resta. October 25.

———. 1994b. Distruggeremo la targa a Pinelli. November 3.

Giraudi, G. 1982. *A Cefalonia e Corfù si combatte. Testimonianza di un superstite della leggendaria Divisione Acqui.* Milan: Cavallotti editore.

Giusti, M. T. 2000. Dalle marce del "davaj" ai campi di prigionia. I militari italiani caduti e dispersi in Russia durante la seconda guerra mondiale. *Nuova Storia Contemporanea* 4 (6): 43–80.

Giustolisi, F. 2004. *L'armadio della vergogna.* Rome: Nutrimenti.

Gobetti, E. 2007. *L'occupazione allegra. Gli italiani in Jugoslavia 1941–1943.* Rome: Carocci.

Gombač, B., and D. Mattiussi, eds. 2004. *La deportazione dei civili sloveni e croati nei campi di concentramento italiani: 1942–1943. I campi del confine orientale.* Gradisca d'Isonzo: Centro Isontino di Ricerca e Documentazione Storica e Sociale "L. Gasparini."

Gordon, R. 2006a. Which holocaust? Primo Levi and the field of Holocaust memory in post-war Italy. *Italian Studies* 61 (1): 85–113.

———. 2006b. The Holocaust in Italian collective memory: Il giorno della memoria, 27 January 2001. *Modern Italy* 11 (2): 167–88.

Gorrieri, E., and G. Bondi. 2005. *Ritorno a Montefiorino. Dalla Resistenza sull'Appennino alla violenza del dopoguerra.* Bologna: Il Mulino.

Gotor, M., ed. 2008. *Aldo Moro. Lettere della prigionia.* Turin: Einaudi.

———. 2008–2009. *Il Diario della Settimana.* Milan: Il Saggiatore.

Grande, T. 1997. La ricostruzione in positivo di un'esperienza di internamento: il campo di Ferramonti di Tarsia. In *Responsabilità e memoria. Linee per il futuro,* ed. D. Barazzetti and C. Leccardi, 139–52. Florence: La Nuova Italia.

———. 1998. Dopo 55 anni una lapide ricorda i crimini fascisti nel campo di Arbe. *Triangolo rosso* 12.

Grayling, A. C. 2006. *Among the dead cities: The history and moral legacy of the WWII bombing of civilians in Germany and Japan.* London: Bloomsbury.

Gribaudi, G. 1999. Guerra, violenza, responsabilità. Alcuni volumi sui massacri nazisti in Italia. *Quaderni Storici* 34 (1): 135–50.

———, ed. 2003. *Terra bruciata. Le stragi naziste sul fronte meridionale.* Naples: l'ancora del mediterraneo.

———. 2004. Memorie private e discorsi pubblici. La "guerra totale" sul fronte meridionale. Italia 1943–44.

———. 2005. *Guerra totale. Tra bombe alleate e violenze naziste. Napoli e il fronte meridionale 1940–1944.* Turin: Bollati Boringhieri.

Gribaudi, M. 1987. *Mondo operaio e mito operaio. Spazi e percorsi sociali a Torino nel primo Novecento*. Turin: Einaudi.

Gubinelli, P. 2005. *Il paese più straziato. Storie di marchigiani nella grande guerra*. Ancona: affinità elettive.

Guccini, F., and L. Machiavelli. 2007. *Tango e gli altri. Romanzo di una raffica, anzi tre*. Milan: Mondadori.

Guerrieri, A. 1996. *La città spezzata: Foggia, quei giorni del '43*. Bari: Edipuglia.

Guidi, A. 1996. Sant'Anna di Stazzema: la visita. In *Un percorso della memoria*, ed. T. Matta. 75–81. Milan: Electa.

Gundle, S. 1996. La "religione civile della Resistenza": Cultura di massa e identità politica nell'Italia del dopoguerra. In *L'immagine della Resistenza in Europa: 1945–1960*, ed. L. Cigognetti et al., 1–39. Bologna: Il Nove.

———. 2000. The "civic religion" of the resistance in post-war Italy. *Modern Italy* 5 (2): 113–32.

Gundle, S., and L. Rinaldi, eds. 2007. *Assassinations and murder in modern Italy: Transformations in society and culture*. New York: Palgrave.

Habermas, J. 1988. *Legitimation crisis*. Cambridge: Polity.

Happacher, L. 1979. *Il lager di Bolzano: Con appendice documentaria*. Trento: Comitato provinciale per il 30 anniversario della resistenza e della liberazione.

Hass, K. A. 1998. *Carried to the wall: American memory and the Vietnam Veterans Memorial*. Berkeley: University of California Press.

Heer, H., et al., eds. 2008. *The discursive construction of history: Remembering the Wehrmacht's war of annihilation*. London: Routledge.

Herf, J. 1999. *Divided memory: The Nazi past in the two Germanys*. Cambridge: Harvard University Press.

Hickey D., and G. Smith. 1989. *The star of shame: The secret voyage of the Arandora Star*. Dublin: Madison.

Horwitz, G. 1994. *All'ombra della morte: la vita quotidiana attorno al campo di Mauthausen*. Venice: Marsilio.

Huyssen, A. 2003. *Present pasts: Urban palimpsests and the politics of memory*. Stanford: Stanford University Press.

Insolvibile, I. 2004. *La resistenza di Cefalonia tra memoria e storia*. Rome: Edizioni ANRP.

Isnenghi, M., ed. 1967. *I vinti di Caporetto nella letterature di guerra*. Venice: Marsilio.

———. 1970. *Il mito della grande guerra*. Bari: Laterza.

———. 1989. *Le guerre degli italiani. Parole, immagini, ricordi 1848–1945*. Milan: Mondadori.

———. 1994. *L'Italia in piazza. I luoghi della vita pubblica dal 1848 ai giorni nostri*. Milan: Mondadori.

———. 1990. La guerra civile nella pubblicistica di destra. In *Guerra, guerra di liberazione, guerra civile*, ed. M. Legnani et al., 231–44. Milan: FrancoAngeli.

———. 1994. L'esposizione della morte. In *Guerre fratricide: Le guerre civili in età contemporanea*, ed. G. Ranzato, 330–52. Turin: Bollati Boringhieri.

———. 1996. *L'Italia del Fascio*. Florence: Giunti.

———. 1997a. Conclusione. In *I luoghi della memoria. Personaggi e date dell'Italia unita*, ed. M. Isnenghi, 427–74. Bari: Laterza.

———. 1997b. La Grande Guerra. In *I luoghi della memoria. Strutture ed eventi dell'Italia unita*, ed. M. Isnenghi, 273–309. Bari: Laterza.

———. 1997c. La Marcia su Roma. In *I luoghi della memoria. Strutture ed eventi dell'Italia unita*, ed. M. Isnenghi, 311–30. Bari: Laterza.

———. 1999. *La tragedia necessaria. Da Caporetto all'8 Settembre*. Bologna: Il Mulino.

Isola, G. 1990. *Guerra al regno della guerra! Storia della Lega proletaria mutilati invalidi reduci orfani e vedove di guerra 1918–1924*. Florence: Le Lettere.

———, ed. 1997. *La memoria pia. I monumenti ai caduti della I guerra mondiale nell'area Trentino Tirolese*. Trento: Editrice Università degli Studi di Trento.

Italiani, amici nemici. Norberto Bobbio, Renzo De Felice, Gian Enrico Rusconi. 1996. Rome: Donzelli.

Johnson, P. 2008a. *Dietrologia: un passato che non passa*. Unpublished dissertation, University College London.

———. 2008b. What lurks behind: *Dietrologia* and the Italian State. *Journal of Politics & Society* 19: 104–24.

Jones, T. 2003. *Il cuore oscuro dell'Italia. Un viaggio tra odio e amore*. Milan: Rizzoli.

Judt, T. 2002. The past is another country: Myth and memory in post-war Europe. In *Memory and Power in Post-War Europe. Studies in the Presence of the Past*, ed. J. Müller 157–83. Cambridge: Cambridge University Press.

———. 2007. *Postwar: A history of Europe since 1945*. London: Pimlico.

Kersevan, A. 2003. *Un campo di concentramento fascista. Gonars 1942–1943*. Udine: Kappa Vu Edizioni.

Kertzer, D. 2001. History as it really wasn't: The myths of Italian historiography. A roundtable with Ruth Ben-Ghiat, Luciano Cafagna, Ernesto Galli della Loggia, Carl Ipsen, and David I. Kertzer. Introduction by Mark Gilbert. *Journal of Modern Italian Studies* 6 (3): 402–19.

Klinkhammer, L. 2006. *Stragi naziste in Italia, 1943–44*. Rome: Donzelli.

———. 2008. Congiunture della memoria. La riscoperta degli eroi di Cefalonia. In *La morte per la patria. La celebrazione dei caduti dal Risorgimento alla Repubblica*, ed. O. Janz and L. Klinkhammer, 175–88. Rome: Donzelli.

Lastraioli, G., and C. Biscarini. 2001. *La Prova. Un documento risolutivo sulla strage nel Duomo di San Miniato*. S. Miniato: FM Edizioni, Centro di Documentazione Internazionale Storia Militare, S. Miniato Bass.

———. 2007. De Bilia. Ultima ripassata sulla strage nel Duomo di San Miniato 22 luglio 1944. *Le Memoriette* 3.

Leed, E. 1979. *No man's land: Combat and identity in World War One*. Cambridge: Cambridge University Press.

Leoni, D., and C. Zadra, eds. 1986. *La grande guerra. Esperienza, memoria, immagini*. Bologna: Il Mulino.

Levi, C. 2000. *Le mille patrie*. Rome: Donzelli.

Levi, G. 1993. On microhistory. In *New perspectives on historical writing*, ed. P. Burke, 93–113. Bari: Laterza.

Levi della Torre, S. 1994. Raccontare per ricordare. In *Le ragioni della memoria. Interventi e riflessioni a vent'anni dalla strage di Piazza della Loggia*, ed C. Simioni, 109–23. Brescia: Grafo.

Lüdtke, A., ed. 1995. *The history of everyday life: Reconstructing historical experiences and ways of life*. Princeton: Princeton University Press.

Luzzatto, S. 1998. *Il corpo del duce. Un cadavere tra immaginazione, storia e memoria*. Turin: Einaudi.

———. 2004. *La crisi dell'antifascismo*. Turin: Einaudi.

———. 2005. Perche non è assurdo festeggiare l'8 Settembre. *Corriere della Sera*, September 17.

———. 2007. R4. In *Annisettanta*, ed. M. Belpoliti, G. Canova, and S. Chiodi, 402–3. Milan: Skira.

———. 2008. *Sangue d'Italia. Interventi sulla storia del novecento*. Rome: Manifestolibri.

Madden, J. 2001. *Captain Corelli's Mandolin*. Feature film.

Maida, B. 2002. *Prigionieri della memoria. Storia di due stragi della Liberazione*. Milan: FrancoAngeli.

Maione, G. 1975. *Il biennio rosso*. Bologna: Il Mulino.

Malaparte, C. M. Biondi, ed. 1995. *Viva Caporetto! La rivolta dei santi maladetti*. Florence: Valecchi.

———. 2002. *La pelle*. Milan: Mondadori.

Malvezzi, P., and G. Pirelli, eds. 1952. *Lettere di condannati a morte della Resistenza italiana: 8 settembre 1943 – 25 aprile 1945*. Turin: Einaudi.

Mancini, E. 2003. L'impegno per la conservazione della memoria dell'eccidio. In *Tra storia e memoria*, ed. M. Palla, 193–99. Rome: Carocci

Mangiafico, A., and P. Gurrieri. 1991. *Non si parte! Non si parte! Le sommosse in Sicilia contro il richiamo alle armi*. Ragusa: Sicilia Punto L.

Mantovani, V. 1979. *Mazurka Blu. La strage del Diana*. Milan: Rusconi.

Marchesoni, P., and M. Martignoni, eds. 1998. *Monumenti della grande guerra. Progetti e realizzazioni in Trentino, 1916–1935*. Trento: Museo Storico in Trento.

Marino, L. 1992. *La verità di piombo. Io, Sofri e gli altri*. Milan: Edizioni Ares.

Marrucci, R. A., et al., eds. 2004. *Bombe sulla città, Milano in guerra 1942–1944*. Milan: Skira.

Marsalek, H. 1977. *Mauthausen*. Milan: La Pietra.

Martini, V. 2007. *Dante Castellucci "FACIO" . . . in nome del partito comunista*. Unpublished theatre play.

I martiri di Cefalonia. Esumazione dei Caduti in Grecia. 1960. Genova: Scuola tipografica opera.

Mason, T. 1995. The Turin strikes of March 1943. In *Nazism, fascism and the working class: Essays by Tim Mason*, ed. J. Caplan, 274–94. Cambridge: Cambridge University Press.

———. 1998. Gli scioperi di Torino del Marzo 1943. In *L'Italia nella seconda guerra mondiale e nella resistenza*, ed. F. Tosi et al., 399–422. Milan: FrancoAngeli.

Matta, T., ed. 1996. *Un percorso della memoria. Guida ai luoghi della violenza nazista e fascista in Italia*. Milan: Electa.

Mayda, G. 2002. *Storia della deportazione dall'Italia 1943–1945. Militari, ebrei e politici nel lager del terzo Reich*. Turin: Bollati Boringhieri.

———. 2008. *Mauthausen. Storia di un lager*. Bologna: Il Mulino.

Mazower, M. 2000. The cold war and the appropriation of memory: Greece after liberation. In *The politics of retribution in Europe: World War II and its aftermath*, ed. I. Deák et al., 212–32. Princeton: Princeton University Press.

McBride, I., ed. 2001. *History and memory in modern Ireland*. Cambridge: Cambridge University Press.

Meletti, J. 2008. Quei 500 italiani dimenticati in fondo al mare. *La Repubblica*, July 2.

Menchetti, M. A., W. Lammoni, C. Weisberg, and V. de Grazia. 1991. The witnesses of Civitella. *Cardozo Studies in Law and Literature* 3 (2): 171–95.

Meneghello, L. 1998. *I piccoli maestri*. Milan: BUR.

Mezzalira, G., and C. Romeo, eds. 2002. *Mischia l'aguzzino del Lager di Bolzano: dalle carte del processo a Michael Seifert*. Bolzano: Circolo Culturale ANPI Bolzano.

Mignemi, A. 2006. Per le strade e nelle piazze: il racconto pubblico della storia. Monumenti e lapidi ai caduti nelle guerre del Novecento. In *Monumenti ai caduti in guerra. Nella provincia di Novara e nella provincia di Verbano Cusio Ossola*, ed. S. Franzolini, 13–61. Novara: Associazione Nazionale Combattenti e Reduci, Federazione Interprovinciale di Novara, Verbano, Cusio, Ossola.

Milani, M. 1994. Non vittime, ma caduti consapevoli. In *Le ragioni della memoria. Interventi e riflessioni a vent'anni dalla strage di piazza della Loggia*, 17–22. Brescia: Grafo.

Minniti, F. 2000. *Il Piave*. Bologna: Il Mulino.

Minucci, P. T. 2000. *Combattenti dell'Onore. Così caddero gli uomini e le donne della Rsi*. Milan: Greco & Greco.

Mondini, M. 2004. La festa mancata. I militari e la memoria della Grande Guerra, 1918–1923. *Contemporanea* 7 (4): 555–78.

———. 2006a. Le sentinelle della memoria. I monumenti ai Caduti e la costruzione della rimembranza nell'Italia Nord Orientale 1919–1939. In *Annali della Fondazione Luigi Einaudi* 40: 273–93.

———. 2006b. *La politica delle armi. Il ruolo dell'esercito nell'avvento del fascismo*. Bari: Laterza.

———. 2008. *Alpini. Parole e immagini di un mito guerriero*. Bari: Laterza.

Monni, R. 2000. Mandolini per una strage. *Diario della settimana*, September 8.

Montaldi, D. 1994. *Bisogna sognare. Scritti 1952–1975*. Milan: Cooperativa Colibrì.

Moranino, L. 1991. La "guerra contro le lapidi" nel Biellese antifascista. *L'impegno* 11 (3): 12–18.

Morelli, P., ed. 2002. *Relazione della commissione di studio sulla figura del vescovo Ugo Giubbi 1928–1946*. San Miniato: Tip. Palagini.

Morgan, S. 2000. The Schio killings: A case study of partisan violence in post-war Italy. *Modern Italy* 5 (2): 147–60.

———. 2002. *Rappresaglie dopo la Resistenza. L'eccidio di Schio tra guerra civile e guerra fredda*. Milan: Bruno Mondadori.

Morucci, V. 1994. *A guerra finita, sei racconti*. Rome: Manifestolibri.

Mosca, C., and R. Rossanda, eds. 1994. *Mario Moretti. Br una storia italiana.* Milan: Anabasi.

Moscardelli, G. 1945. *Cefalonia.* Rome: Tip. Regionale.

Moss, D. 2004. *Il Caso Moro 1978–2004:* Witchcraft, oracles and magic. Working papers, Dipartimento di studi sociali e politici, University of Milan.

———. 2007. From history to mystery: The parliamentary inquiries into the kidnapping and murder of Aldo Moro, 1979–2001. In *Assassinations and murder in modern Italy: Transformations in society and culture,* ed. S. Gundle and L. Rinaldi, 101–15. New York: Palgrave.

Mosse, G. 1979. National cemeteries and national revival: The cult of the fallen soldiers in Germany. *Journal of Contemporary History* 1: 1–20.

———. 1991. *Fallen soldiers: Reshaping the memory of the World Wars.* Oxford: Oxford University Press.

Muir, E., and G. Ruggiero, eds. 1991. *Microhistory and the lost peoples of Europe.* London: John Hopkins University Press.

Il Museo monumento al deportato a Carpi. 1997. Milan: Electa.

Nazione Pontedera. 2008. Campane a distesa per la lapide. Ma le discussioni non si placano. July 19.

Negri, M. 2004. Il bisogno di una casa della memoria. In *Bombe sulla città, Milano in guerra 1942–1944,* ed. R. A. Marrucci et al., 115–27. Milan: Skira.

Nizza, E. 1996. Presentazione dell'editore. In *Monumenti alla libertà. Antifascismo, Resistenza e pace nei monumenti italiani dal 1945 al 1985,* ed. L. Galmozzi, 9–12. Milan: La Pietra.

Nora, P. 1984. *Le lieux de mémoire.* Paris: Gallimard.

Nucci, L., and E. Galli della Loggia, eds. 2002. *Due nazioni. Legittimazione e deligittimazione nella storia dell'Italia contemporanea.* Bologna: Il Mulino.

Odorico Tempesta, P. 1995. *Foggia nelle ore della sua tragedia.* Foggia: Edizione del Rosone.

O'Leary, A. 2007. *Tragedia all'italiana: Cinema e terrorismo tra Moro e Memoria.* Angelica: Tissi.

———. 2008. Dead man walking: The Aldo Moro kidnap and Palimpsest history in Buongiorno, notte. *New Cinemas: Journal of Contemporary Film* 6 (1): 33–45.

Oliva, C. 1987. Il potere e una lapide: dimenticare Pinelli. *A* 151: 10.

Oliva, G. 2007. *"Si ammazza troppo poco." I crimini di guerra italiani 1940–1943.* Milan: Mondadori.

Onofri, N. S. 2007. *Il triangolo rosso 1943–1947. La verità sul dopoguerra in Emilia-Romagna attraverso i documenti d'archivio.* Rome: Sapere 2000.

Orlandi, C. 2005. Rappresaglia o fatalità? La strage del Duomo di San Miniato del 22 luglio 1944. In *Poetiche e politiche del ricordo,* ed. P. Clemente and F. Dei, 134–62. Rome: Carocci.

Orwell, George. 1987. *1984.* London: Penguin.

Padoan, G. 1965. *Abbiamo lottato insieme. Partigiani italiani e sloveni al confine orientale.* Udine: Del Bianco.

Paggi, L., ed. 1996a. *Storia e memoria di un massacro ordinario. La memoria divisa. Civitella della Chiana 29 giugno 1944–94.* Rome: Manifestolibri.

————. 1996b. Antifascism and the reshaping of democratic consensus in post-1945 Italy. *New German Critique* 67: 109–10.

————, ed. 1997. *La memoria del nazismo nell'Europa di oggi.* Florence: La Nuova Italia.

————, ed. 1999. *Le memorie della Repubblica.* Florence: La Nuova Italia.

————. 2004a. Storia di una memoria antifascista. In *L'eccidio del Duomo*, ed. L. Paggi, 13–38. San Miniato: Comune di San Miniato.

————, ed. 2004b. *L'eccidio del Duomo di San Miniato. La memoria e la ricerca storica 1944–2004.* San Miniato: Comune di San Miniato.

Palla, M., ed. 2003. *Tra storia e memoria. 12 agosto 1944: la strage di Sant'Anna di Stazzema.* Rome: Carocci.

Palumbo, B. 1997. Retoriche della storia e conflitti di identità in una città della Sicilia. *Meridiana* 30: 135–68.

Panorama. 2000. August 17.

Pansa, G. 2003. *Il sangue dei vinti. Quello che accadde in Italia dopo 25 Aprile.* Milan: Sperling and Kupfer.

————. 2005. *Sconosciuto 1945.* Milan: Sperling and Kupfer.

————. 2006a. *La grande bugia.* Milan: Sperling and Kupfer.

————. 2006b. *Prigionieri del silenzio.* Milan: Sperling and Kupfer.

————. 2007a. *I gendarmi della memoria.* Milan: Sperling and Kupfer.

————. 2007b. *Ma l'amore no.* Milan: Sperling and Kupfer.

Pantozzi, A. 2002. *Sotto gli occhi della morte.* Trento: Museo Storico in Trento.

Paoletti, P. 1998. *Sant'Anna di Stazzema. 1944: La strage impunita.* Milnan: Mursia.

————. 2000. *1944, San Miniato, tutta la verità sulla strage.* Milan: Mursia.

————. 2003. *I traditi di Cefalonia. La vicenda della Divisione Acqui.* Genova: Fratelli Frilli Editori.

Parsons, G. 2007. Fascism and Catholicism: A case study of the Sacrario dei Caduti Fascisti in the crypt of San Domenico, Siena. *Journal of Contemporary History* 42 (3): 469–84.

Passarin, M., and G. M. Sandrini, eds. 1995. *Obiettivo Vicenza. I bombardamenti aerei sulla Città 1943–1945.* Vicenza: GM Sandrini.

Passerini, L. 1987. *Fascism in popular memory: The cultural experience of the Turin working class.* Cambridge: Cambridge University Press.

————. 1988. *Storia e soggettività. Le fonti orali, la memoria.* Florence: La Nuova Italia.

————. 1996. *Autobiography of a Generation: Italy 1968.* Middletown: Wesleyan University Press.

————. 1999. Memories of resistance, resistances of memory. In *European memories of the Second World War*, ed. Helmut Peitsch et al., 288–96. New York: Berghahn Books.

————. 2001. La visita di Mussolini a Mirafiori. In *Introduzione alla storia orale.* Vol. 2, ed. C. Bermani, 95–118. Rome: Odradek.

————. 2003. *Memoria e utopia. Il primato dell'intersoggettività.* Turin: Bollati Boringhieri.

Patricelli, M. 2007. *L'Italia sotto le bombe. Guerra aerea e vita civile 1940–1945*. Bari: Laterza.

Pavone, C. 1991a. *Una guerra civile. Saggio storico sulla moralità nella resistenza*. Turin: Bollati Boringhieri.

———. 1991b. Le tre guerre: patriottica, civile e di classe. In *Guerra, guerra di liberazione, guerra civile*, ed. M. Legnani and F. Vendramini, 25–36. Milan: Franco Angeli.

———. 1999. The general problem of the continuity of the state and the legacy of fascism. In *After the War*, ed. J. Dunnage, 5–20. Hull: Troubadour.

———. 2008. 1943. L'8 settembre. In *Novecento italiano. Gli anni cruciali che hanno dato il volto all'Italia di oggi*, 89–112. Bari: Laterza.

Peli, S. 2004. La memoria pubblica della Resistenza. *Italia contemporanea* 237: 639–41.

———. 2006. *Storia della Resistenza in Italia*. Turin: Einaudi.

Pertini, S. 2001. Prefazione, in *Bandiera Bianca a Cefalonia*, by M. Venturi, 5–8. Milan: Mondadori.

Pes, L. 1998. Descrivere il territorio: il punto di vista storico. *I viaggi di Erodoto* 12 (34): 48–51.

Petrizzo, A. 2005. Il "discorso della strage" tra verità storica e biografia individuale. Il caso di San Miniato. In *Poetiche e politiche del ricordo*, ed. P. Clemente and F. Dei, 163–90. Rome: Carocci.

Pezzino, P. 1997, 2007. *Anatomia di un massacro. Controversia sopra una strage tedesca*. Bologna: Il Mulino.

———. 2002. *Senza stato. La radici storiche della crisi italiana*. Bari: Laterza.

———. 2003. Una strage senza un perché? Indagine su Sant'Anna di Stazzema. In *Tra memoria e storia*, ed. M. Palla, 34–85. Rome: Carocci.

———. 2005. The Italian resistance between history and memory. *Journal of Modern Italian Studies* 10 (4): 396–412.

———. 2007a. The German military occupation of Italy and the war against civilians. *Modern Italy* 12 (2): 173–88.

———. 2007b. Trascrizione della Relazione pronunciata dal Prof. Paolo Pezzino a Sarzana, il 16 marzo 2007. http://www.faciovive.it/recensioni/pezzino-pollicino .htm (accessed January 16, 2009).

———. 2008. *Sant'Anna di Stazzema. Storia di una strage*. Bologna: Il Mulino.

Pfeifer, B. 2005. Il Polizeiliche Durchgangslager Bozen 1944–1945. In *Uomini, donne e bambini nel lager di Bolzano*, ed. D. Venegoni, 381–91. Milan: Mimesis.

Pirani, M. 1999. Cefalonia una strage dimenticata. La storia senza memoria. *La Repubblica*, September 15.

Pisanò, G. 1964. *Sangue chiama sangue*. Milan: Edizione pirola.

———. 1965. *Storia della guerra civile in Italia*. Milan: Edizioni Val Padana.

Poggio, P. P., ed. 1986. *La Repubblica sociale italiana, 1943–1945*. Brescia: Annali della Fondazione Micheletti.

———. 1994. *La memoria della strage. Piazza della Loggia 1974–1994*, ed. C. Simoni, Brescia: Grafo.

Pollak, P. 1995. Il campo di concentramento di Urbisaglia. http://www.eclettico .org/israele/urbis/pollak.htm (accessed November 14, 2008).

Ponzani, M. 2003. Il mito del secondo Risorgimento nazionale. Retorica e legittimità della Resistenza nel linguaggio politico istituzionale: il caso delle Fosse Ardeatine. *Annali della Fondazione L. Einaudi* 37: 199–258.

———. 2004. L'eredità della Resistenza nell'Italia repubblicana tra retorica celebrativa e contestazione di legittimità 1945–1963. *Annali della Fondazione L. Einaudi* 38: 259–308.

Portelli, A. 1985. *Biografia di una città. Storia e racconto: Terni 1830–1985.* Turin: Einaudi.

———. 1991. *The death of Luigi Trastulli and other stories: Form and meaning in oral history.* New York: State University of New York Press.

———. 1996. Lutto, senso comune, mito e politica nella memoria della strage di Civitella. In *Storia e memoria di un massacro ordinario,* ed. L. Paggi, 85–110. Rome: Manifestolibri.

———. 1997. *The Battle of Valle Giulia: Oral history and the art of dialogue.* Madison: University of Wisconsin Press.

———. 1999, 2005. *L'ordine è già stato eseguito. Roma, le Fosse Ardeatine, la memoria.* Rome: Donzelli.

———. 2003a. Perché ci ammazzano? Ambiguità e contraddizioni nella memoria dei bombardamenti. L. Piccioni ed. *Roma moderna e contemporanea* 11 (3): 649–70.

———. 2003b. *The order has been carried out: History, memory, and meaning of a Nazi massacre in Rome.* Basingstoke: Palgrave.

———. 2005. Roma tra guerra, Resistenza e liberazione: storia, memoria e immaginazione in un'ottica contemporanea. http://www.italia-liberazione.it/it/ 60moliberazione/RELATORI/PORTELLI.RTF (accessed June 5 2007).

———. 2006. So much depends on a red bus, or, innocent victims of the liberating gun. *Oral History* 34 (2): 29–43.

———. 2007. *Storie orali. Racconto, immaginazione, dialogo.* Rome: Donzelli.

———. 2008. Nessuna matrice politica: la Roma di Alemanno. *Il manifesto,* May 28.

———. (n.d.). Un lavoro di relazione. Osservazioni sulla storia orale. http://www .memoteca.it/upload/dl/E-Book/Alessandro_Portelli.pdf (accessed February 3, 2006).

Prandstraller, A. 2005. *Anatomia di un massacro.* Documentary film.

Preston, P. 1995. The Great Civil War: European politics, 1914–1945. In *The Oxford history of contemporary Europe,* ed. T. Blanning, 148–81. Oxford: Oxford University Press.

Procacci, G. 1981. Repressione e dissenso nelle Prima Guerra Mondiale. *Studi Storici* 22 (1): 119–50.

———. 1999. *Dalla rassegnazione alla rivolta. Mentalità e comportamenti popolari nella Grande Guerra.* Rome: Bulzoni.

———. 2002. The disaster of Caporetto. In *Disastro!,* ed. J. Dickie et al., 141–64. New York: Palgrave.

———. 2005. Italia 1915–18: Il fronte interno. In *La memoria della Grande Guerra nelle Dolomiti*, ed. I. Bossi Fedrigotti et al., 126–39. Udine: Gaspari.

Pupo, R. 2006. I caduti di piazza Sant'Antonio Nuovo e di piazza Unità d'Italia. In *Istituto Regionale per la Storia del Movimento di Liberazione nel Friuli Venezia Giulia, Un percorso tra le violenze del novecento nella Provincia di Trieste*, 109–18. Trieste: IRSMLFVG.

Quazza, G. 1967. Prefazione, in *Guerra partigiana tra Genova e il Po. La Resistenza in provincia di Alessandria*, by G. Pansa. Bari: Laterza.

———. 1979. Prefazione, in *8 Settembre. Lo sfacelo della quarta armata*. Turin: Book Store.

Ranieri, A. 2007. Partigiano Facio, il rovescio della memoria. *L'unità*, February 13.

Ranzato, G., ed. 1994. *Guerre fratricide. Le guerre civile in età contemporanea*. Turin: Bollati Boringhieri.

———. 1997. *Il linciaggio di Carretta. Roma 1944. Violenza politica e ordinaria violenza*. Milan: Il Saggiatore.

Rastelli, A. 1994. I bombardamenti aerei nella II guerra mondiale. *Italia Contemporanea*, 195: 309–42.

———. 2000. *Bombe sulla città, gli attacchi alleati: le vittime civili a Milano*. Milan: Mursia.

Rastello, A., and Opezzo, L. 1981. Vercelli: 1922–1927. Nascita e organizzazione del fascismo. *L'impegno* 1: 24–33.

Ratti, M., ed. 2006. *Non mi avrete. Disegni di Mauthausen e Gusen. La testimonianza di Germano Facetti e Lodovico Belgiojoso*. Milan: Silvanaeditoriale.

Residori, S. 2007. *Il massacro del Grappa. Vittime e carnefici del rastrellamento 21–27 settembre 1944*. Verona: Istrevi, Cierre edizionierona.

Restelli, G. 2006. *Viaggio in un mondo fuori dal mondo. Dachau, Ebensee, Hartheim, Gusen, Mauthausen*. Legnano: IPSIA, Raccoltoedizioni.

Rev, I. 2004. *Retroactive justice: Prehistory of post-communism*: Palo Alto: Stanford University Press.

Revelli, M. 1996. *Le due destre: le derive politiche del postfordismo*. Turin: Bollati Boringhieri.

Revelli, N. 1966. *La strada del Davai*. Turin: Einaudi.

———. 1993. *La guerra dei poveri*. Turin: Einaudi.

———. 1997. La ritirata di Russia. In *I luoghi della memoria*, ed M. Isnenghi, 365–79. Bari: Laterza.

Ricci, G. 1978. *Storia della Brigata Matteotti-Picelli: brigate partigiane delle 4 zona operativa*. La Spezia: Istituto storico della Resistenza Pietro Mario Beghi.

Rigoni Stern, M. 1993. *Il sergente nella neve*. Turin: Einaudi.

Rizzi, P. 1988. Pinelli, quella lapide non è ancora da museo. *L'unità*, September 7.

Rochat, G., and M. Venturi, eds. 1993. *La divisione Acqui a Cefalonia. Settembre 1943*. Milan: Mursia.

———. 1997. La prigionia di guerra. In *I luoghi della memoria*, ed. M. Isnenghi, 381–402. Bari: Laterza.

———. 2006. Ancora su Cefalonia, settembre 1943. In *Studi e ricerche di storia contemporanea* 35 (65): 5–21.

Rodogno, D. 2003. *Il nuovo ordine mediterraneo. Le politiche dell'occupazione dell'Italia fascista in Europa 1940–1943*. Turin: Bollati Boringhieri.

Romano, S. 2001. Cefalonia, una pagina nera della storia militare italiana. *Nuova storia contemporanea*: 133–36.

Ropa, R. 2008. *Prigionieri del Terzo Reich. Storia e memoria dei militari bolognesi internati nella Germania nazista*: Bologna: CLUEB.

Rosati, C. 1990. La memoria dei bombardamenti. Pistoia 1943–1944. In *Linea Gotica 1944. Esercito, popolazioni, partigiani*, ed. G. Rochat, 409–34. Milan: FrancoAngeli.

Rossi-Doria, A. 2000. Una storia di memorie divise e di impossibili lutti. *Passato e presente* 18 (49): 133–40.

Rough Guide to Cephallonia and the Ionian Islands. 2001. London: Rough Guides.

Rousso, H. 1991. *The Vichy syndrome: History and memory in France since 1944*. Cambridge: Harvard University Press.

———. 2002. *The haunting past: History, memory and justice in contemporary France*. Philadelphia: University of Pennsylvania Press.

Rovatti, T. 2004. *Sant'Anna di Stazzema. Storia e memoria della strage dell'agosto 1944*. Rome: Deriveapprodi.

Ruffini, E. 2008. Un silenzio rumoroso. In *Gli ultimi fuochi. 28 aprile 1945, a Rovetta*, ed. A. Bendotti and E. Ruffini, 135–277. Bergamo: Il filo di arianna.

Rusconi, G. E. 1993. *Se cessiamo di essere una nazione. Tra etnodemocrazie regionali e cittadinanza europea*. Bologna: Il Mulino.

———. 1995. *Resistenza e postfascismo*. Bologna: Il Mulino.

———. 2004. *Cefalonia 1943. Quando gli italiani si battono*. Turin: Einaudi.

Sabbatucci, G. 1974. *I combattenti nel primo dopoguerra*. Bari: Laterza.

———. 2002. La Grande Guerra come fattore di divisione: dalla frattura dell'intervento al dibattito storiografico recente. In *Due nazioni. Legittimazione e deligittimazione nella storia dell'Italia contemporanea*, ed. L. Nucci and E. Galli della Loggia, 107–25. Bologna: Il Mulino.

Salotti, G. 2001. La tragedia di Cefalonia: un referendum per un massacro. *Nuova storia contemporanea* 5 (4): 93–106.

Salvatores, G. 1996. *Mediterraneo*. Feature film.

Samuel, R., and Thompson, P. 1990. Introduction, to *The myths we live by*, ed. R. Samuel and P. Thompson, 1–22. London: Routledge.

Santarelli, L. 2004. Muted violence: Italian war crimes in occupied Greece. *Journal of Modern Italian Studies* 9 (3): 280–99.

Santomassimo, G. 2001. La memoria pubblica dell'antifascismo. *Italia Contemporanea* 225: 549–72.

———. 2004. Da Aldo Moro al caso Moro. In *Antifascimo e dintorni*. Rome: Manifestolibri.

Satta, S. 1980. *De Profondis*. Milan: Adelphi.

Scalarini, G. 1920. *La Guerra davanti al tribunale della storia*. Milan: Avanti!.

Scaramucci, P. 1982. *Licia Pinelli. Una storia quasi soltanto mia*. Milan: Mondadori.

Schreiber, G. 1992. *I militari italiani internati nei campi di concentramento del Terzo Reich 1943–1945. Traditi, disperati, dimenticati*. Rome: Stato Maggiore dell'Esercito, Ufficio Storico.

————. 2000. *La vendetta tedesca, 1943–1945. Le rappresaglie naziste in Italia.* Milan: Mondadori.

Sciascia, L. 1989a. *La Sicilia come metafora.* Milan: Mondadori.

————. 1989b. *L'affaire Moro.* In *Opere 1971–1983*, ed. C. Ambroise. Milan: Bompiani.

————. 2007. *L'affaire Moro.* Milan: Adelphi.

Scoppola, P. 1995. *25 aprile. Liberazione.* Turin: Einaudi.

Seghettini, L. 2006. *Al vento del Nord. Una donna nella lotta di Liberazione.* Rome: Carocci.

Il segno della memoria. 1945–1995 BBPR Monumento aui caduti nei campi nazisti. 1995. Milan: Electa.

Sessi, F. 2000. *Nome di battaglia: Diavolo. L'omicidio don Pessina e la persecuzione giudiziaria contro il partigiano Germano Nicolini.* Venice: Marsilio.

Sfiligoi, E. 1993. *Qui Marina Argostoli Cefalonia: Il contributo della Marina nella eroica difesa dell' isola jonica e la via crucis di alcuni marinai sopravvissuti all'immane massacro consumato dalla Wehrmacht.* Monfalcone: Edizione della Laguna.

Simonazzi, D. 2004. *Azor. La resistenza "incompiuta" di un comandante partigiano.* Reggio Emilia: Age.

Snowden, F. 2002. From triumph to disaster: Fascism and malaria in the Pontine Marshes, 1928–1946. In *Disastro!*, ed. J. Dickie et al., 113–40. New York: Palgrave.

————. 2008. Latina Province, 1944–1950. *Journal of Contemporary History* 43: 509–26.

Sofri, A. 1993. *Memoria.* Palermo: Sellerio.

————. 2009. *La notte che Pinelli.* Palermo: Sellerio.

Sorcinelli, P. 1996. *Il quotidiano e i sentimenti. Introduzione alla storia sociale.* Milan: Bruno Mondadori.

Sponza, L. 2000. *Divided loyalties: Italians in Britain during the Second World War.* New York: P. Lang.

Stern, S. 2006. *Remembering Pinochet's Chile. On the eve of London 1998.* Durham and London: Duke University Press.

Storchi, M. 1992–1993. Violenza, tradimento, territorio. Riflessioni e ipotesi di lavoro sul dopoguerra reggiano. *Ricerche Storiche* 71: 5–14.

————. 1995. *Uscire dalla guerra. Ordine pubblico e forze politiche. Modena 1945–1946.* Milan: Franco Angeli.

————. 1996. Ordine pubblico e violenza politica nel Modenese e nel Reggiano. *L'Impegno* 16 (1): 48–51.

————. 1998. *Combattere si può vincere bisogna. La scelta della violenza fra Resistenza e dopoguerra. Reggio Emilia 1943–1946.* Venice: Marsilio.

————. 2001. La memoria della violenza fra Resistenza e dopoguerra. *L'impegno* 21 (2): 29–37.

————. 2005. *Sangue al bosco del Lupo. Partigiani che uccidono partigiani. La storia di "Azor."* Reggio Emilia: Aliberti editore.

————. 2007. Post-war violence in Italy: A struggle for memory. *Modern Italy* 12 (2): 237–50.

La strage di stato. Controinchiesta. Savelli, 1970.

Suzzi Valli, R. 2000. The myth of squadrismo in the fascist regime. *Journal of Contemporary History* 35 (2): 131–50.

———. 2008. Il culto dei martiri fascisti. In *La morte per la patria. La celebrazione dei caduti dal Risorgimento alla Repubblica*, ed. O. Janz and L. Klinkhammer, 102–20. Rome: Donzelli.

Tasca, A. 1965. *Nascita e avvento del fascismo*. Bari: Laterza.

———. 2002. *Nascita e avvento del fascismo*. Florence: La Nuova Italia.

Taviani, P. E. 1982. Prefazione. In *A Cefalonia e Corfù si combatte*, by G. Giraudi, 5–7. Milan: Cavallotti editore.

Thaler, F. 2003. *Testimonianze dai lager*. Bolzano: Citta di Bolzano, Archivio Storico.

———. 2006. *Commissione parlamentare d'inchiesta sulle cause dell'occultamento di fascicoli relativi ai crimini nazifascisti*. Rome: Parlamento Italiano. http://www.camera.it/_bicamerali/nochiosco.asp?pagina=/_bicamerali/leg14/crimini/home.htm.

Thompson, P. 2000. *The voice of the past: Oral history*. Oxford: Oxford University Press.

Tibaldi, I. 1994. *Compagni di viaggio. Dall'Italia al Lager nazisti. I "trasporti" dei deportati 1943–1945*. Milan: Franco Angeli.

Il Tirreno. 2008a. Nuovi dibattiti sulle due tesi. July 19.

———. 2008b. Il sindaco spieghi quelle due lapidi. July 20.

Tobagi, W. 1973. *Gli anni del manganello*. Milan: Fratelli Fabbri Editori.

Tobia, B. 1998. *L'altare della patria. L'Italia monarchica, fascista, repubblicana nella storia di un monumento*. Bologna: Il Mulino.

———. 2002. *"Salve o popolo d'eroi . . ." La monumentalità fascista nelle fotografie dell'Istituto Luce*. Rome: Riuniti.

Todero, F. 2002. *La metamorfosi della memoria. La Grande Guerra tra modernità e tradizione*. Udine: DelBianco editore.

Todorov, T. 1995. *Una tragedia vissuta. Scene di guerra civile*. Milan: Garzanti.

———. 2003. *Hope and memory. Reflections on the twentieth century*. Princeton, NJ: Princeton University Press.

Tonkin, E. 1992. *Narrating our past*. Cambridge: Cambridge University Press.

Torino 1938/45. Una guida per la memoria. 2000–2001. Settore Musei della Città di Torino, Istituto piemontese per la storia della Resistenza e della società contemporanea, Città di Torino, Turin.

Toscani, O., ed. 2003. *Sant'Anna di Stazzema—12 agosto 1944. I bambini raccontano*. Milan: Feltrinelli.

Tota, A. L., ed. 2001. *La memoria contesa. Studi sulla rappresentazione sociale del passato*. Milan: FrancoAngeli.

———. 2003. *La città ferita. Memoria e comunicazione pubblica della strage di Bologna, 2 agosto 1980*. Bologna: Il Mulino.

———, ed., with Marita Rampazzi. 2007. *La memoria pubblica. Trauma culturale, nuovi confini, identita' culturali*. Turin: UTET.

Tremlett, G. 2006. *Ghosts of Spain: Travels through a country's hidden past*. London: Faber and Faber.

Triarius. 1945. *La tragedia di Cefalonia*: Rome: Ugo Pinnarò editore.

Ugolini, W. 2004. Communal myths and silenced memories: The unremembered experience of Italians in Scotland during the Second World War. In *Memory and memorials: The commemorative century*, ed. W. Kidd and B. Murdoch. London: Ashgate.

L'Unità. 1979. Quella morte di Pinelli in questura. December 15.

Venegoni, D., ed. 2005. *Uomini, donne e bambini nel lager di Bolzano. Una tragedia italiana in 7809 storie individuali*. Fondazione Memoria della Deportazione Biblioteca-Archivio "Aldo Ravelli." Milan: Mimesis.

Ventresca, R. 2006. Mussolini's ghost: Italy's duce in history and memory. *History and Memory* 18 (1): 86–119.

Venturi, M. 1963. *Bandiera Bianca a Cefalonia*. 2nd ed. 1972, with an introduction by Sandro Pertini. Republished in 2001, Milan: Mondadori.

———. 1966. *The white flag*. New York: Vanguard.

Verbali del Consiglio dei ministri. Luglio 1943 – maggio 1948. 1994, edizione Critica, Vol. 2, Rome: Presidente del Consiglio dei ministri.

Vergani, G. 2004. Dal cielo, la morte che "insudicia." In *Bombe sulla città, Milano in guerra 1942–1944*, ed. R. A. Marrucci, 107–13. Milan: Skira.

Versolato, G. 2001. *Bombardamenti aerei degli alleati nel Vicentino. 1943–1945*. Novale-Valdagno: Gino Rossato Edizioni.

Vidal-Naquet, P. 1993. *Assassins of memory*. New York: Columbia University Press.

Vidotto, V., B. Tobia, and C. Brice, eds. 1998. *La memoria perduta. I monumenti ai caduti della Grande Guerra a Roma e nel Lazio*. Rome: Argos.

Vietti, G. 1980. *L'Alta Val Taro nella Resistenza*. Parma: ANPI.

Villani, C. 2006. La persecuzione degli ebrei in Alto Adige. In *Tra Roma e Bolzano. Nazione e Provincia nel ventennio fascista*, ed. A. Bonoldi and H. Obermair, 138–48. Bolzano: Città di Bolzano.

Villani, S. 1994. *L'eccidio di Schio: luglio 1945, una strage inutile*. Milan: Mursia.

Virgili, F. 2002. *Shorn women: Gender and punishment in liberation France*. Oxford: Berg.

Vivarelli, R. 1991. *Storia delle origini del fascismo. L'Italia dalla grande guerra alla marcia su Roma, Volume II*. Bologna: Il Mulino.

———. 2000. *La fine di una stagione. Memoria 1943–1945*. Bologna: Il Mulino.

Volpe, F., ed. 1990. *Ferramonti: un lager del Sud, atti del convegno internazionale di studi, 15–16 maggio 1987*. Cosenza: Edizioni Orizzonti Meridionali.

Von Boeschoten, R. 2007. Broken bonds and divided memories: Wartime massacres reconsidered in a comparative perspective. *Oral History* 35 (1): 39–48.

Winter, J. 1995. *Sites of memory, sites of mourning: The Great War in European cultural history*. Cambridge: Cambridge University Press.

———. 2006. *Remembering war. The Great War between memory and history in the twentieth century*. New Haven and London: Yale University Press.

Young, J. E. 1994. *The texture of memory: Holocaust memorials and meaning*. New Haven: Yale University Press.

Zaghi, V. 1990. "Con Matteotti si mangiava": simboli e valori nella genesi di un mito popolare. *Rivista di Stora Contemporanea* 19 (3): 432–46.

Zangrandi, R. 1995. *L'Italia tradita L'8 settmbre 1943*. Milan: Mursia.

Index